T0307001

THE DIGITAL FRONTIER

THE DIGITAL FRONTIER

HOW CONSUMER COMPANIES CAN CREATE MASSIVE VALUE THROUGH DIGITAL TRANSFORMATION

AJAY SOHONI

WILEY

Library of Congress Cataloging-in-Publication Data

Names: Sohoni, Ajay, author. | John Wiley & Sons, publisher.
Title: The digital frontier : how consumer companies can create massive
    value through digital transformation / Ajay Sohoni.
Description: [Hoboken, NJ] : Wiley, 2021. | Includes index.
Identifiers: LCCN 2021008534 (print) | LCCN 2021008535 (ebook) | ISBN
    9781119803249 (cloth) | ISBN 9781119803256 (adobe pdf) | ISBN
    9781119803263 (epub)
Subjects: LCSH: Business enterprises—Technological innovations. | Customer
    relations.
Classification: LCC HC79.T4 S736 2021 (print) | LCC HC79.T4 (ebook) | DDC
    658.4/06—dc23
LC record available at https://lccn.loc.gov/2021008534
LC ebook record available at https://lccn.loc.gov/2021008535

Cover Design: Wiley
Cover Image: © Getty Images

Set in 11/14pt, MinionPro by SPi Global, Chennai, India.
Printed and bound by CPI Group (UK) Ltd, Croydon, CR0 4YY

C803249_270421

To my parents, for accidentally engineering a hyper-curious and free-spirited professional and giving me the twin gifts of language and humor. I think it worked out okay this time, but I highly doubt that it is repeatable.

CONTENTS

CONTENTS

WHY I WROTE THIS BOOK AND WHY YOU SHOULD READ IT

It was early July in 2020 and we were just emerging from the COVID-19 lockdown in Singapore, termed the "circuit breaker" here. A six-week period of closure, distancing and disciplined social behavior which saved the city from the pandemic. A little after 8 am and I was sitting with my wife at the beautiful outdoor seating at a café in Singapore's quiet, green and modern media district, having just dropped my five-year-old off for Day One of her arts camp nearby. The wide-open space and the understated grandeur of the Fumihiko Maki-designed Mediapolis was further magnified this morning by the fact that my wife and I were the only people there. I was meant to take two weeks off from work, people had stopped taking days off since the pandemic started and the company had urged us to take time off and look after ourselves.

"I am concerned about two things", I told my wife. I wasn't sure about how to use the two weeks productively. I was also at an inflection point in my career, having spent the last six years in the digital and technology-enabled business space I was looking to move on to something else. But I loved the space I was in and I felt like I still had a lot to offer; it worried me that I would allow everything I knew to just fall into obsolescence if I left "the scene". My wife is much smarter than me, and I am not just saying that to demonstrate my own humility, we don't do that in my generation anymore. That question was settled 11 years ago when she outscored me on the GMAT and she likely had a better GPA than I did at INSEAD where we met. But we will never know, because we have continued INSEAD's grade non-disclosure policy in our household.

"Write a book", she said. So, I did.

This book is an aggregation of my understanding and my opinions about driving digital transformation in consumer-facing business. For me, specifically, that comes from my experiences in digital during my startup tenure at Lazada, in transformations during my time at McKinsey, and in consumer-facing business at the Coca-Cola company. In my fourteen-year career so far, I've been lucky enough to have worked in most corners of the world in a variety of companies that have given me an incredible array of experiences. The number of times there has been a day which ended in a high (or a low) and I've wished I could just tell everyone about it! So, this here is my chance to share with you readers some of what I have learnt so far. But before we get into the main body of this book, I want to share three distinct memories with you from three of the many events in my career so far that have made an impression, all three involving three admirable leaders.

The year was 2010 and it was starting to get cooler in Amsterdam, around November. Little did we know that we'd end the year in a snow-storm that would close the airport for a few days. But, on that cold November day I was helping put together the final edits on a presentation in one of the meeting rooms in McKinsey's beautiful office on the picturesque Amstel river. Our client was a large consumer products conglomerate and the recently appointed CEO was holding a gala event to end the year at the 300+-year-old Amsterdam Hermitage museum. Top business leaders from around the world were assembled here in a beautiful space and, while the light and sound engineers were rigging the place up, we were conferring with the CEO on some nuances of his speech and presentation. That night he launched a transformational journey that has spanned a decade, taking this multi-country and multi-category business, splitting and carving and buying and stitching it together into a completely new form, while at the same time changing the way the company operated from inside out. Looking back at that evening on the Amstel, thinking about the moves that were then mere bullet points on a PowerPoint slide, and looking at the ensuing actions two qualities of this transformational leader shine through: Courage and commitment.

Five years later, and this time it was November again and also very cold in Hangzhou, China. Still groggy from the short overnight flight and drive from Shanghai I walked into a conference room at the sprawling and impressive

Alibaba campus. We were here to meet Daniel Zhang, the CEO of Alibaba. Lazada group, one of Southeast Asia's leading e-commerce companies, was discussing an investment from Alibaba and I was running Lazada's payments company, which would then be acquired by Alipay. A few months later Alibaba acquired a controlling stake in Lazada, but we were still in the midst of negotiations in November 2015. Mr. Zhang had an intense aura about himself. He spoke in a calm collected way, every word measured to make a specific incisive point. We spent maybe 30 minutes talking about what consumers value, what merchants value, and what brands value. No complex tech terminology, no mention of buzzwords like fintech and, worse still, blockchain. Daniel Zhang is an incredibly impressive leader and, looking back at that interaction, I realized the core idea, that you'll see me repeat several times in the book, is that the objective is to create commercial value using technology, *not* to apply technology for the sake of it and then find associated commercial value in some way. Two transformational qualities: Pragmaticism and focus.

Four years on, it was early September and this time I was at a conference room near downtown Singapore. It was warm as usual, as it is all year round in Singapore, and the neighborhood was bustling with road closures and the signs of impending activity in preparation for the Formula 1 Grand Prix, which was a couple of weeks away. For a weekend, the downtown streets transform into a racing track for some of the world's fastest and loudest cars, nothing short of a modern-day marvel. On one of the higher floors of this 70+ storey hotel, some of the Coca-Cola company's brightest and most creative minds were gathered to talk about, among other things, what the brand ought to mean for consumers. There were presentations and ideas galore, and constructive debate, and then in the midst of it all – the most senior leader in this meeting rolled up his sleeves and walked over to the flipchart. What followed was an unforgettable 30-odd minute one-on-one on brand Coke, its history of campaigns, its changing role in consumers' lives over the last few decades, the product's chemical composition and the role each ingredient played physiologically, the different ways in which the brand's own identity and ethos was inextricably linked to the science of the product but extended far beyond the product itself, the implicit lifestyle choices and personal statement a consumer made when he selected that can from the shelf. It was almost like he was reminding us to make choices that lived up to the 130+ year history of the company.

I remember thinking why they hadn't taught us that in business school and there was a lesson in this too. There is simply no substitute for experienced leadership, and an understanding of the ways of the world accumulated over decades of experience. We stand to gain much more from bringing our senior leaders up to speed on digital than from putting "guys who can code, who read *Wired* magazine and whose LinkedIn status says serial entrepreneur" into leadership roles. Transformation qualities learnt: Deep consumer understanding and corporate legacy.

Knowledge and understanding are distinct and different but often used interchangeably. This book is not about knowledge, it's about understanding. Epistemologically, knowledge has an obligation to be rooted in truth, and in a marketplace for goods and services which is now made especially complex by fast-changing and hard-to-fathom technology, it's impossible to discern the truth. If it exists that is. So, I can't necessarily share any knowledge on digital transformation; I can, however, offer my own understanding of it and that is what this book is about. As I went through the chapters I took on one topic at a time and just wrote up how I understood it. And, in writing it up I am passing it on to you for you to take and process and to develop your own understanding on the topics I write about. Success for this book would be you feeling a lot more at ease with the changes involving digital transformation after you're done reading it.

And then there is fun, I want you to have fun reading this book. I love a dark joke, a good meal, a shocking movie, an emotional song, a stiff drink, a long run, a convoluted story, and most importantly I love not taking serious things seriously. So, I've tried to make this severe-sounding topic of digital transformation fun to digest and I want you to get a good laugh out of it. So go ahead and dive right in!

ACKNOWLEDGMENTS

I would like to start off by thanking my wife Eun Joo for suggesting writing this book in the first place and for her continued counsel as I worked through it. My little daughter Ira, for her wide-eyed curiosity for what Baba was up to, hammering away at his laptop early morning and late night. The thought of walking her into a bookstore someday and showing her the book that her daddy wrote has been motivation enough!

I'd like to thank my father, who was the first person to read the drafts and who suggested I write bits of fiction within the book, which I did, my mother and my sister for the constant positive reinforcement. My brother-in-law Yashodeep, and close friends Mihir and Leslie for taking the time to read through the draft in meticulous detail and for making game-changing suggestions.

In my Coca-Cola family, I'd like to acknowledge Iain McLaughlin for pushing me to publish the book, Claudia Lorenzo for allowing me to spend the time I needed on the book, Belinda Ford for reading through and surfacing questions I would not have seen otherwise.

And finally, I would like to thank the leaders and colleagues at Coca-Cola, Lazada-Alibaba and McKinsey for being incredible teachers and allowing me to learn the things that formed the foundations of this book.

CHAPTER 1
SETTING THE CONTEXT

Let There Be Value Creation

We need to stop pretending

It was another early morning in the Sohoni household, for me at least. I have been waking up at 5:30 am every morning and my wife thinks I am getting old. I am in fact, or was on this specific morning, only 38 years old but I guess the mind does age faster these days considering how much more information and how many more situations it needs to process.

So, on this morning in September 2019, in a world before COVID-19, where the only problems facing the world were stuff like climate change, religious fundamentalism, racism and prejudice etc., I was doing my morning read of the papers. This, in my world of course, takes the shape of sipping on a nice long black while lounging on the living room sofa and mindlessly scrolling through a couple of news websites and Reddit. And there it was in the headlines:

"WeWork's Adam Neumann Steps Down as CEO"[1]

This event had followed months of intrigue around bad executive behavior, a failed IPO and a broken business model. Here we go again, I thought, now we must all pretend this was shocking because come on, the company was destined for such great heights. That this was toxic management culture making a mess out of a perfectly amazing and investable asset. That this was not the norm but an accident. An accident of somewhat colossal proportions, but an accident, nevertheless. We have to all pretend, all over again, just like we did when Travis Kalanick resigned as the Uber CEO in 2017[2], or when Elizabeth Holmes was charged with wire-fraud at former-company Theranos in 2018[3]. Or even when big name tech company IPOs like Snapchat, Lyft or Slack did not result in the response everyone expected. If an IPO were sort of like the finish line at a marathon, this is the equivalent of not caring about who finishes or wins but just celebrating the ones that sprint like hell in the first few kilometers.

Fast forward, or more like fast backward – does that exist? to December 2019 and it is another morning albeit somewhat cloudy. I am in pretty much the same position and other than the weather the only thing that's different is my coffee – this time I'm drinking a special Colombia bean edition coffee from my trusted capsule coffee brand which tastes almost exactly the same, but I have the pleasure of paying a bit more for a slightly more attractive packaging. This time I am on LinkedIn, doing my monthly ritual of reading about success stories from my connections to feel like a complete failure myself. The Forbes 30 under 30 has just been published and features 30 millennials with a ton of courage who have started companies with catchy names made up of five letters, like ZIPSY and FRIXO (I made those up), that have raised tens of millions of dollars. And we have to all start pretending again, that this is the new model of success we and our children need to aspire to – raise funding, more and more and many times over.

This time its early 2019, I am in the United States in a workshop and we are about to kick off a 3-day Agile session (Yes, I said A****, more about that in Chapter 7). There's coffee here as well but this is a corporate office in America so it's scalding hot water which is gently scented with coffee beans. There are a couple of bean bags thrown in the corner for effect, we have a little gig running where we record vertical videos à la Tik Tok so someone can make a collage later – because digital. A senior leader stands up and thanks us profusely for our commitment to discuss this important topic and then says the words, "We need to start acting and thinking like a startup". And we all start pretending again, that this is indeed the one thing we need to do, think like a startup. And we pretend to know what it means to think like a startup.

This is what keeps me awake at night, and I figured I would write this book so I can sleep in peace. We need to stop pretending, seriously we do. Sitting inside large traditional companies we need to figure this out now. What is really happening out there and how can we understand it better? What should we do, and will it help us make more money? How do we all agree on a way forward together instead of pulling in many different directions? How do we stop attending webinars and start getting stuff done?

Value creation is at the root of it all

Companies make money because they create value, individuals make money because they create value. Now that is one thing we can all get behind, making money. Of course, there will be those amongst us that do not believe in the capitalist model and do not subscribe to it, but this book is not building a case for or against capitalism. This book takes the current market situation as a reality that companies need to operate in and tries to unpack the situation to build a shared understanding and a practical way to succeed. Success in this world is about profits, and profits in turn are about value creation.

I am not a trained economist, neither am I a university professor but I wanted to make an attempt to lay out my internal dialogue and reflection here in words and see if it helps you as readers to understand what is happening just as it did for me. In doing so I am going to dramatically simplify things but hopefully it will not take away from the validity of my thesis.

I would define the act of Value Creation as the undertaking of an activity by an individual that produces an outcome (say a product) that has value to someone else. In performing the activity, the individual has created something of value to someone – value creation. Say, as an example, Person A finds out that he is sitting on top of an oil well and decides to drill for it, takes out a barrel of oil and it costs him 10$ to do so. Person B needs said oil and is willing to pay person A 15$ to buy that barrel of oil off him. Person A has created 15$ of value by deciding to extract that oil, value that would not have been created had he chosen not to do anything and just sit at home and binge-watch *The Witcher*.

And in that process, he has earned 5$ of profit, a compensation he got paid for performing the activity of drilling the oil out of the ground.

If now there were a lot more Persons A and a lot fewer Persons B, because there was a lot more oil discovered, or because the uses for oil just disappeared as the world woke up to the grim realities of climate change, then the demand for oil would drop. Consequently, the world would not "value" the activity of drilling for oil as much anymore and Person B will likely only pay 12$ for a barrel. It would still cost Person A 10$ to drill and they will now only earn 2$ instead of the original 5$. Less profit for A because the world does not value what they do as much anymore. Less value created.

We need to imagine the world and our economy as an incredibly complex, layered and interconnected web of individuals and companies that wake up every day and set about performing activities that result in value being created for other individuals and companies. And if you are creating something that has value for someone else you will get paid for it and make money. How much money you make will depend on how badly people need what you are making and how many others are making something similar. The opposite is then also true, if you are not making any money or enough money then you are likely not creating any value or not creating enough value to deserve a fair compensation for your activities.

So, this begs the question, are startups creating value?

Let us delve into this taking five of the most popular use cases of the last decade as an example: Ride hailing, Co-working spaces, Food delivery, e-commerce and Digital payments.

Ride hailing – Back in 2009, while I was getting my MBA, a bunch of us went to Kuala Lumpur to watch the Formula One Grand Prix at the Sepang circuit. Getting a cab in KL was a nightmare, you were constantly getting overcharged, refused and on one occasion threatened with a knife. Ten years on, ride hailing in KL is a breeze and by bringing absolute transparency in the supply–demand equation of the urban transportation market, ride hailing companies have truly performed a valuable activity for us consumers. But what they have failed to do, over their entire history of existence, is to make any profits at all from this venture. In other words, they are being paid 8$ for their barrel of oil when it is costing them 10$ to drill the oil out. And the reason for that is quite straightforward. To make sure they continue to get massive funding and huge valuations in a fiercely competitive context they have had to sell more and more rides and acquire more and more consumers at a loss. All with the promise of monetizing this consumer base in the future – a promise that has yet to materialize. Some have diversified into other use cases, like food delivery and payments, all of which are also loss-making and, as one might expect, putting several loss-making businesses under one company makes for a bigger loss-making company.

Co-working spaces – The key question on my mind about co-working spaces has always been who is the company creating value for? WeWork's failure can be attributed to many things, and there were far too many, but they also got the answer to this fundamental question wrong. Airbnb creates obvious value for the hosts as well as the travelers as most of you have doubtlessly experienced. A co-working model creates a lot of value for real estate asset owners as they get the chance to earn a better return on their asset as it becomes available to a larger consumer base and gains higher occupancy. But WeWork took that out of the equation by owning the real estate and then renting it out cheaply, so they took value from the real estate asset from their own pockets and handed it to consumers. On the consumer side, other than the obviously severely attractive pricing, it was unclear if consumers really needed this product. There was no endemic lack of office space in our cities and a startup employee's willingness to accept dilapidated office infrastructure is way higher than a traveler's willingness to accept a decrepit Airbnb accommodation. I once spent a whole week during my startup tenure sitting on a chair which only had three legs. Oh, and you can work in a Starbucks for free.

Food delivery – Food delivery is not a new phenomenon, pizza delivery started in the 60s, first taking orders on the phone for a couple of decades and eventually through the internet in the mid-90s. Can you believe it? Actually picking up the phone and having a conversation with another human being! Ugh! The value here was already obvious to the consumer, the convenience of staying at home and getting a meal delivered to you. Food-delivery apps merely extended this value to a larger set of restaurant operators and a larger installed base of consumers, and now the proposition included a much wider variety of meals. And delivery players rightfully charged both consumers as well as the restaurants for the value provided. The industry however went through a couple of interesting turns. First, players geo-fenced their delivery radius and improved operations in general, so food was delivered in 20 minutes, thus providing more value to consumers. And second, some players realized that they were not able to make delivery operations work at acceptable costs in some markets and actually started shrinking and exiting specific cities. And this was, so far, perfectly acceptable conduct as the industry was becoming more normalized. Just as this was starting to happen, ride hailing giants and more competitors entered this business and started allowing consumers to get free deliveries and major discounts. As a result, we have now ended up with another unprofitable use case which will only start making sense once consumers are asked to pay for the service they are getting. This is not always easy, if that barrel of oil were always handed to you for free, you would be up in arms when you are told to shell out 15 USD for it.

e-Commerce – There are many different forms of e-commerce today but regardless of the size of the assortment a platform carries, or the delivery and fulfilment model, the two main value creating elements of e-commerce are improvement in availability or visibility and the convenience of shopping from home. Products that were only possible to be browsed by those who were lucky enough to live in big cities near retail locations are now available for everyone everywhere. I remember the first time my mother bought a microwave oven or a rice cooker growing up in small-town India and she had a total SKU choice of one and at a price that she had absolutely no reference to evaluate. When my dad bought a coffee machine last year, he had virtually endless choice and was able to make a very informed decision that he feels quite proud of. The convenience of not having to lug stuff home is obvious and I do not need to explain it here. There are many other elements that make e-commerce exciting but there are also some value destroyers, the lack of in-store experience for example. But unfortunately for e-commerce, too many brands and platforms have treated it like a discount channel in their desperation to show short-term progression in sales, and consumers have started thinking of it that way as well. The value is endangered, but I am confident that this will change. The benefit for me as a consumer is too compelling for me to forego just because I am not used to paying shipping fees on my purchases.

Digital payments – This is an interesting one and I personally wrestled with this a lot some time ago when I was running a payments company. There is the broader world of Fintech, perhaps a topic for another book, but the much narrower definition around consumers using non-cash instruments to pay conveniently is what I want to address here. Payment companies have rightfully always touted the convenience for consumers to do contactless, one-click, no-click etc. payments without having to withdraw cash and handle change, as a key benefit. And for merchants there is the potential to turn anonymous cash payments into useful consumer data together with the promise of lower cash handling costs and interchange fees. But has that value truly materialized? In our less developed cities cash is still very widely used and consumers do not really care as much about that non-cash convenience yet. In our larger cities credit cards and banks have started offering similar convenience and consumers are using digital payment apps mostly for the rebates and discounts which is not a sustainable model. I still believe there is value to be created in digital payments, but unlike during Alipay's rise in China from 2005 to 2015 which was fueled by a lack of personal financial products available to consumers from the retail banks or PayPal's rise in the US around the same time, propelled by its captive transactions from eBay, payment instruments from traditional banks and credit card companies have vastly improved in access and quality. And the incremental value gained by moving to a new payment instrument might not be compelling enough for consumers or merchants.

So, what can we learn from this little tour of the most popular start-up cases of the last decade?

For one there is clear value to be created for consumers or buyers and merchants or sellers. Companies embarking on a digital transformation need to start there and pin down what value they are creating for their consumers and for other partners in the ecosystem which might include suppliers, retailers, manufacturers, employees or any other entity which the company has a financial relationship with. It is important to have explored all these aspects of value creation, as often the real beneficiaries of a new way of doing business are not the most apparent ones.

And secondly, this pursuit of value needs to be relentless and quite frankly the only reason why we embark on a digital transformation. Too often the waters get muddied by fundraising objectives, more about that later in this chapter, personal agendas from leaders who want to build a reputation rather than a profitable franchise, unnecessary urgency which doesn't allow companies to properly educate the consumers on the long-term value economics of a new business model, and shock and awe type of narratives from thought leaders who keep throwing new terminology into the mix and constantly distract unsuspecting executives from the focus on generating profits.

But if these companies are not always creating value how is it that they have such insane valuations? Why can't traditional companies do the same and benefit from amazing share price increases? These are very pertinent questions to answer and I want to spend some time reflecting on these.

Enter the capitalists with too much money

May 2017, Masayoshi Son announced the first close of his 100 USD billion Vision fund with committed investment sourced in a big part from middle eastern sovereign wealth funds, the Saudi sovereign wealth fund contributing up to a staggering 45 USD billion[4]. With the breadth of investments in companies big on discounting, we can all revel in the fact that we have benefited from Saudi oil money since 2017. 100 USD billion, I ruminated on that number and I was thinking how it is impossible to dimensionalize these numbers for me as an individual and quite frankly also for most companies. Perhaps it would be easier if they start expressing the figures in Swimming pools or Football fields. Like Softbank just raised 50 Olympic sized Swimming pools full of 100 USD bills in their Vision fund, you would be able to imagine then how much money that is. And there are more funds and more investors and more swimming pools full of money, lots and lots of money which governments just cannot stop printing.

At this point it is important to go back and understand the market for capital, again using my overly simplified analogy of a dude drilling oil out of the ground. So, Person A has been creating value by digging out oil at the cost of ten USD a barrel and selling to Persons B at 15 USD a barrel. Person A now realizes that there is a lot more demand for oil and consequently there is a lot more demand for the act of extracting the oil. So, he decides to spend 100 USD on a truck to move the barrels around but realizes he does not have that kind of money. Enter Person C – the investor. Person C gives the money to Person A for buying that truck and in return is promised a share of the company and a corresponding cut of Person A's future profits. The higher the profits generated, the higher will be the cut earned by Person C and the keener Person C would be to lend that money to Person A. In this simple world investors will always seek out a bigger cut and companies that create more value will be the ones that attract the most funding. So why is reality different?

Say Person A's company keeps getting bigger as demand increases and keeps getting more efficient with scale and operational innovation, consequently the value of his company or the size of a cut of his future profits continues to increase. Today, there is a lot of money in the hands of a lot of Persons C or investors keen on investing their money to make more money for themselves. They want to make money quick without waiting for profits to materialize, and so they are constantly buying company stakes off each other and making money as a result of the increase in valuations. This would still be fine if there were only a limited amount of money in the hands of Persons C to go around. But is there? This is where it starts to fall apart.

There is altogether too much money in the world right now and has been for the last decade. This is not a book on macroeconomics and even if it were, there is no version of what is right and what is wrong which has absolute global consensus. But leaving aside right and wrong, my simple version of causality goes a bit like this:

Economy tanks > Everyone freaks out > People stop buying stuff > Companies stop making stuff > People lose jobs > People freak out more > Governments get nervous > Governments print more money > Governments give away free money > Companies get money to continue to grow > Companies hire people back. But hang on, demand has not actually gone up and companies are not creating more value than they were before, so the extra money just mollifies the general population by creating jobs and causes massive perversion in the capital markets.

Why do economies tank in the first place, should governments react like this, what might happen if they don't and there is endemic unemployment etc. are of course HUGE questions and a lot of them are rooted in our human nature and animal instincts and they are FAR beyond the scope of this book. So, let us just say that a chain of events spanning several decades and especially the events of the last decade have resulted in us ending up in a world where there is altogether too much money.

This money desperately flows into assets that likely did not deserve it in the first place. Couple this with the incredible expectation of always earning a super high return on all investments all the time and you have a recipe for blind speculation. Bring in the young founders in a quest for fame and money and likeminded professionals who are compensated with stock options who will do anything it takes to increase the valuation of the company. Add a smattering of investment bankers who are all too keen on making up methodologies to value companies that do not make any money at all. Investment banks will essentially tell an investor group A to buy stock in a company at a certain valuation and then a year later tell another investor group B to buy the same stock in the same company for twice the valuation. They have in this process doubled the investment of group A and can claim to group B what incredible advice the bank gives. The bank makes extremely attractive fees, and no one seems to question if the underlying company actually doubled in value or point out the glaring conflict of interest in the fact that the same banker arbitrarily increased the valuation of a company between two subsequent fundraising rounds.

So this all seems like some kind of crazy Ponzi scheme where the poor sod, who ends up holding the stock when some event allows for the true value (or lack of it) to be exposed, ends up footing the bill, as we saw in failed IPOs and dead Unicorns. Of course not all start-ups are like this and we have seen tech behemoths like Facebook and Google who have found incredible value creation models and have demonstrated that it is possible to do well, without all the smoke and mirrors. And by the way, public markets are in no way immune to this, just seeing the way loss making companies have had IPOs for example Uber or Lyft. This does not mean they will fail, perhaps investors are buying the story on future returns and a path to profitability, after all Facebook and Amazon were also loss making when they listed. But today's tech unicorns that built businesses in the cheap-money environment have never had the discipline to actually generate returns and are likely in a rush to list to satisfy private investors hungry for an exit, driven by clauses clearly worded in previous funding rounds.

Startups are built mostly for investors, sometimes for consumers

Phew, what a mess. But I would maintain that there is nothing wrong with this situation and there are market forces at work here too. We ended up with too much money and there was a need for someone to create assets to have this money invested in, and a way for investors to make more money off the investments. Start-ups are merely fulfilling that need and, in the process, they are creating value for the investors who are making profitable exits. They might not be creating value for consumers or other stakeholders in the ecosystem, but they are creating shareholder value and there is nothing wrong with that. I would even hazard a guess that beneath the veneer of "changing the world" and "making the world a better place" most founders and senior leaders in the start-up space know that there is a dual game at work here. We want to make money for the company by making good products, but we also want to make money for the investors by ensuring our valuation keeps increasing.

Okay, what does it mean for us? For the corporates who are wanting to think like a startup.

For starters we need to acknowledge that there are two different games being played and we need to decide which game we want to play so we can play it wholeheartedly. Are we operators that will use technology and innovation to find new ways of creating value for consumers? Or are we agents who will build investable assets to serve as a vehicle for future investments from outside, so an eventual exit will create more shareholder value? Or can we actually do both?

Let us start with the innovative operator answer: There are of course a lot of examples of companies innovating in-house and in fact that is how we still have several iconic companies represented in the Fortune 500 today that have been around since more than 50 years ago. But these innovations are often buried inside the company's core business, shielded from external capital markets and find it harder to shine through earnings calls and analyst reports into the stock market for valuation gains to accrue. Worse still, a company's internal market for funding and the rules by which it is governed just doesn't allow for breakthrough innovation to be supported the way it does in a startup.

Let us look at the pure investor angle: There are some examples of traditional companies acting as successful investors, going back to DuPont's 1914 investment in General Motors or Microsoft's 2007 investment in Facebook[5]. But these are hard to find, because corporations are in general not in the business of investing. Some corporations are operationalizing this by setting up incubators. This is neither here, nor there. It is part investment, but never enough investment and part company related innovation but never completely relevant. Corporate venture capital has had mixed success in the past because companies have found it hard to play the investor role, because the sheer ticket size for entry into the space is far too big for traditional companies because of the insane amounts of VC money that fuels it. Traditional companies have more traditional investors to answer to and proceed, thankfully, with much more caution.

But I think this does not mean that corporates are not allowed to play, and I think the time is right for us to conceive a new kind of startup. One that is linked to our core business and might even be majority owned, but through specific mechanisms allows us to preserve the incentives and ways of working in a startup that give it the opportunity to make extraordinary gains for our business and our shareholders. In the last section of this book I will speak about how companies can go about architecting this middle ground in digital transformation to both create value for consumers and deliver sustainable returns for existing shareholders.

Maybe it's right to do a sports analogy here. Traditional companies can likely never be the Michael Jordan of digital business, we cannot afford to be so mercurial and high risk all the time because it does not matter if we win the MVP title in every season, what matters is that we win. And Scottie Pippen won too. Let us learn to be like Scottie.

So, what exactly do you do?

A question I have been asked repeatedly, and one that has had widely varying answers depending on when the question was asked. Around the time that I exited the start-up phase and decided to make my entry into the corporate world the job market was flush with roles that had the term "Digital" in them, including my own. And these roles came with different suffixes: Digital integration lead, Digital commerce lead, Digital marketing lead, Digital transformation lead, Digital business management, Digital business development, Digital this and Digital that – but Digital. Each job description essentially containing the same vague narrative around technology, data, connected-ness, innovation, start-ups, blockchain etc. but with extraordinarily little concrete information about what the person was actually supposed to do.

I have met several of my peers, agents of Digital change in traditional organizations, and the story is the same. We were hired, and then as the first task, asked to figure out what we were exactly hired for. I do not want to belittle this, apart from the obvious fact that it provided employment to the likes of me, it does demonstrate courage on behalf of companies. It is not easy to go hire people without knowing what they ought to do but trusting your instincts on the fact that something indeed needs doing. So, in my early days I set about trying to pin down a definition of digital transformation and came up with a definition here:

Digital transformation is **the journey** of creating **incremental value** by deploying **technology choice-fully** and **sustainably** into the **business operations** of the organization, so it becomes part of the **new normal**.

There are seven parts of this definition, marked in bold font, which warrant further explanation, starting with the fact that digital transformation is a journey and not just an end state. A digital transformation executive assumes responsibility to channel technology-based innovations into the organization and if there is new technology there will be the opportunity to affect a transformation using it. So this role is one which likely will not go away for the foreseeable future because there will always be new technology. The ever-accelerating pace of tech development makes it important to have this role in the company to continually filter, synthesize and inject ideas into the organization.

The transformation is only successful if it has created incremental value for the organization it is serving. Value can of course be a vague and often mis-used term because many things can have value to a company, but it helps to think of value creation in terms of incremental profits. The link might not always be very straightforward e.g., installing a new digital app to allow employees to photo-capture and expense travel and meal receipts will create convenience for employees and potentially save time which employees are able to spend on more value-adding topics which should in some form improve the company's profits. We do not always need to find out how much exactly, but it helps to know there is a profitability implication. Initiatives with easily and clearly demonstrable impact on company profits will rightfully tend to get more attention and more prioritization.

Digital transformation should primarily be about technology. How this relates to innovation, if such a function exists in the organization, is a very pertinent question which a lot of companies struggle with. In my opinion digital transformation is a sub-set of innovation but in today's environment has the potential to contribute a substantial share of all innovation. Perhaps there was a time when most breakthroughs in the world came through the discovery of new fuels or new materials or new production methods or management philosophies or new ingredients and flavors. But a large share of innovations in the past decade and in the next decade will come from technology, and the digital transformation function will take the responsibility to bring this to the organization. Of course, there is a need to unpack what this broad catch-all term of technology could contain, and we will do that in the next chapter.

Digital transformation ought to be choiceful about which technologies to channel into the organization. Some technologies have no use to a specific business situation, others are not developed or mature enough to make a difference, and some are just too expensive to scale. The transformation executive needs to be able to tell the ones that make sense apart from the ones that do not at that specific point in time. One excellent example of this is the euphoria around Blockchain that has come and gone over the last three to five years without making a noticeable impact on most consumer facing companies. Executives have struggled to understand blockchain, struggled to find applications for it in their organizations but in the meantime blockchain evangelists have continued to preach at conferences and panel discussions creating a FOMO (fear of missing out) in companies and wasting valuable time and mind space. Its time will come, just not yet.

Digital transformation needs to be sustainable – meaning the company needs to be able to maintain a new state of being for a significant enough period to be able to cash in the purported value created by the technology. This also relates to the patience needed in such a transformation to allow for the new business model to run through a few cycles and iterations before it starts delivering value. Too often the organization demands immediate results and the only thing this drives is short-term thinking which could completely compromise the long-term value creation potential. e-Commerce "flash sales" have provided the perfect opportunity for companies to lose money in the short-term to show amazing sales while doing pretty much nothing for the longer-term prospects of the channel. Flash sales are amazingly effective in driving awareness and trial but are more often used to kick up sales numbers with completely unsustainable pricing.

Digital transformation can and should touch any and every part of the business operations and organization. Most of the main body of the book, Chapter 2 onwards, will focus on how digital could impact different aspects of a consumer facing business. Quite often true potential can only be realized with a seamless end-to-end implementation which speaks against restricting the digital function to be siloed inside the traditional functions in an organization most notable marketing and commercial. The most discussed structural problem of the times as pertaining to digital transformation has been the blurred lines between brand marketing, shopper marketing and actual purchase (leave aside manufacturing). It helps massively to take an end-to-end view of the digital consumer journey, but our existing organizations make it virtually impossible to do that.

Digital transformation does not end until a new normal has been achieved. Often companies end up with a bunch of "ideas guys" who come in from the outside, acting as thought leaders to inspire change but with little empowerment to make change happen. It is important that the role of the transformation executive is not seen to stop at strategy but is seen to include actually steering the organization into making the right investments and resource allocation to make the new reality come to life. This would need companies to be much bolder in putting more resources at the transformation executive's disposal. The measure of success should not be bragging rights for who has managed to hire the most exciting millennial digital guys who know all the terminology but who has driven clear profits from doing the hard work of embedding something new into the business.

In summary thus, digital transformation is about finding and embedding the right technology into the company to change the business to make more profits. (See Figure 1.1.) But what are these technologies? Are there any broad governing trends that makes these current times more exciting and riper for change?

Alright, now that you've stuck with me through this 20-odd page rant and heard all my complaints, it's time to be less opinionated and a bit more factual in the next section, where we will look at some cool technologies that will likely shape the decade ahead.

The Technology That Powers It

During my consulting years there was always an archetypical change management guru at the firm, who had all the trappings of being a guru. He said obnoxious things in senior meetings, he changed plans the night before a big presentation, he had ketchup stains on his dress-shirt and a sprinkling of dandruff on his coat. He was also full of great ideas as you would imagine and would repeatedly urge leaders to Get to The Bottom of The Iceberg

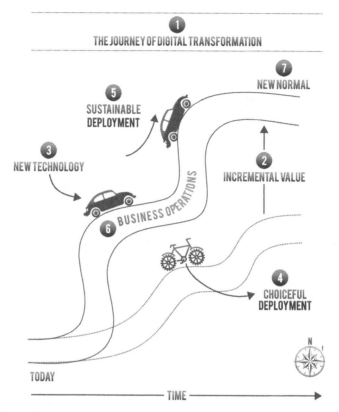

FIGURE 1.1 What is digital transformation?

or Peel the Onion or Climb Down the Ladder of Inference. Where I am trying to go to with this is the following – underneath all the incredible use cases and value creation opportunities confronting us, there are, there must be some broad underlying evolutions in technology or in the state of being of the world. And how great would it be to uncover the perfect underlying formula for change and then get back on top of the iceberg, unpeel the onion and climb up the ladder of inference to end up with endless value creation opportunities.

However, it is quite impossible to understand everything that is going on, and even if one did it would change pretty soon after. But, here below, I am going to make a start and try listing out the big underlying shifts as I see them. I would encourage you to reflect on these and think up some more if there are indeed.

Later in this book, I will try to link these shifts to actual use cases, particularly in the consumer goods and services space.

Accuracy and accessibility of geospatial intelligence

It was sometime in the fall of 2011 and my wife and I discovered the "Find my phone" app. Apple had launched their Find my iPhone app a year before and we were ecstatic that now we could also find my Android phone with this app. After proceeding to download it, we went ahead and connected to each other on the service so we could each find the other's phone if it were misplaced. It did not take us long to realize that this also meant we would both know exactly where the other person was at all times and being still in the first year of our marriage it felt like a pretty major commitment. A week into using it we had a somewhat short dinner conversation.

"Babe, should we delete the app?" "Yes".

The official reason was that it takes too much battery. Ten years on it's becoming very clear that the ability to know with accuracy, where you are, where anyone else (who allows you to know where he/she is) is, where any place is, who is at that place (if that person has consented) or where an object is (like a bus or a delivery rider), could bring incredible value to businesses. This is what I term as Geospatial intelligence. I am writing this in the middle of a COVID-19-induced semi-lockdown out of Singapore and the Safe-entry service, which allows you to check-in and -out of places, and the Trace-together service that tracks who else you have been in close proximity to so as to keep track of your risk of infection, have been valuable assets for the community to stay safe[6]. Park the thoughts on privacy, I will address those later.

Over the next decade, this space will continue to evolve: as more and more Geospatial information is generated by many more devices, either personal or business-owned, with improvements in the accuracy of pinpointing where a specific device is, with better ability to analyze incredibly large amounts of geospatial data, and with the ready availability of services for businesses and consumers to utilize this intelligence. While Google maps, Ride hailing, or even Pokémon Go, have already become indispensable services for us today we have yet to see large-scale application of Geospatial Intelligence in the consumer goods industry. Imagine a world where companies provide consumers with a differentiated value proposition based on a location they have been to in the past or a location that they currently find themselves at in the present.

Total availability and commoditization of personal devices

In early 2016, an unknown company took the smartphone market in India by storm, or threatened to do so, by announcing the launch of the Freedom 251 phone, to be priced at 251 INR[7]. What followed was pandemonium and then a series of Fyre Festival[8]-style cringeworthy events which ended in arrests and controversy and – no phone. But there was an interesting learning underneath this controversy, the fact that personal devices were fast becoming a commodity and almost complete penetration was inevitable. And in that environment, being a first mover and having ownership over a massive installed base would allow you to become a gatekeeper for anyone who wanted to reach that installed base of consumers. Giving away a device for free in the near term would pay itself back in the long-term as you are able to monetize the consumer base.

Later that same year Reliance launched the Jio 4G service; with aggressive pricing it gained 100 million subscribers in less than six months and is now the leading telecom operator in India[9]. The strategy was the same, except this time executed by a far more reputable and resourceful company. Jio now controls access to 100s of millions of subscribers and is monetizing these well with a slew of use cases. But right now, it all comes down to the smartphone. And the smartphone did not really have much penetration ten years ago. So, what is likely to happen ten years from now?

Interestingly, if we look at adoption of technologies over the last several decades in the US, the path to >80% adoption shrank from say 20-odd years for the Color TV, to ten-odd years for the smartphone[10]. We will see more household and personal devices emerge over the next decade, potentially replacing the smartphone completely. This ability to be a constant companion of every consumer in ways that are more and more passive and in the background (think something that tracks your mood and recommends an activity based on that), as scary as it sounds, could become the norm and would have immense applicability for consumer-facing businesses.

Artificial intelligence and machine learning

In 2017, Netflix dropped the AlphaGo documentary. It chronicled the journey of the Deepmind[11] owned AlphaGo computer program as it competed against Lee Sedol, the world's best Go player, ending in a 4–1 defeat of Lee and his subsequent retirement from the game. Go is more complicated for a computer to learn than chess, after the first two moves there are only ~400 possible moves in chess compared to the ~130,000 moves possible in Go. While a computer can analyze all possible chess moves and their outcomes with accuracy, it would be practically impossible for all the world's computing power to analyze all possible moves in Go. AlphaGo uses deep learning, meaning it studies past games and plays against itself, and in the process teaches itself to recognize patterns to come up with moves that eventually end in Lee Sedol's defeat. Especially interesting is move 37 in one of the games, which everyone initially thought was a mistake, but which later proved to be a tactic too complex for the human mind to fathom, which the AlphaGo program had taught itself.

This whole universe full of terms and technologies, including: Artificial intelligence, Advanced analytics, Big data, Machine learning, Deep learning, Data mining, etc. are used interchangeably all the time. This area represents an underlying trend which is already making our lives better, but we have only begun to scratch the surface. Broadly, let us think of this trend as being made up of four elements: First, the improved ability to capture more data from diverse sources like location data from personal devices that we discussed earlier. Second, our ability to connect it to data acquired from a variety of other sources e.g., Person X who has been in location Y also used his credit card to pay for item Z in store Q. Third, our ability to make sense of this information and, more importantly, predict future events based on it e.g., Person X is likely to be in same location next week and in high likelihood will buy item Z again. And finally, our ability to layer usability on top of it all by providing

SETTING THE CONTEXT

applications and dashboards etc. for individuals and businesses to actually make use of.

This example is, of course, far too easy: Imagine a world where you have millions of data points generated from hundreds of different data sources which are completely disconnected, by hundreds of millions of consumers every day. Imagine the effort needed to ensure this data is captured, connected, analyzed and presented and you begin to understand the level of difficulty and the reason why data scientists are hard to find and so well paid. Over the next decade this will become easy and accessible for companies and the applications and value creation from this technology will become more obvious. There is a version of the future where many human decisions will be made by computers using deep learning, and like most of the technologies I speak about here, this is a scary possibility but also a very exciting one if you choose to look at it that way.

Automated content creation and rendering

My five-year-old just finished the second season of *Paw Patrol* (or was it the third?). For the unaware, *Paw Patrol* is a Canadian animated series featuring a young boy and his team of six pups, who all have different skills, which they use to solve problems. Each season has 26 episodes with two segments in each episode. With five seasons already aired and a couple more in the works we have got 300 stories aired so far. The amazing thing about this show is that each segment has the same storyline. Someone gets into trouble and calls the *Paw Patrol* which deploys two pups with their skills to the rescue. During the rescue it is realized that one additional pup is needed who is then summoned. The problem is solved, and the pups get a treat. The storyline is so uniform that it would lend itself very well for a computer to write it and this anecdote is but a small introduction to the vast world of possibilities and pitfalls of synthetic media.

Synthetic media is a catch-all phrase which essentially refers to the ability to generate stories, images, videos, speech, sounds or any other type of media automatically from scratch. The technology is itself quite strongly linked to

21

AI and machine learning as discussed earlier. An easy way to understand it is to think of a program which understands all the different structural elements that make up a piece of media at an extremely detailed level of granularity; e.g., an image of a face. The program then trains itself by looking at millions of images of faces, deconstructing each into its individual structural components and learning how the different bits go together in forming a real image. With this learning, the program can then create hyper-realistic combinations of randomly chosen sub-elements to make up a piece of media, in this case a face, that looks very real.

The possibilities for this technology are exciting to say the least, not just for the media and entertainment industry but also for the consumer sector which relies heavily on rich media to drive awareness and preference for its products and services. Unfortunately, the technology has gotten itself a bad name with its ventures in pornography and totalitarian politics and it will continue to be seen with suspicion in a world where creative genius is considered to be almost exclusively a human endeavor and there is value attributed to authenticity. Perhaps we will see a world where artists will unionize and strike against synthetic creative shops! But like all things this too will change, and I expect there to be ample value creation based on synthetic media over the next decade. Say one day you wake up to find out that Emma Watson is not real, and all her imagery has been synthetically put together in a production house, would it matter? She is still awesome, and it is not like you were ever going to meet her.

Implants and sensors

My wife, at some point in her career, worked in the diabetes care and blood sugar monitoring space where the very successful incumbent technology involves making a small prick in your finger and allowing a tiny strip to absorb a droplet of blood which then gets analyzed in a handheld device. She told me back then that their key disruption risk came not from other medical device companies, but from Google. Back in 2014 Google was working on developing contact lenses that would measure blood sugar levels from tears[12], that project seems to have not yielded desired results. But research continues; including on lenses that can measure blood sugar levels in blood vessels behind the eyelids. This example is just one of several ways of extracting information from the human body either actively as in the case of haptics and touch-based technology or passively as in the case of smart watches. Add to this the ability of adding sensors on products or machinery and we can visualize an interesting map of the world where there is incredible trackability of triggers, needs and responses that can be beneficial to companies.

As far as wearables go, the technology will continue to evolve along three key dimensions: The actual device itself, the level of integration with the human body, and as a consequence what the device reads the ability of the device to alter human behavior. The device itself could take many different form factors and will most likely be a combination of several including Earbuds, Glasses, Clothing, Gloves, Implants, Patches, Jewelry (that includes Watches), Motion detection, Voice detection (e.g., Alexa) etc. We will see devices passively gathering more and more information directly and suggesting actions to us. Especially in the medical diagnostics space this has obvious uses, but we will also see applications in the recreational space. Wearables, in the form of exoskeletons for example, could also provide real time physical feedback to our bodies for applications that involve coaching on specific movements or in gaming.

RFID technology and IOT technology are two different environments which will both see useful advancements. RFID essentially means putting tags on items which when triggered with a signal, respond with the identity of the item the tag is stuck on. This technology will improve in terms of cost per tag going to low single digit cents per tag, in the ability of the tag to relay more complex information back when triggered, and improvement in the range. IOT technology is more advanced both in terms of the sensor and the network which connects with it. It is different from other wireless networks that we use today, because of its lower power usage, longer range and lower device costs. In all three areas of power, range and sensor costs we will see major advancements in the coming years and as the world aligns on specific protocols and standards, think GSM vs. CDMA phones in the 2000s, this will become financially feasible for companies to adopt on a large scale.

It's easy to see that the ability to embed a sensor on every consumer and every asset in the supply chain that puts together the product that is eventually delivered to the consumer, will unlock an opportunity for companies to get a much better handle on predicting demand for products, capturing the demand at the right time and fulfilling it in the most efficient way possible through the value chain.

5G and connectivity

I am sure most of us remember all too well the mid–late 90s when getting on the internet involved struggling with a dial-up modem which relied on patchy networks, not to mention the likelihood of power blackouts if you were lucky enough to grow up in an emerging market. Every time a friend sent you an image or a short video, you would watch it frame by frame as data tumbled along at impossibly slow speeds. How lucky we are to be living in a world where internet speeds are quite amazing and data costs at least not as exorbitant as they used to be. So, this begs the question, with 5G coming, where do we go from here and which new opportunities will be unlocked as a result of it?

As we delve into this notion of connectivity there are three key points we need to understand and acknowledge about 5G. How is 5G better than 4G? What use cases would that improvement unlock? Is there a 6G? Let us start by dimensionalizing the improvement that 5G brings in connectivity. If your uninformed answer to this is that 5G is better than 4G because it is faster, then you are right. But how much faster is it? An average two-hour movie could take us six minutes to download on 4G, 5G will allow us to make that download in four seconds. That is incredible, and perhaps not entirely necessary if all you are doing with 5G is downloading movies. But beyond the speed, 5G also has several other critical advantages, most important of which is the total capacity of the network and the latency or the time lag between data transfer which could be as low as one millisecond.

And herein comes the utility. A lot of the technologies we discussed earlier around IOT and connected devices and connected people would rely on billions of pieces of hardware and devices constantly communicating with each other and such a dense network of communication can only function effectively with the high capacity and high speeds that 5G offers. Think autonomous vehicles, smart cities, smart manufacturing, connected homes and all other use cases popular culture and tech magazines have been touting as the next best thing to watch next year for the last five years. All of these will start coming true much faster than they have in the past.

So, all this sounds great, but we must be realistic about the timelines. 5G was only just introduced to the world in 2019. Countries, cities and telecom providers will take time to have it made available to consumers and it will take time for its penetration to grow to a point where the use cases we speak of will be possible. This is partly because 5G needs nodes (think of it as cellphone towers) that are far more densely packed in the geography than 4G does to offer the same service, and it would also take the entirety of the world's installed base of devices to be changed into 5G compatible devices. By some estimates it could take us until the middle of the next decade to reach an installed base on 5G that lends itself to adoption of 5G dependent use cases and by that calculation this next decade will most likely belong to 5G. That answers the next question – we do not need to think about 6G yet. Period. So, if you are a person or a company in one of the early adopter markets for 5G, you have definitive reason to rejoice.

Efficiency and modularity in software development

"The greatest trick the devil ever pulled is to convince the world that he does not exist" – so went the famous line from that amazing movie *The Usual Suspects*. Likewise, one of the greatest tricks that start-ups, particularly late-stage start-ups have pulled is to convince the world that, somehow, they do things more efficiently than big corporates. I am flashing back to my time in the start-up world and as the owner of a business line within the group, the annual product-planning process was easily the most critical and also the most intrigue-filled event of the year. We all submitted heavily loaded-up requests on what features we needed built in our part of the app and what followed was a three-day-long pow wow, sometimes with real objects and strong words thrown all around. In the end there was never enough software development capacity, and everyone came away slightly unhappy. Oh, and whatever was indeed agreed to be fit into the product backlog hardly ever made it out in time and as agreed. The whole thing definitely did not make us feel like we are at the cutting edge of the tech world.

So, what changes are we likely to see in software and application development and operations? I am personally far too much of a non-techie to write about specific new technologies and coding languages, but I will highlight what I think are the broad directions in which a recipient of or an enterprise user of software can expect the world to move in. To start with, let us consider modularity. Applications have started over the last several years to be built into smaller and smaller component modules or services that all interact with each other via APIs[13]. This trend will continue, and while breaking down a monolithic application into sub-units adds complexity of managing communication between the sub-units, it is a far more efficient way to build and update applications. Next, let us consider AI assisted development. I say assisted because I have seen firsthand how the genius of one incredible developer is worth at least ten average developers and it is hard for me to believe that AI can take over development completely. But there are parts to the application development process, like testing or also development of some rather straightforward services or modules, which will become completely automated and would help increase the efficiency of existing development teams.

Computational power could see a major revolution, as would new more effective forms of data storage. Both the ability to compute a large amount of data and store large amounts of data are necessary for us to have any of the other technologies highlighted above (IOT, AI) to become fully feasible in their entire potential. Technologies like quantum computing or DNA data storage[14], which are either being tried out or being heavily researched, will need to see the light of the day and gain massive adoption for this to be possible.

Finally, we will also see evolution in the way the enterprise buyer and software provider relationship works with several new commercial models. Like increasing usage of low-code application development where companies build their own applications by essentially using a drag-and-drop type approach without having to write a single line of code, with server-less offerings where companies pay for actual usage rather than for blocked-out capacity, which often goes underutilized. Or, almost all companies adopting a hybrid cloud model, with most of the data stored and applications run in multiple cloud solutions.

Personal data privacy and security

July 2015, and the world woke up to the news of some self-righteous hacking group of vigilantes threatening to release user details of thousands of adulterers or potential adulterers from the Ashley Madison website[15]. For those in the unknown, Ashley Madison was a sort of a match-making site for married folks who were looking for some side action. What followed was nothing short of carnage, with data dumps into the dark web, lawsuits and counter-lawsuits, and blackmails, suicides, opinion pieces – the whole works. And this pattern has repeated itself, both before and after 2015, in several high-profile data leaks; including platforms we all use (assuming Ashley Madison is not one of them) like Adobe, eBay, LinkedIn, My Fitness Pal and Yahoo, in case anyone still uses Yahoo. And these days you won't even need to be a talented hacker to find out enough about pretty much any person you'd want just by being smart about how to use social media and search to scrape everything about a person off the public domain. So that begs the question, where is all this heading to over the next decade?

This is not a question merely about technology, although technology is one key part of the answer. As important are the consumers' changing attitudes to personal data privacy, the value equation and economics around personal data exchange and of course the evolving legal framework which governs it. These four elements of technology, attitudes, economics and regulation will push and pull at each other as the world haphazardly progresses to a new normal on data privacy over the next few years. A bit like how man-buns went from being a shocking affront to decency, to a kind of interesting look, to a much sought after "steal-yo-girlfriend" look, to no one really caring about them anymore. As far as data privacy goes, we are still in the shocking affront stage, but I think this will change.

First and simple, technology. Of course, there will be better ways to encrypt personal information and there is a lot of progress happening on anonymizing personal data but with the advent of AI and machine learning this progress is made null as algorithms are once again able to pinpoint the identity of the person behind all the anonymity based on behavioral pattern recognition. Technology will keep trying to make it harder to decipher real identities behind a digital footprint by enabling computation and services to be rendered on encrypted data without having to decrypt it so the identity is never revealed in the first place and by splitting the services to be performed across multiple providers so no-one ever sees the whole identity. But personally, I think this is a losing battle, and perhaps there is just no way to be entirely data secure anymore. Unless the cost of committing a data breach is just much bigger than the potential benefit, data breaches will continue to happen. Blockchain might play a role here and more on that later in this section.

Consumers' attitudes will change too and, in a way, this will reduce the potential benefit a data breach might provide to a criminal. As an example, one of my many bad habits is that I absolutely love to dig my nose, many times in public, and my wife can vouch for the fact that this is very disgusting behavior. By virtue of writing this here I have taken away any monetary value a fraudster might have extracted from me by threatening to make this information public and I have now reduced the value of this privacy infringement to zero. Stretch that to even difficult things like infidelity, financial distress or chronic health conditions. Difficult to imagine but not impossible, remember we got used to man-buns pretty fast.

From an economics point of view, companies will finally start paying for consumer data in real currency and stop fleecing consumers into believing that amazing services like social media are "free". Consumers on the other hand will make that independent evaluation of the price of privacy and most likely allow for data sharing in exchange for value. Regulation in this case is unfortunately going through a "US war on drugs" type of situation. Where instead of legalizing and controlling the industry, we banned it and made it violent, opaque and profitable and essentially no-one benefited. Not even the criminals because most of them die early or rot in prison. Over-regulation in this space is likely going to incentivize criminals to think of more nefarious ways of stealing data, drive up cost of data protection and disallow market forces to just let the value exchange around personal data privacy stabilize around a comfortable point. But just as weed is slowly getting legalized, we will see a gradual lifting of over-regulation and a data marketplace will establish itself.

Blockchain and distributed ledger

Amazon.com started selling for the first time in July 1995, I will let it sink in that this was 25 years ago. In the first five years the sales grew to ~3 USD billion and then the dot-com bubble burst. What followed was a somewhat less exciting 3x growth from 2000–2005 and sales have continued to grow 3–4x every five years since then, albeit on a much higher base. In hindsight the 2000–2005 period appears like a bit of a lull when the world was kind of "over the internet" post bubble and was just sorting itself out and catching up. When the world was finally ready though, the assets that were built, for example the installed capacity in bandwidth for internet usage, were right there to be utilized at low cost and that majorly helped use cases like Amazon.com to prosper. As reference, 76% of total digital wiring was laid down in the US during the dot-com era, cost of bandwidth dropped to 90% by 2004, and, as late as 2005, as much as 85% of the broadband capacity in the US was still unused.[16] I think we are in this lull period when it comes to Blockchain, that started a couple of years ago after the insane bitcoin price peak of around 15k USD around end of 2017. Massive interest and excitement, followed by speculation, followed by realization that work still needs to be done on getting the world used to it, followed by a 2.5-year-odd lull. Perhaps this might make way for profitable use cases to emerge and gain traction in due time, we will have to see.

Now, I am not going to answer the "What is blockchain?" question in all technicality, there are hundreds of resources on the internet to understand the nitty gritty details. I think what is more important is to understand what it is about blockchain that makes it exciting and then to think about how this could gain momentum and service the world better over the coming decade. The basic underlying notion here is decentralization of authority and that has the potential to improve operational efficiency, security and market efficiency which I will explain here. What blockchain does is it stores information about, say historical transactions in any given market, in blocks of information which are attached to each other in a chain, copies of which are stored on multiple nodes (or in multiple places). So, to start with there is no central authority where you have to get your transaction registered, stored or retrieved and this drives a lot of operational efficiency. Think about today's constraint of not being able to make transactions over the weekend because banks are closed. Because there is no central authority storing your information it is harder to hack and change it, you would essentially have to change it on all the nodes, or 51% theoretically, which would be impossibly expensive when there are millions of nodes. This makes it more secure. Just with these two benefits, blockchain can find a lot of application in the banking, healthcare, government sector etc. – any place where a central authority handles confidential personal information and there is an opportunity to make service provision less time and resource constrained.

The more interesting part of blockchain is this, to become a node you must earn the right to be one by doing some work to prove yourself, and you get compensated in the process. So, copies of this historically accurate record of transactions will sit with entities that have earned the right to qualify additional transactions and update that record. To make it more practical let us take TripAdvisor as an example. This application has essentially taken away the right to qualify hotels from some certification agency or the hotel brands themselves, and given it to the people, of course to rate a hotel you have to earn the right to rate it by staying at that hotel. Now stretch your imagination to think what if: The price of the hotel room was completely dependent on the TripAdvisor rating, there was no TripAdvisor company running the platform in the first place, and to close the loop the price available to you as a consumer was dependent on the quality and usefulness of your reviews to other consumers. And soon you would start to understand the potential of a decentralized model – more on this in subsequent chapters of this book.

Robotics and 3D printing

As soon as the lockdown restrictions in Singapore lifted, after the first serious wave of COVID-19, my wife, daughter and I unanimously agreed that we must make way to the closest Haidilao hotpot restaurant[17]. For those who have not been to one yet, please do find your way to one, the food is amazing, the service top-notch and it really exemplifies the points I made about real value creation in the first chapter. So, in this post-COVID world we made our order through a tablet, which is quite commonplace these days; but lo and behold a robot delivered our food to our table and the whole restaurant was buzzing with food-carrying robots who politely stayed out of each other's, and other people's, ways and delivered your food to your table. There was someone waiting a small cluster of tables who actually served the food but besides being just fascinating for my five-year-old, and for me admittedly, it focused the employee on the more important bit of customer service rather than the transport of food from the kitchen to the table. Everybody wins.

Over the next decade we will start seeing more practical applications of robotics in our lives in part made possible by previously mentioned technologies like IOT sensors and connectivity but also from the ever-decreasing sizes of appliances and devices. Miniaturization of hardware has been driven primarily by the development of smaller PCBs (printed circuit boards) and 3D printing has opened up a plethora of possibilities in cramming as much circuitry in as little a physical space as possible by making possible multiple layers, smaller components, liquid ink with electronic functionalities and more effective embedding of components. Reducing size and cheaper component and manufacturing costs will open more practical applications for robotics including drones in all sizes and a variety of other personal and household gadgets. Add to it the layer of AI and these gadgets will take on more and more complex jobs to our benefit.

In an overly simplified way, any mechanical operation is essentially physically changing the position of an object from point A to point B – this might be installing a part on an assembly line, delivering an e-commerce order to the doorstep, a food item to a restaurant table, or people from one destination to another. By the end of the next decade there will be very few menial tasks left where there is no robotic alternative available to human effort at an acceptable cost. The facility of performing a lot of these operations remotely will also change the location strategy of our supply chains as the traditional paradigm of mass manufacturing for economies of scale might not hold true anymore. All in all, we will end up in a world where we spend our time waiting tables rather than bringing food out from the kitchen, or in other words we will focus human attention on areas which require a human touch; what those areas exactly are is left to be seen.

So, there you have it, my somewhat imperfect list of the ten technologies, the evolution of which will create value creation opportunities for the world. It is not exhaustive for sure and it is also not static, so maybe there are technologies I missed and perhaps there are new ones that will emerge. Some from this list will just fall off and maybe some will get morphed into something else. But this is a good start, and I would suggest any executive who is looking to get started on a digital transformation journey to keep a pulse on these and similar technologies as breakthroughs happen and applications are found. Understanding this is really at the foundation of keeping the idea factory alive.

Applications are everywhere in all sectors, including energy and finance and healthcare and telecom. But I meant for this book to be about the consumer goods and services space and beyond technology there will be mid-long-term shifts in consumers, both in the practicalities around their lives and the attitudes consumer adopt towards their environment. Next, I will walk through what I think are the most interesting of these consumer shifts to be mindful of.

The Key Consumer Trends of The Next Decade

"Every new generation adds a new lifetime", if you ever end up with me in a whiskey bar, you will hear me say. And I will start off by explaining it here. I am in my late thirties, my father is in his late sixties and my grandfather, if he were still alive, would likely be in his nineties. My grandfather had a childhood spent in the rural Konkan region on the western coast of India and then re-invented himself as a student in my hometown of Nashik where he also started his career and was an established professor before he died. Three lifetimes, a childhood, a formative student-hood plus early career and a distinguished professional life as a professor. My father did all that and a couple of years ago faced the question, "What now?". He has recently taken on his fourth lifetime in a quest to rethink how architecture should be taught, starting with an online learning asset called Ideamoocs. Do check it out, it's nifty and rich.

I will likely face the "What now?" question a good 15–20 years before my father did and already now, I am starting to try to transition into my fourth lifetime.

A wonderful childhood in Nashik, student-hood and early career in Europe, a professional career in Singapore and hopefully something different to start over the next few years. I will pursue my fourth lifetime until, say, I am in my late fifties then I will need a fifth and then a sixth when I am in my eighties. Things have changed so much since my father was my age that it is not possible anymore to simulate how your life would be when you reach your next lifetime purely based on parental reference.

In other words, the past is now an insufficient reference for predicting the future. But we must see the clues and try to think up a future to benefit from it by staying ahead of it. In this chapter, that's what I am going to do by highlighting the ten major consumer trends that are identifiable today which will stay with us for the next decade, and also examine the implications of these trends and the opportunities they will create in launching digitally enabled value-creating businesses. Some of these talk about the practicalities of being a person in tomorrow's world and some talk about the spirituality of being a person, but they all eventually end up in shaping consumption, which is what us businesses look to profit from. These businesses could be online or offline businesses and after each of the consumer trends below, I will list a couple of apps that are capitalizing on the trend today. This is for illustration only and I am sure there are more and better examples out there for you to find.

The changing shape of households

Alone-ness over Loneliness. A couple of years ago I came across the Korean concept of "Honjok", probably something my Korean wife mentioned in passing. It is a word made up of two component words, "Honja" meaning alone and "Gajok" meaning family; so, essentially a single person family. You have likely heard of the Japanese term of "Hikikomori" which refers to people who choose to withdraw themselves from society and spend months, and sometimes years, locking themselves into their homes. Honjok is different from Hikikomori, in the sense that its accepted as a pretty normal way of choosing to be, and there is an entire plethora of commercial activity surrounding a Honjok person, including eating out alone, going to karaoke alone, watching movies alone and so on, and it's a perfectly acceptable way of living one's life in Korea as it should rightfully be.

I think there are four main ways in which the shape of the average household will change over the next couple of decades. The first one that we all know about, as it's much talked about, is the ageing population, which by 2030 will be 1.4 billion strong[18], defined as people over 60 years of age. This age group also has more money to spend and less need for having a high investment or saving rate. Secondly, single person households will grow across the world with an expected 120 million single person households added between 2016 and 2030[19]. Thirdly, more and more children will continue to live with their parents longer into adulthood than they do today because of the rising cost of home ownership and the personal financial situation of new entrants into the job market not allowing for easy affordable access to homes. Over the last decade, after the Great Recession, the percentage of adults in the age 25–34 in the US who live with their parents went up, and thanks to COVID now 52% of young adults in the US lived with one or both of their parents[20]. And this trend will continue over the next decade[21]. Finally, female headship, households where the woman is the primary decision maker is becoming more and more explicit and accepted. Today, in approximately one out of three heterosexual dual-income marriages in the US, the wives earn more than the husband and I see this number only growing over the next decade.

These trends in the changing household profiles bring with them a host of opportunities to create value for the newly shaped households. Apps and use cases designed with older people in mind including easily navigable UX but allowing for richer post-retirement lives like Audible[22] with its audiobooks, or Epicurious[23] with recipes will enjoy easy popularity. Hopefully, I will not see the day my Mom gets onto Tik Tok, because she will have her own set of platforms to go to. Platforms designed for single persons focused on allowing consumers to enjoy life on their own or letting them connect with other individuals, beyond Tinder of course, such as Meetup[24] will also continue to emerge.

The changing personal financial situation

Slumdogs and Millionaires. During my business school summer, back in 2009, a bunch of us did a course titled "Building business in India" and as a part of the course, we had an organized excursion into the slum of Dharavi. Dharavi, with its population of over a million residents is one of the largest slums in the world and entering into the roughshod borders of the slum I was amazed to see that it was an entire completely self-sufficient city within a city. There was a residential part of the slum where hundreds of thousands lived quite amicably with each other under dire conditions but respectful of each other's right to survive. And there was an entire commercial section of the slum with thousands of businesses, including a major export business in recycled plastic. That night we celebrated the end of the two-week course in a newly opened upscale bar, shelling out 15 dollars for a cocktail. That has been the irony of Mumbai for decades and that is turning out to be the reality the world over as we head into the next decade.

Three important trends will mark the rich–poor equation over the next decade starting with the simple fact that the rich will get richer and the poor will stay poor. The rich, defined as households with expenditure of over 110 USD per day, while making up only 4% of the global population will account for a quarter of the household consumption. In North America, all the growth in expenditure over the next decade will be driven by rich households while the share accounted by the middle class will stay stagnant, the same in Europe. Secondly, a large middle class will fuel growth and expenditure in Asia which, by 2030, will make up a significant part of the global middle class population of 5.5 billion souls[25]. While China's "Upper" middle class drives spending for the first half, India's current "Lower" middle class could fuel this expenditure in the second half of the decade and beyond. Thirdly, the savings rate which had risen post the Great Recession has declined over the last few years, especially for the middle class, and will continue to decline over the next decade after perhaps a short-lived recovery post-COVID19. The average savings rate in the US after overall expenditure, has declined 16.6 percentage points since 2010 and is now in the low single digits[26], and this trend will result in ever lower rates in asset and wealth accumulation.

Technology and digital transformation can play a role in providing value to consumers as they undergo these changes. As the rich get richer and spend more, it creates room for a host of online services and e-commerce, which is rooted primarily in convenience and variety and not in price discounting like the boutique hotel platform Mr. and Mrs. Smith[27]. The explosion of middle class spenders in China has already spawned a revolution of digital transformation there, and there is a clear opportunity to innovate for the middle class in countries like India with use cases that are tailor made for the local environment, such as Dunzo[28] which took the traditional errand-boy occupation and made it go digital. On the flip side, as the middle class in Europe and North America looks to make the most of the stagnation, we will see unprecedented price and discount seeking behavior which will create opportunities for marketplaces rooted in creating price transparency. Finally, with lower appetite for asset accumulation overall we will see more demand for a sharing economy, be it rides or homes or office space or kitchens.

A growing sense of responsibility

Turning rags into riches. Social and environmental responsibility seems to have skipped two generations, or at least where I am from. My grandfather, an incredibly gentle and generally optimistic personality always re-used everything. Those of you who grew up in India in the 80s and 90s would know the annual ritual of buying new books and then crafting paper covers for all of them. Notebook and textbook covers in school for me were pages from annual reports of companies he invested in. Every half-liter pouch of milk was carefully emptied, snipped, washed and then used to pack lunch sandwiches for school. Fast forward 30 years and I am unpacking a 3 USD-worth charger cable shipped from China in a plastic bag, inside a box with bubble wrap, inside another plastic bag with three A4-sized sheets of paper with all sorts of documentation. But there is still hope. My five-year-old, who was a "planet protector" in school for a week, regularly reminds me not to waste water and keeps switching off everything in the house behind me. So maybe awareness skipped a couple of generations, but it is back.

This underlying trend of consumers being more mindful of the impact of their consumption on the environment and society will get reinforced by a few facilities the next decade will provide. Social media has made expression of displeasure a lot easier and a lot more visible, people quickly find other fellow displeased personalities and an opinion very quickly turns into a movement. Consumer sentiment on plastic pollution including on reusable straws for example, first emerged in 2017 and within two years, related Google searches grew 20x and we are facing plastic straw bans in several countries today.[29]

There is also a lot more visible research available in the public domain and consumers get educated very fast on key topics. Pro-vegan documentary, *The Game Changers* became the best-selling documentary of all time on iTunes – within a week after its release, even if it was widely criticized as being selective in the facts presented, and this was even before it was released on Netflix. Companies, in turn, are able to read consumer feedback relatively quickly and more often than not tend to do the right thing to deal with it, as brushing things under the carpet has become difficult and has proven to backfire rather direly. In 2015, Apple famously apologized and changed its policy for not paying artists and musicians during the three-month free trial period for Apple Music after Taylor Swift tweeted her displeasure to her now 85 million+ followers.[30] Perhaps most interestingly, bad behavior has started to be priced more and more accurately and marketplaces are popping up which allow companies and individuals to buy the right to behave badly within limits. Just in the second half of last year, carbon offset company Cooleffect reported a 700% growth in individuals buying offset credits.[31]

After a confusing first few years of antivaxxers, climate change deniers, flat-earthers and other irrational groups getting an undeserved voice, we will see emergence of reliable, independent and fact-based platforms for consumers to build valid points of view based off of. Tracking, seeding and shaping consumer attitudes in the right way will become an important use case for companies and other entities using social sentiment analysis tools like Mention.[32] By far the big opportunity will lie in setting up marketplaces to buy bad behavior credits or get rewarded for good behavior in terms of real money like Cooleffect mentioned earlier.[33] This is an interesting development I think where as a consumer you could literally "pay the price" for doing the wrong thing.

An acceptable form of homelessness

Out of work dad. A couple of years ago I took a couple of months off between jobs and after doing the satisfactory amount of travel and a couple of weeks' worth of doing absolutely nothing I started getting tired of staying at home. My solution was to hit a nice cafe and spend literally the whole day there, and I was just blown away by the fact that all cafes were full all the time. People working, studying, reading, sleeping, meeting, dating, eating, drinking, drawing, drafting, baby-sitting, gossiping etc. all day in this cafe. Ten years ago, I remember things a bit different and twenty years ago far more so. Of course, things have changed since COVID19, but I am confident that the minute the world opens up again, we will all make a beeline to spend all our money in restaurants and bars.

Consumers are spending a lot more time outdoors than at home. Eating out is outgrowing eating at home, and in the US as an example, expenditure on food away from home surpassed that on food at home in 2007 and the gap has widened ever since, with food away from home representing 54% of expenditure a couple of years ago.[34] This trend will continue for food and for other activities. Community spaces, too, are getting more and more complex, where a place would earlier either be a cafe or an office or a barber shop now it can be all the above and a lot more. Co-working spaces which combine an office space with a cafe and a meeting point are expected to grow users 2.5x just in the coming three to four years.[35] As real estate prices skyrocket, homes are getting smaller and shared. In metropolitan India, for example, apartment sizes shrank by 27% between 2014 and 2017, with Mumbai seeing a 45% reduction in size.[36] Co-living, which is a more glamorous take on "having a roommate" is on the rise and the number of beds available in the US is expected to triple in the coming few years.[37] Finally a bit of an unexpected trend, thanks to COVID will be a trend towards de-urbanization. I have heard anecdotes of families moving out of Mumbai to homes a hundred kilometers away in smaller towns with good connectivity and retail availability. This trend precedes COVID though and in key metropolitan areas in the US annual population growth rates have been declining and have even gone negative for New York, LA or Chicago with a move to Exurbs, meaning prosperous areas beyond a city's suburbs.[38]

These trends create opportunities in helping consumers make the most of their smaller homes through for example, co-living platforms like Common[39] or Ollie.[40] And as consumers spend more time outdoors, platforms that help consumers decide where and how to spend their time outside will continue to provide great utility as Yelp[41] and similar platforms have done for the last decade and more.

Accepting defeat in the war on privacy

Tinder. An unbelievably disruptive platform but hardly every spoken about in the same vein as an Uber. It started a few years after I met my wife, so I have had no use for it personally, but it had clearly taken over the lives of many a single friend. A couple of years ago, a buddy of mine shared a demonstration, where to deal with the risk of photos being considerably more attractive than the person in real life, he would use a combination of Facebook, Instagram, LinkedIn and just pure old web search to find out virtually everything about his Tinder match even before he met her. I guess everybody does this and it just goes to show how much of us is already out there on the public domain and how little we can do to avoid this. The only thing someone needs is your name and everything else is out there, so perhaps the most privacy conscious of us should stop sharing their names publicly and choose to remain eternally anonymous. I routinely use a fake name, especially when I am travelling and need to book a car or something as it just does not seem right to allow personal access to the taxi mafia in some foreign city.

So, to start with there is just too much personal information already available and searchable out there and it's growing exponentially every minute beyond control. Every day more than 300 million photos are uploaded on Facebook by over 1.73 billion daily active users,[42] this unprecedented window into the lives of the entirety of the world's consuming population is not something that can be shut instantaneously, the war on privacy is thus already lost. Consumers are starting to take an active interest in this topic, with one in three adults worldwide saying they care about privacy and are willing to act. These consumers are younger and more affluent so this trend of awareness will continue. But awareness does not mean reluctance, two out of three of these aware consumers are willing to share purchase history in return for personalized products and services. Awareness means confidence in the consent and control offered to them, with two out of three aware consumers saying they felt they could protect their privacy well today.[43]

So, over the next decade the alarmism over data sharing will give way to a more confident approach if companies are able to provide control, take consent and most of all provide real value in return. For the still worried there will be "clean-up" services like DeleteMe,[44] which only work to an extent and for the more comfortable there lies the access to a rich variety of services in return for allowing the data to be resold, a great example being 23andme[45] which provides valuable DNA analysis to consumers for a mere 99 USD but also shares the data with the likes of GSK for drug research.

Plurality of thought and habits

Garibaldi and Abortion. No, those are not connected. This first anecdote is from the time I was just starting my career in a consulting firm in the Amsterdam office. There was a secretive club in the office called the Garibaldi club, for people who had an incredible appreciation for the Italian general from the 1800s, Giuseppe Garibaldi. To become a member of the Garibaldi club you had to answer an incredibly difficult quiz about his life. There were only two members in the Garibaldi club. Perhaps today it would be easier, Garibaldi has a Facebook page, and 55 people follow that page when I last checked. On a more somber note, *Reversing Roe*, a Netflix documentary about the flips and flops of the pro and anti-abortion regulation and debate in the US, aired in 2018. Setting aside my own point of view on this topic, what really got to me was the length to which an entire almost half of a country's population was willing to go to decide and impose a way of life or a personal choice on a completely unrelated individual. And this is, of course, not merely an American phenomenon, you would only need to refer to parenting in most Asian countries in the 80s and 90s to know what I am talking about.

But there is hope that this might change with the Millennials in a big way, where perhaps in the future everyone can do and live as they please, as long as it does not hurt anyone else. For starters, people are more confident today in just being the way they want to be and making the lifestyle choices they want to make. In the US, the number of reported same-sex couples in the 2019 census was close to a million, up considerably from the 2010 census of ~650k. Incidentally, a much higher percentage of same-sex couples are now also married than merely ten years ago.[46] Consumers' attitudes towards plurality of thought and lifestyles have also changed substantially, with the live-and-let-live philosophy becoming more and more inclusive. Sticking to same-sex couples, the percentage of Americans who favored it reversed from 40% in 2004 to 60% in

2019[47] and this trend of acceptance will continue in the next decade. Regardless of who you are and what you choose to be like, it is a lot easier today to find likeminded individuals and have a reference for how to make the most of your specific condition. In April 2019, Facebook said there were around 400 million consumers participating and engaging in various Facebook groups.[48]

Companies can make the most of this consumer trend to build digitally enabled use cases that serve niche consumer needs but also allow for massive personalization, so every consumer gets exactly what he or she wants. As an example, you could shop for male fashion at 2Tall[49] if you were 6ft3in and taller or Peter Manning[50] if you were 5ft8in and under. Or if you were a sneakerhead, you might be interested in designing your own custom shoe online and having it delivered to you within three weeks on Nike By You.[51]

Value of experience and appetite for complexity

Pizza. There was a time 30 years ago when Pizza night at home in small town India was a standard issue flatbread with ketchup lathered on it, bits of shredded chicken, way too much capsicum heaped with grated Amul cheese shoved in the oven. There were no types of cheeses, cheese was just cheese that came in a can. A few years later in college, pizza had to be Dominoes or Dr. Oetkars with generous amounts of Sriracha. Then something started changing, soon it had to be thin crust, wood fired with Prosciutto from Parma and fresh Rucola and dollops of Ricotta. And now it's all of that but the dough needs to be made from flour from Puglia and there have to be roasted capers for sure and the setting needs to be reminiscent of a slightly left-wing neighborhood in Florence with bathroom tiles halfway on the side walls and graffiti on one wall and backless stools and people drinking wine by the carafe and a waitress who smells faintly of weed and La Municipal playing on repeat. That is what it takes to make a good pizza.

Consumers are not satisfied with mere products anymore; they need an experience to go along with that. There is a need to make sure a somewhat unidimensional product like a pizza is now offered to us in the form of a multi-sensory pizza-eating experience. Three out of four consumers would rather spend money on an experience than a material item.[52] But it does not just stop there, of course with us humans it never just stops anywhere. Consumers want to ladder up the experiences into more and more complex and extreme forms. I started noticing more and more friends over the last few years signing up for an Ironman triathlon so I looked it up and from 2005 to 2017 the number of registered runners for the middle-distance Ironman went up from 5000 to 130,000 finishing with an average time of a little over six hours.[53] And these "experienced" consumers more than the experience quite often want to be able to show off some badge of honor for having had this experience. A somewhat loosely related statistic, but perhaps not so much, is the growing popularity of tattoos which are sort of a product and an experience and a statement and a badge all in one. One in three Americans has a tattoo and this number increased 20% from 2012 to 2019 and[54] it's becoming so mainstream that I once attended a session on how to react appropriately to an interview candidate if he or she had a very visible neck tattoo (the right answer is to not react at all).

So there is an obvious value in companies offering more and more experiences over products and Airbnb's foray into offering experiences is an excellent example of this, they even offered online experiences during COVID.[55] And then, of course, platforms that recognize consumers for the experiences they have had and potentially create celebrities in the process will find followership, something gaming companies have achieved great success with their surrogate leagues like, for example, League of legends e-Sports and the thousands of local, regional and even neighborhood leagues[56] that have spawned around the LOL playing experience.

Overwhelming availability, choice and transparency

OJ in SF and Diamonds from HK. I am talking about the other OJ, meaning orange juice and the year was 2010. I was visiting my then girlfriend and now wife in San Francisco and she decided to show me the three most shocking bits of American excess in her five-mile radius, starting with a stack of pancakes, doused in butter and bathed in syrup at iHOP, then the endless pain medication aisle at a CVS and then Wholefoods where I had a come to Jesus moment in front of the Orange Juice section. Never in my life had I been confronted with so much choice on such a trivial purchase and yet I left the store feeling cheated that I had never been offered this totally deserved assortment before. A year later I was in Hanoi, hatching a plan to propose marriage to her and was introduced to the very difficult world of selecting the right diamond, a multivariate analysis with six key variables trying to optimize for an intangible outcome of happiness, loosely connected to a pretty binary yes or no decision. I panicked and called my brother-in-law who gave me the phone number of "his diamond guy" in Hong Kong, I do not want to generalize so let us call him Moshe. So, I called Moshe and he said, "Don't worry, tell me where she is from, your budget, and I'll buy you the optimal diamond". Later I found out that her being South Korean, the only thing that mattered was the size, so it was an easy pick, but I really needed Moshe to tell me that.

Consumers are just absolutely overwhelmed by availability especially now with the concept of an endless shelf-space. I remember in my time at an e-commerce startup merely five years ago, we had a target of crossing 4 million SKUs on the platform and the same platform today has 300 million SKUs onsite. The choice is just staggering.[57] For most purchases and particularly more complex purchases there is also just way too much unorganized information out there. So, it is taking longer and much more effort to decide which ones of the 300 million SKUs to buy and consumers are doing more research and using more consultation, like Moshe, than ever. 80% of consumers use online search and video before making purchases and 71% even do this research while standing in front of the shelf.[58] And even after this decision has been made there is FOMO, Fear Of Missing Out and consumers are in need for reassurance that they have indeed made the right decision or perhaps the flexibility to reverse a decision if indeed it was the wrong purchase. Almost one out of three apparel and footwear items ordered online are returned, and this facility of no-regret buying is one of the key reasons why this channel is seeing explosive growth[59] within fashion and apparel.

One obvious value creation opportunity which has been out there for several years is price comparison where consumers are offered free transparency, and comparison platforms monetize the traffic sent to retail through affiliate marketing commissions. This space will continue to evolve, more so with giants like Google[60] and I will speak more about this further in the book. Providing consumers with the convenience of trying out products before paying for them, through services like BNPL, Buy Now Pay Later, is another key enabler for digital commerce, with several digital payments companies playing in this space, like, for example, Klarna.[61]

Changing attitudes to education and employment

Engineer or YouTuber. Growing up there were only two career choices for me and my friends back in India, you would either become a Doctor or an Engineer. Once you were a little older and realized that it takes about a decade of intense study to become a doctor you landed on engineering. As an engineering applicant you funneled yourself into a college whose primary value proposition was seldom the education but more its selectiveness based on the level of difficulty getting in which over time had stopped having much to do with the quality of education itself. Years later, it was the same at business school. There was learning but there was also the brand and beyond selectiveness there was the ability to pay incredible sums of money as fees. So, education was about learning, about branding, about financial mettle and about selectiveness, with schools offering up branded, smart kids from moneyed families who had undergone some learning to prospective employers. A friend's 10-year-old told him recently that he wanted to grow up to be a YouTuber and so did most of his friends. My friend then proceeded to try to understand what it meant to be a YouTuber and found some examples of 20 something year old millionaires, which gave him some comfort that it was indeed a valid career path to take. But he was also terrified to know that there was no formal education available to become a YouTuber and that he was condemned to supporting his child in an endeavor where his own wealth, the kid's grades in school or his ability to get into a well renowned college had pretty much no role to play!

Consumers are getting fast accustomed to unconventional routes to career building and participating wholeheartedly in the gig economy. A couple of years ago, in the US already 36% of workers participated in the gig economy, with alternative work arrangements being their primary job.[62]

Traditional higher education structures as a result of this are being challenged as the link between a college degree and the ability to get and sustain employment starts becoming weaker and weaker. In the US, for instance, since 2010, the enrolment levels in higher education institutions have dropped consistently.[63] Far more than a centralized certification, employers are starting to rely on recommendations and ratings as a more accurate representation of a person's capability to do a specific job or provide a certain service with eight out of ten HR executives consistently contacting references for experienced positions.[64] And finally, the time limit on education is going away as consumers sign up for lifelong learning and up skill themselves many times over later in life as personal renewal becomes the norm. In spite of the narrative surrounding entrepreneurs in their mid-20s striking big, the reality is that several startup millionaires made their first million well in their 30s, and more often than not in a field that had nothing to do with their university education, or with how they started their careers.[65]

Digitally enabled marketplaces allowing learning access to consumers, like Coursera[66] have been around for a while and will continue to gain traction over the decade at the expense of formal education. Freelance marketplaces like Upwork[67] too have been around for a while, although they have changed and pivoted a few times, but this type of platform will continue to expand in its scope to include more and more complex jobs.

Social media for life reference and for self-actualization

"What's the Craic?" Five years ago, my personal trainer and good friend would shout out as he came into the gym before proceeding to destroy me in the subsequent 60 minutes. And he would spend in-between sets talking about his "Insta" where every detail of his day was carefully chronicled. Fast forward a few years and I finally got onto it myself and I unabashedly, absolutely love it. It is hard work though and I have close friends who are definitely much more devoted to it than I am where literally nothing gets done every day, no matter how mundane or special it is without snapping a picture of it and posting on Instagram. I know that conventional wisdom is to look on this sort of behavior as some sort of desperate showmanship in search for actualization and there is a sea of intellectuals passing judgement on influencers and the hollowness of it all. But let us acknowledge the fact that it is a phenomenal social movement and perhaps look under the hood to understand why it is what it is and how this can serve us well in the coming decade or more. I distinctly remember when 20+ years ago ICQ and MySpace first broke through, parents around the world were concerned as hell about kids breaking through the social barriers of family and community and actually having a conversation with people outside that immediate circle. The same parents are now making strongly worded comments about someone on the other side of the world not taking good enough care of their Rhododendrons.

Allowing to share their life experience constantly has given consumers a way to perhaps stay motivated to live fuller lives and I think this trend will continue unabated, even after the initial euphoria around some of these platforms wears off. Over 1.7 billion people worldwide are active on Facebook, a large majority of these using the platform to share what they did that day.[68] The ability to be party to someone else's daily life choices is an important reference for consumers to make richer decisions for themselves every day. Almost three out of four Instagram users make purchase decisions based on something they might have seen on the platform, and it's mostly not about paid ads but about emulating your peer group.[69] I think when people complain about this phenomenon, it's actually the lack of authenticity of paid influencers and posters who then set unrealistic personal expectations in the minds of impressionable consumers that bothers them. A comforting statistic here is the fact that your immediate circle of friends and regular folks with less than 5000 followers are four times more likely to drive engagement than celebrities with over a million followers or definitely self-styled paid influencers with over a 100k followers.[70]

So, this trend of consumers using social media as a reference for their lives will continue, and we will see amazing growth in platforms that make posting about your own life and managing social media easier and more seamless like Hootsuite[71] has done for a few years now for companies. And on the other hand, tools and platforms that allow companies and eventually individuals to find the right people to follow and right influencers to connect with like Traackr[72] will also continue to become relevant.

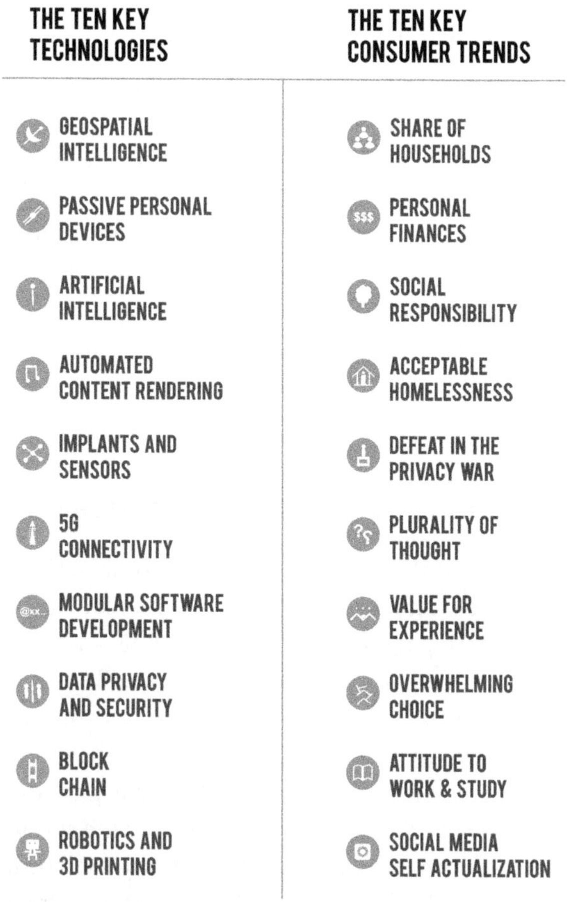

THE TEN KEY TECHNOLOGIES

THE TEN KEY CONSUMER TRENDS

THE TEN KEY TECHNOLOGIES	THE TEN KEY CONSUMER TRENDS
GEOSPATIAL INTELLIGENCE	SHARE OF HOUSEHOLDS
PASSIVE PERSONAL DEVICES	PERSONAL FINANCES
ARTIFICIAL INTELLIGENCE	SOCIAL RESPONSIBILITY
AUTOMATED CONTENT RENDERING	ACCEPTABLE HOMELESSNESS
IMPLANTS AND SENSORS	DEFEAT IN THE PRIVACY WAR
5G CONNECTIVITY	PLURALITY OF THOUGHT
MODULAR SOFTWARE DEVELOPMENT	VALUE FOR EXPERIENCE
DATA PRIVACY AND SECURITY	OVERWHELMING CHOICE
BLOCK CHAIN	ATTITUDE TO WORK & STUDY
ROBOTICS AND 3D PRINTING	SOCIAL MEDIA SELF ACTUALIZATION

FIGURE 1.2 Top ten technology and consumer trends

So, there you have it, the ten consumer trends and technology trends that I find most interesting for the coming decade. (See Figure 1.2.) Some very tactical and pragmatic, some more emotional and spiritual but all of them with the potential to shape consumption and the future of building and running businesses. In the next and final section of this introductory chapter, we will take another step back and reflect on what we talked about so far, before once again diving back into this exciting world of change.

Stepping Back Before Diving In

So, what have we discussed so far? Digital transformation needs to create value, digital transformation is motivated by change in Technology and digital transformation finds utility when it tracks Consumer trends. In this chapter, we will start discussing what an organization or an executive should do with all this information. We will discuss uncertainty and absurdity as one tries to build for the future. And finally, while we acknowledge the broad applicability for digital transformation, we will narrow our focus down to the consumer goods and services industry and get introduced to the key areas of attention that the next set of chapters in this book talk about.

Oh my God, this is already too much. Where do I start?

If you are asking yourself this, fear not, you have come to the right place. As I started working in consulting back in 2006, my first few weeks and months were all devoted to getting up to speed with the skills and tools that need to be in any consultant's arsenal. I believe this is probably the case with most professional services firms where you need to start off by learning the language that the company uses to speak to its clients. They introduced me to the seven-step problem solving process, and the firm was confident that no problem was ever too complicated or too difficult for the seven-step problem solving process. The seven steps in itself are nothing extraordinary: Define, Structure, Prioritize, Work-plan, Analyze, Synthesize and Present and I have to commend the rigor and discipline the firm builds around going through these steps implicitly or explicitly to deliver a solution to the client every single time. So, if this were so straightforward, why are some consulting projects more successful than others, why are some consulting firms more successful than others, why are some start-ups more valuable than others and why are some corporates returning better gains to shareholders than others? Can't we all just follow the seven steps and solve all our problems?.

What no one tells you is that there is a magic step in the middle, invisible, like the platform nine and three quarters from Harry Potter. Having spent the first five steps defining the problem, structuring the space you're trying to understand, deciding which parts to understand first and understand better, planning the team's time and analyzing the space, or in short having spent the first five steps improving your understanding of the situation at hand, you take a pause. And maybe just let it sink in. Take a long weekend, disengage, run a marathon, get wasted, play counter strike for 12 hours straight, make a 5000-piece jigsaw puzzle with your five-year-old. Just do not think about the problem anymore. Then walk back into the office on Monday morning stand on a chair and loudly proclaim to everyone what the answer is. And that step of changing between a reactive stance of internalizing material to a proactive and confident story-teller stance is the magic step. Then it is up to the process of synthesis and presentation, but the magic step makes or breaks the solution and there is no short answer for the magic step. It is just a reflection of who you are as a person, how you interpret a given reality, how you establish connections between different bits of insight and drive an exciting inference from it all.

For a simple problem, say adding two single digit numbers together, there is a finite amount of computational power needed, and you get a definitive answer which is always absolutely the right one. Corporate issues like "What to do in a digital transformation" are a lot more complex I am afraid, with technology changing, consumers being impacted, people's personal agendas, the stock market's expectations on returns, and the fragility of relationships with retailers and suppliers. So, although there might be an optimal and exhaustive approach for a company, it is virtually impossible to spell it out with absolute confidence. And that's where people come in, and great people can create great magic with the same understanding of a situation as everyone else. In the absence of a definitive answer to a complex problem a well informed and street-smart executive's best guess is the way to go, if the executive is actually well informed and street-smart.

My recommendation is to do this in four stages: Understand, Articulate, Argue and Commit, simple as that. We need to start our attempts at digital transformation by trying to understand as much as we can about what is happening in this world. The earlier section of this book started doing that for you by giving you snippets of the technology and consumer trends, I assume you understand your company and the industry you operate in and the people who work there. But take the time before jumping to conclusions to deepen your understanding of all these dimensions; the better you know your way around these topics the better your ability to chart a path will be. Stage 2 is for you to stand on the chair and articulate a plan for your business, much as uncomfortable as it might make you feel, as you foray into the scary and hard to fathom world of technology, you need to put that stake in the ground. And if you are well informed and street-smart, which is likely why you were hired, your narrative will be almost on point. Stage 3 is for you to argue with everyone you think might have something to add, to adjust and iterate your narrative. There is so much to be gained from constructive conflict and especially from tweaking your approach to make it more robust when people throw issues at it. And then finally Stage 4 is for you to just commit to the plan, maintain flexibility to an extent but mostly just lock it in and do not look back. Our organizations, even if we would like them to, are not built to change course within a financial year and the loss of momentum in attempting that will far outweigh the loss of committing to what might end up being only a slightly sub-par initiative.

I will dedicate the entire final chapter of this book to the "How to" of fleshing this out in much more detail. There I will provide you a blueprint and some more concrete ideas on how to build and operate this digital transformation engine in your organization. For now, I would say just walk with me and argue with me. Let me be the transformation executive who has spent time under-standing the context and let me articulate what I think the storyline is likely to be in the coming decade or so, based on but limited by what I know. And then let us argue, perhaps not in person but hopefully as you reflect on this book, in your mind at least.

The six frontiers of change in the consumer goods and services sector

The idea of the six frontiers first took seed in my mind a couple of years ago as I was starting to think through the long-term digital transformation strate-gic plan for an iconic company and brand that was set in its ways, but also had amazing people who wanted to hear how to break into the new world. There was a lot of talk about being present forward and working on things we know were happening right now but also being future back so as to trans-plant yourself into say 2035, imagine the world and start thinking about what it would take you in five-year increments to get to this idea of the future. I thought this was a very powerful way of crafting a roadmap into the future but it quickly became a somewhat esoteric exercise because either not enough time was spent on understanding the context, so we ended up with more science fiction stuff like jet packs and bionic implants or not enough allowance was given to argue on things because that just didn't fit into the culture of the company. But the concept stuck to me and I started thinking about 2035 and trying to break it down into sizeable chunks which would lend themselves well to explaining to the organization.

So that's where the six frontiers came from; I call them frontiers because I imagine a bubble of digital enablement that grows on all sides, along these six frontiers and keeps encroaching on more and more space and in the process becomes bigger and bigger and provides ever increasing value. Within each frontier I started thinking about the most exciting use cases where a collision of technology advancement and consumer behaviors would create value-adding opportunities for consumer facing companies. I restricted myself to four use cases under each frontier and made sure I could always think up four, mostly because I am a bit OCD that way. So as a result, you might find that there are some in the 24 use cases that are perhaps not as compelling, or you might think of a couple of use cases that I did not think to include. Send me a note, let's argue and I will include it in the next edition. The six chapters in the next section are organized along the six frontiers, and here they are (see Figure 1.3):

Frontier 1 – How companies reach consumers. We will look at the future of TV advertising, Out-of-home advertising, understand how personal devices and therefore the nature of social media will change and anticipate disruption in the ad creative space

Frontier 2 – How companies engage with consumers. We will understand how companies will harness their consumer base, the future of loyalty programs and how new value propositions and intangibles could create consideration in the future

Frontier 3 – How consumers transact. We will look at how At-home purchases, On-the-go purchases, Browse purchases and Consultation transactions will evolve in the future

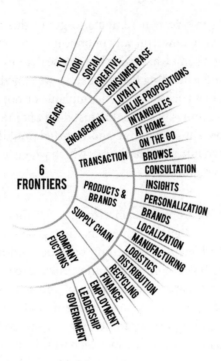

FIGURE 1.3 The six digital frontiers

Frontier 4 – How companies create products and brands. We will discuss how companies will source consumer insights and use that to create meaningful brands, personalized products and localized offerings

Frontier 5 – How supply chains get configured. We will discuss Industry 4.0 in the context of manufacturing, logistics, and distribution and also explore the emergence of reverse logistics for recycling

Frontier 6 – How companies function. We will study how some of the key stakeholders for a company including investors through the finance function, employees through the HR function, leadership in general and government services will change

This is going to be absurd, but in a good way

I was born in a Hindu family to somewhat liberal parents who were not keen on religion but also never really attempted to get me to believe in a specific religious ideology, huge advantage for me growing up. Later in life I spent several years in Berlin and Amsterdam, perhaps the two leading urban centers of social liberalism and then a decade ago I married into a conservative Christian Korean family. So, life's been a bit of a mixed bag when it comes to beliefs and I don't spend time reflecting on it much. The one thing that has struck me repeatedly and the one firm belief I do have is the fact that life is just absurd. Good things do not always happen to good people and bad things do not always happen to bad people. Of course, one can make sure to understand the present and anticipate the future well so as to put oneself in the best position to deal with it, but eventually things are going to happen in the most absurd of ways.

There is Fate and there is Karma perhaps, but if anything, it's most likely just a result of a causal chain of events that is far too complex and long for the human mind to understand. Imagine that, AI will finally expose Karma for what it really is by exposing all the complex patterns on why things eventually happen to us. And in all of this we will find that a significant majority of events are just absurd coincidences.

The reason I want to end this first section on this note is that I want you to know that the world is likely not going to progress along these frontiers with uniformity and integrity. Events will happen along the way, some of you will work in different companies, some of your employers will cease to exist, there will be new regulation or de-regulation, you might have grandchildren or you might get a divorce, there might be a technological breakthrough or another protracted war or pandemic will consume the world's resources and everything will just stop for a bit, some of us might not be around to experience this world in 2035 and some of us might win the lottery and choose to withdraw to a remote island.

The journey of digital transformation, much like life itself, is going to be absurd and there is no set path laid out for us through blockchain and AI and wearables, which has all the answers. As Albert Camus said, there are really three possibilities for us, literal Suicide, Philosophical suicide, or Embracing the absurdity. Suicide in this case would mean we give up on the topic entirely and just accept our fate and perhaps be left behind, philosophical suicide would be to ignore the absurdity and do something symbolic like start an incubator, attend a webinar, hire a consulting firm and just believe it's going to solve the digital transformation issue. Camus and I reject both options and highly recommend you get comfortable with the absurdity and do four things really: Understand, Articulate, Argue and Commit.

Notes

1. https://www.wsj.com/articles/neumann-expected-to-step-down-as-we-ceo-11569343912?mod=breakingnews
2. https://www.wsj.com/articles/uber-ceo-travis-kalanick-resigns-1498023559
3. https://www.wsj.com/articles/u-s-files-criminal-charges-against-theranoss-elizabeth-holmes-ramesh-balwani-1529096005
4. https://www.wsj.com/articles/softbank-saudis-to-launch-100-billion-tech-fund-1495270854
5. https://www.wsj.com/articles/SB119323518308669856
6. https://www.tracetogether.gov.sg/
   The TraceTogether Programme is a programme to enhance Singapore's contact tracing efforts, in the fight against COVID-19. It comprises the TraceTogether App and TraceTogether Token.
   https://www.safeentry.gov.sg/
   SafeEntry is a national digital check-in system that logs the NRIC/FINs and mobile numbers of individuals visiting hotspots, workplaces of permitted enterprises, as well as selected public venues to prevent and control the transmission of COVID-19 through activities such as contact tracing and identification of COVID-19 clusters.
7. https://www.wsj.com/video/indian-company-launches-4-smartphone/4A5800CA-EFF9-41BF-B7D1-3D3D5121C28E.html
8. https://www.wsj.com/articles/fyre-examines-a-failed-festivals-ashes-11547563442
9. https://www.wsj.com/articles/two-years-ago-india-lacked-fast-cheap-internetone-billionaire-changed-all-that-1536159916
10. https://ourworldindata.org/technology-adoption
11. https://deepmind.com/
    "We're a team of scientists, engineers, machine learning experts and more, working together to advance the state of the art in AI"
12. https://www.wsj.com/articles/BL-DGB-32076
13. "A set of programming tools that enables a program to communicate with another program or an operating system, and that helps software developers create their own applications (= pieces of software) (the abbreviation for 'application programming interface')" – Oxford Advanced Learners Dictionary

14. Great articles on Quantum Computing and DNA Storage:
    https://www.wired.co.uk/article/quantum-computing-explained
    https://www.wired.com/story/the-rise-of-dna-data-storage/

15. https://www.wsj.com/articles/affair-website-ashley-madison-hacked-1437402152

16. https://ideas.ted.com/an-eye-opening-look-at-the-dot-com-bubble-of-2000-and-how-it-shapes-our-lives-today/
    As late as 2005, as much as 85% of broadband capacity in the United States was still going unused.

17. https://www.haidilao.com/sg/
    By the end of 2019, Haidilao has opened 768 chain restaurants in China, Singapore, U.S., South Korea, Japan, Canada and Australia with over 54 million members and 100,000 + employees

18. https://www.un.org/en/development/desa/population/publications/pdf/ageing/WPA2015_Highlights.PDF
    Between 2015 and 2030, the number of older persons – those aged 60 years or over – in the world is projected to grow by 56%, from 901 million to more than 1.4 billion

19. https://blog.euromonitor.com/households-2030-singletons/
    Over 2016–2030, single-person households will see faster growth than any other household type globally, with around 120 million new single person homes to be added over the period.

20. https://www.pewresearch.org/fact-tank/2020/09/04/a-majority-of-young-adults-in-the-u-s-live-with-their-parents-for-the-first-time-since-the-great-depression/
    In July, 52% of young adults resided with one or both of their parents

21. https://www.npr.org/local/305/2020/02/18/807050015/more-couples-are-embracing-female-breadwinners-despite-decades-old-stigma
    Nearly 30% of American wives in heterosexual dual-income marriages earn more than their husbands, according to 2018 data from the Bureau of Labor Statistics

22. https://www.audible.com

23. https://www.epicurious.com

24. https://www.meetup.com

25. https://www.brookings.edu/blog/future-development/2020/01/16/who-gained-from-global-growth-last-decade-and-who-will-benefit-by-2030/
    In 2030, the rich will account for 4% of the world's population and one-quarter of household consumption.
    Indeed, the middle class could swell to over 5.5 billion people, predominantly in Asia.

26. https://www2.deloitte.com/us/en/insights/economy/spotlight/economics-insights-analysis-08-2019.html
    Average savings has contracted during this period – the narrower AS1 measure by 16.6%

27. https://www.mrandmrssmith.com/
28. https://www.dunzo.com
29. https://www.businessgreen.com/opinion/3061143/is-meat-the-next-plastic
    Plastic pollution: Trends in campaigning vs
30. https://mobile.twitter.com/cue/status/612824625345511425
31. https://www.nationalgeographic.com/science/2019/12/what-are-carbon-offsets/
    Carbon offset vendor Cool Effect says individual purchases of their carbon offsets
    have risen 700% since May
32. https://mention.com/en/
33. https://www.cooleffect.org
34. https://www.fb.org/market-intel/u.s.-food-expenditures-at-home-and-abroad
    Food-away-from-home spending first surpassed food-at-home purchases in
    2007, with 581 USD billion spent
35. https://www.coworkingresources.org/blog/key-figures-coworking-growth
    We estimate that almost 5 million people will be working from coworking spaces
    by 2024, an increase of 158% compared to 2020
36. Average apartment sizes have shrunk by 27% over the past five years
    https://www.hindustantimes.com/real-estate/real-estate-moving-towards-
    smaller-homes-across-india-report/story-rv8B9uQ74TrajfB3JVaLNO.html
37. The number of units offered by major co-living companies in the US is going to
    triple to about 10,000
    https://www.vox.com/recode/2019/5/29/18637898/coliving-shared-housing-
    welive-roommates-common-quarters
38. In fact, America's three largest cities – New York, Los Angeles, and Chicago – saw
    their populations actually shrink by the end of the 2010s
    https://sparkrental.com/de-urbanization-americans-fleeing-cities/
39. https://www.common.com/
40. https://ollie.co/
41. https://www.yelp.com/
42. 1.73 billion people on average log onto Facebook daily and are considered daily
    active users
    https://zephoria.com/top-15-valuable-facebook-statistics/amp/
43. 32% of respondents – who said they care about privacy, are willing to act
    When asked whether they felt they could protect their privacy today, 67% of
    privacy actives responded that they would be willing to provide their purchase
    history in exchange for personalized products and services, 62% of privacy
    actives were comfortable with the trade-off
    https://www.google.com/amp/s/hbr.org/amp/2020/01/do-you-care-about-
    privacy-as-much-as-your-customers-do
44. https://joindeleteme.com/
45. https://www.23andme.com/en-int/
46. There are 543,000 same-sex married couple households and 469,000 households
    with same-sex unmarried partners living together.

https://www.census.gov/newsroom/press-releases/2019/same-sex-households
.html
From the 2010 Census, there were 131,729 same-sex married couple households
and 514,735 same-sex unmarried partner households in the United States.
https://www.census.gov/newsroom/releases/archives/2010_census/cb11-cn181
.html
47. The majority of Americans (61%) support same-sex marriage
https://www.pewforum.org/fact-sheet/changing-attitudes-on-gay-marriage/
48. In April 2019, Facebook said that there were more than 400 million people in
groups that they find meaningful.
https://www.cnbc.com/2020/02/16/zuckerbergs-focus-on-facebook-groups-
increases-facebook-engagement.html
49. https://www.2tall.com/
50. https://www.petermanningnyc.com/
51. https://www.nike.com/nike-by-you
52. 76% of all consumers would rather spend their money on experiences than on
material items
https://www.prnewswire.com/news-releases/76-of-consumers-prefer-to-spend-
on-experiences-than-on-material-items-new-study-finds-300937663.html
53. In 2017 almost 68k people registered for full Ironman, and 130k people registered
for middle distance
https://instarea.life/so-how-many-ironmans-there-is-8223a1de33d5
54. Three in ten (30%) of Americans have at least one tattoo, an increase from 21% in
2012
https://www.ipsos.com/en-us/news-polls/more-americans-have-tattoos-today
55. https://www.airbnb.com.sg/s/experiences?_set_bev_on_new_domain=
1596783152_MjhjMGRmZWNkOTI3
56. https://lolesports.com/teams/j-team
57. Currently, there are 300 million stock keeping units (SKUs) on the site
https://blog.splitdragon.com/our-guide-to-selling-on-lazada-international-
seller/
58. People move through the purchase journey on their own terms, seamlessly
shifting between search and video
https://www.thinkwithgoogle.com/advertising-channels/search-video-
purchase-journey/
71% of consumers use their mobile phones to do additional online research while
standing at the shelf
https://www.automat.ai/resources/majority-of-beauty-consumers-struggle-
making-purchases-would-value-assistance-from-virtual-beauty-advisors-new-
market-research-study-finds/
59. Estimates for returns of online purchases range from 15 to over 30%, with items
such as apparel and footwear at the high end of that range
https://retailwire.com/discussion/are-return-rates-out-of-control/

60. Shopping.google.com
61. https://www.klarna.com/us/what-is-klarna/
62. 36% have a gig work arrangement in some capacity.
    https://www.smallbizlabs.com/2018/08/gallup-says-36-of-us-workers-are-in-the-gig-economy.html
63. A decrease of 6% between 2010 and 2017.
    https://nces.ed.gov/fastfacts/display.asp?id=98
64. Eight out of ten HR executives consistently contact references for professional (89%), executive (85%), administrative (84%), and technical (81%) positions
    https://www.forbes.com/sites/85broads/2013/05/30/what-linkedin-users-ought-to-know-about-job-references/#501078092cf1
65. On average the world's richest earned their first million at age 36
    https://slotsia.com/uk/time-to-first-million
66. https://www.coursera.org/
67. https://www.upwork.com/
68. During the first quarter of 2020, Facebook reported over 1.73 billion daily active users (DAU)
    https://www.statista.com/statistics/346167/facebook-global-dau/
69. 72% of users report making purchase decisions based on something they saw on Instagram;
    https://retailtouchpoints.com/resources/72-of-users-make-purchase-decisions-based-on-instagram-content
70. You don't need a celebrity to influence buying behavior
    https://retailtouchpoints.com/resources/72-of-users-make-purchase-decisions-based-on-instagram-content
71. https://hootsuite.com
72. https://www.traackr.com

CHAPTER 2
HOW COMPANIES REACH CONSUMERS

The natural first step for any consumer products company is to try to get the message out there and create awareness and understanding into the consumer's mind that the product exists and has the potential to add value to the consumer's life. I imagine the pre-historic man who created an extra stone tool and then ran around his cave complex yelling out the benefits of his bludgeoning axe in whatever pre-historic language he used. He probably used the "direct to consumer scream" channel with much success with a message that involved slaying a mammoth. He for sure targeted the more enterprising males in the settlement and used his most creative animal sounds to depict the distress such a bludgeoning would put said mammoth under. Fast forward 100,000 years and a lot has changed but the fundamentals of consumer reach have not. Awareness, Reach, Message, Channel, Targeting, Creatives, Benefits etc. are as relevant today as they were then and will continue to be in the future. The difference will be in the "How".

I think the future of advertising will be more driven by science than it is by art. A lot of value will come from being more effective and precise in our reach and while I am sure we will have amazing creativity in the future, the human role will continue to diminish. Today's advertisers and marketing leaders in large organizations are very heavy on strategy and creative experience and somewhat light on science, especially data science. There is also a heavy tendency to rely on agencies for everything because talent has been concentrated in the agencies and innovation has originated in the agencies. This might not continue to be the case in the future as most agencies are playing catch up as much as their clients are. Companies might consider insourcing some of the responsibility only to outsource it again to open marketplaces, so this is not a topic a marketer can afford to ignore.

Four main vectors of evolution underline this Frontier of how companies will reach their prospective consumers. Three of the four specific to channels, the future of Out-of-home media, future of TV advertising and future of personal devices with its implications on social media. The fourth relates to the message itself with an evolution in the way ad creatives are put together. Let's dive in.

Future of Out-of-Home Media

Odin books a holiday

It was 7:30 am on another bitter cold Thursday morning in February, as Odin stepped out of his apartment in Berlin Mitte. Minus twelve degrees today, but they said it was going to get warmer over the weekend and Odin was not sure if that was a good thing or a bad thing. With the snow melting and turning to slush and re-freezing and turning into a skating rink, these ups and downs in temperature were not welcome. "It'll be over soon, just a couple of more months till summer and I'll be partying in Ibiza with the crew", he consoled himself as he walked along Muellerstrasse towards Wedding S-Bahnhof. Little did he know, some 8000 kilometers away, Mahela, with his newly opened five-hut beach hotel on Hikkaduwa beach in Sri Lanka had other plans, as he dropped his daughter off to the local school and headed to his office at the resort. And then it started.

As Odin passed by the bus stop near Reinickendorferstrasse a digital ad at the bus stop flickered to a beautiful view of a hut on Hikkaduwa beach on stilts with the caption – "Not been to Sri Lanka yet? Here is your chance!" "That looks nice", Odin thought as he continued along towards Wedding station. At Wedding station, he breathed a sigh of relief as he climbed aboard the S41 towards Gesundbrunnen; it was finally a bit warmer. With only three stops to go, he stood at the doors and looked up and there it was again, another ad on top of the automated doors – "Hikkaduwa beach, get your advanced PADI certification!" Odin reminisced about the week-long dive trip he took last year in Spain where he got his PADI. He did feel a bit left out on the final day when the more advanced folks in the crew went off for a night dive and his best friend and his wife decided to have a dinner date, leaving him alone at the bar, posting a selfie on social media with the title, "Loving diving. Next up Advanced PADI!".

Six pm, Odin finished a good day's work at the co-working space in Prenzlauer Berg, where he worked as the finance head for a small startup that operated a meal prep and delivery service for vegans; they had the best selection of synthetic meats in Berlin. As he headed to a nearby bar for a quick drink with a freelancer that he worked with, to discuss the financial year closing, he looked up and there it was again, a billboard with a catchy five-second video, sort of a go-pro shot of a group of friends with different ethnicities all running and jumping off a cliff into crystal blue waters – "Travel and make friends in beautiful Sri Lanka!"

10:30 pm. The day was drawing to a close, and Odin was snuggled under a heap of blankets and watching the remake of *Game of Thrones* Season 8, it was a good thing they decided to just redo the whole thing after the disaster that was the original Season 8, he thought. Also, great to be living alone so I do not have to fight about what show to watch every night. There were no ads here, just uninterrupted content but he saw a new title added to his recommended watch-list, "Sri Lankan beaches – paradise on earth". Two days later, Odin had booked a summer week in Mahela's resort and four months later they met and remarked what "good fate" it was that they were having a beer together.

Understanding the evolution of out-of-home media

The evolution and establishment of smart out of home media will bring all the efficiencies associated with digital media today into the traditional world for truly seamless communication with the consumer.

Out-of-home media has had an interesting history with several important pivot points. In the mid-1800s roadside advertising took root in America with merchants putting up painted signs near their businesses and therein lay the birth of this form of media. Within a few decades it was commercialized, with a few of the first sign-making and posting companies coming into existence. The first big evolution happened when, in the early 1900s, standardization of billboard sizes allowed companies to mass produce and put up ads country-wide and by the mid-20s the first outdoor advertising company was listed on the NYSE. In the early 60s, JCDecaux introduced the bus shelter and an additional popular advertising format. Then in the 70s, printing on vinyl became possible and led to a dramatic improvement in the quality of creatives and the efficiency in producing them. In the middle of 2000s, the first digital billboard appeared, and the industry has been on the cusp of change ever since, waiting for technology to catch-up. OOH has been very resilient despite the strong emergence of digital media, growing consistently at +4% per year[1] in the last decade and the next decade is going to be extremely exciting indeed.

Tearing apart this area into its sub-components, there are five main sub-elements worthy of discussion: Ad assets, Supply side networks, Measurability, Demand-side exchanges and a Single view of the consumer through retargeting. (See Figure 2.1.) Let us look at what each of these means and what evolution we can expect in each of them.

Ad assets – By this I mean the actual signs including billboards, bus ads, taxi ads, elevator ads, bus stop ads, ads inside trains, ads on lampposts etc. The cost of installing screens has dropped significantly over the last decade and will continue to fall, prompting a major increase in the installed base of assets. Essentially, we will start seeing screens everywhere where there is room to put up a screen. In addition, a large percentage of screens that are already installed but are today not capable of displaying third party ads, and therefore not monetizing, will become part of the asset base available to display ads to consumers. So, if you have a screen in a public place for some other purpose, you will start displaying third party ads on it and make some money on the side.

Supply-side networks – This is the task of aggregating all the screens in the marketplace, classifying these according to the type of audience and location reached and making these available to advertisers to buy. This also needs creating a backbone for sending ads, and the software for running these ads on the millions of screens in the network. Already companies like Vistar media[2]

AD ASSETS

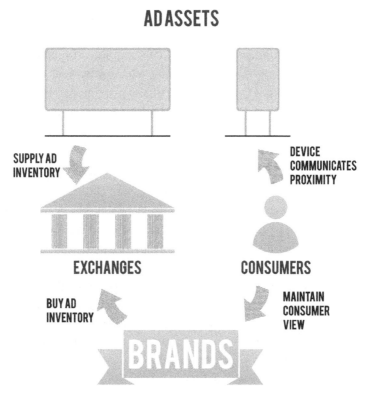

FIGURE 2.1 The digital OOH marketplace

have started offering solutions to asset owners to manage their screens and the content, and in the process have started getting access to a large amount of digital out-of-home inventory. This trend will continue for a few years but for sure we will see a big play by perhaps Google in this space as it forms a natural extension of AdSense to the physical world. AdSense, for the uninformed, was Google's product that allowed website owners to rent out ad space on their websites.

Measurability – Advertisers in OOH today have no idea who is seeing the ad, and if it is really working. Much less so than standard social media advertising where viewability of ads is better reported. Measurability is critical to demonstrate the effectiveness of these media assets over competing channels. Measurability of ad views will improve over time with location data becoming available through IOT and 5G connectivity that tracks a person's device as soon as it is in proximity of a screen. Technology like facial recognition and traffic data will also provide some way of qualifying the ad asset but true measurability will only come when individual location data is available, and sharing is "switched on". In the interim, some qualification system for assets, potentially based on AI could emerge as a reasonable proxy for effectiveness.

Demand-side and exchanges – Once the inventory is assembled and qualified and ready to display ads, it needs an exchange which allows advertisers to bid on the ad inventory or even participate in private deals for specific inventory. An important sticking point for smart OOH media on the demand side has been a much lower demand from advertisers, primarily because of the lack of measurability. Suppliers, too, are reluctant to place inventory on exchanges, worried that pricing might degrade, like it did for social media CPMs in the past and will be difficult to recover in the near-term. Improving measurability will allow auction exchanges to function pretty much like they do on social media marketing today, creating more demand and stabilizing prices. In the meantime, direct deals between advertisers and media owners will likely be more common as this channel emerges.

Single view of the consumer and retargeting – As was the case with Odin, linking specific communication or a chain of messaging to the same consumer through different touch points, while using past interactions as a reference for tailoring future messages opens up amazing possibilities in being targeted and efficient in the way we reach consumers. To begin with we are likely to rely on aggregate data on types of consumers that are found in proximity of the screen based on traffic data and facial recognition etc., but there will come a time when re-targeting on an individual basis through OOH ads will be possible and feasible. Walled gardens like Google and Facebook who are already sitting on huge amounts of data seem like likely candidates to provide this unified consumer view, but there is already substantial consumer data available outside walled gardens and companies will make more and more independent plays in data acquisition for retargeting.

Three practical things you should do now

We are still a few years away, perhaps three years away from digital out-of-home breaking into the mainstream in a noticeable way. This creates an incredible opportunity for tech companies, startups, corporates and investors to start making plays in this space now for creating a position of confidence in three years or achieving great exits if that is your priority.

As corporates and brands trying to make use of this evolution, I would suggest the following:

Build your own screen inventory. Start creating owned media assets wherever possible, even if it's screens in the hallway, or on vending machines or inside elevators. And start working with supply side platforms to monetize this, even if purely for the learning.

Start buying digital OOH inventory. If there is a sizeable media owner in your market, start buying guaranteed inventory now, even if it is just a pilot. Find partners in your ecosystem, perhaps retailers who have screens available who are likely to become future media owners and make guaranteed buys on this asset a part of your existing relationship with them.

Establish basic measurability. As you buy the inventory establish a rudimentary measurement and qualification framework around it. The classification of assets based on location and potential target consumers will likely be no different than how OOH media owners do it today and you can use sources like Google Maps or Telco data to estimate intensity and type of traffic. You might only be 50% accurate but that is already a good start.

Future of TV Advertising

Chick-fil-A at Bhindi-Bazaar

It was 11 am, in the scorching summer heat and humidity in Mumbai, Wahad piled himself into the metro Line 11 at Wadala with his tool bag heading home to Wadi bunder. "Nice 30-minute gig for a good 1000-rupee payout", he thought. The weekend repair pricing worked well for him, with the girls off to hockey practice on Saturday morning, he had nothing worthwhile to do anyway. And he did not mind earning a bit on Saturdays after having missed half a day's worth of jobs on Friday because of Friday prayers. He gets off at Wadi Bunder and makes his way to his rented two-bedroom apartment and feels like he is on top of the world.

Life's been good to him since he moved to Mumbai four years ago, he couldn't have imagined that the skills he built repairing bikes in his dad's bike shop in his hometown would come in handy, as he quickly built a great reputation as a Mr. Fix-it-all on both major handyman platforms in the city. It also helped that he was lucky enough to be married to Wahida who is building a successful career in a recycling startup and makes much more than he does. He wonders if his daughters will be back yet – he promised to take them to the newly opened Chick-fil-A in Bhindi-Bazaar and truth be told, he is looking forward to it as much as the girls.

He heard about Chick-fil-A for the first time a couple of years ago, when he received a free TV from the Indian communications behemoth Reliance Jio. He had to commit to watching a certain number of ads which seemed like a pretty easy thing to do for a free TV. Chick-fil-A had been announcing their entry into Mumbai for a while now and of course, after opening the first outlets in the more affluent neighborhoods, finally Bhindi Bazaar is getting one. He does not mind the ad as much, especially because it features his favorite Cricket star from the Mumbai Indians dressed as a chicken and doing a chicken dance. Incidentally, his wife, who is from Delhi has been seeing the same ad and the same dance being performed by her favorite Delhi Capitals star when she watches her morning show.

Then of course there was their family favorite romantic sit-com *Love in the time of Coursera* where a distance learning teacher falls in love with a Chick-fil-A cashier who is learning how to restore antiques in his small shop in Chandni Chowk. Those chicken sandwiches that she brought him in the show always looked amazing, not to mention the waffle fries. It is hard to find good shows these days because there are just too many, he thought, but lately he has been finding some interesting ones from the Chick-n-watch curated channel of shows, he likes the feel-good vibe that the shows have which they say is a reflection of how it feels to dine in a Chick-fil-A. Oh and of course he has heard that the folks at Chick-fil-A are big on glorifying God and being kind to everyone. And that is something he can get behind.

Understanding the evolution of TV advertising

The first ever TV ad played in 1941; it was a clock-like graphic where the second hand swept around for a full minute, with a logo on the bottom right of the screen. And the industry has grown into a behemoth over the last eight decades with key pivots. But in many ways this last decade has for the first time bunged the spanner into the works forcing the industry to have a reckoning. Color television launched in the 50s, and by the 60s TV surpassed newspapers as the primary source of information for consumers and more viewership meant more ads. In the 80s Apple did that iconic half-million-USD ad spot during Super Bowl, introducing the Macintosh, thus underlining the importance of the medium. Then YouTube launched in 2005 and Netflix streaming in 2007 and by 2018/19 YouTube had 1.9 billion monthly users and Netflix had 150 million subscribers.[3] Incidentally 2007 also brought us Mad Men and Don Draper, romanticizing the agency executive persona, which is not entirely inaccurate from my own experiences of agency folk. But today is a unique moment in time, now that the share of spending on TV ads has fallen consistently in the last few years[4] and continues to decline and will fall even further in absolute terms going ahead.

TV advertising is irreversibly linked to television and content and as such, its lot is tied to the future of content consumption. The traditional advertising model has relied on asking consumers to watch an ad and in return rewarding them with high quality content for free. This exchange of ad consumption as a mode of payment for high quality content in return will remain. Perhaps what will change is how that payment is exactly made and the industry will need to evolve this value exchange model to stay alive. Showing an ad to consumers on TV today is a bit like asking consumers to pay for a product in a currency they do not possess. So, what are the key movements we need to understand, to understand the future of TV ads? (See Figure 2.2.)

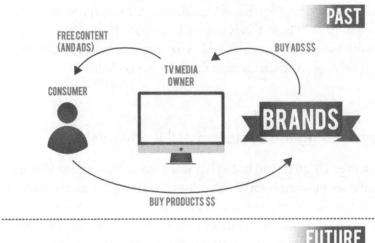

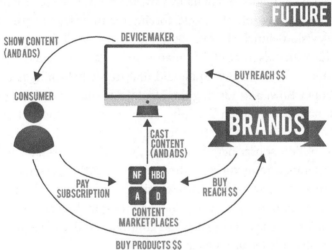

FIGURE 2.2 Value exchange for TV ads

Smart TV penetration – Yes, smart TV, connected TV or Casting device penetration is growing; in the US, 74% of all homes now have a connected TV and the rest of the world is not far behind.[5] Connected TVs, just like the digital OOH opportunity we discussed earlier, allow for being much more targeted in serving the right ad and a different ad to each consumer and allow for much better measurement of ad consumption and performance. Once connected TVs achieve 80%+ penetration, and are actually connected, this space too will go through a reinvention in terms of how ad supply is put on the marketplace and how it is bought programmatically on exchanges based on a cost-per-impression type of pricing. But contrary to what you would expect or read, the key disruption for the future lies not in the Smart TV hardware penetration but in how consumers consume and pay for content and their tolerance for interruption by ads playing a role in that.

Content marketplaces – Imagine a platform where as a consumer you could go and pick and choose the type of content you'd like to watch, a movie, a sports broadcast, news, short form content, music videos, documentaries, whatever you'd want. You decide what to put into your basket, you decide if you want a single serving or a large multi-pack, you decide if you'd want to grab one item and go or you want to dwell and add many more items, you decide if you want to be a loyalty program member and get better pricing, you decide if you want branded content from a reputed production house or private label content like platform originals. Eventually all content providers will converge on this model. Today, we have multiple marketplaces e.g., Netflix, Amazon, Hulu, Fox, HBO, Disney+ each with their own private label content and third-party content and each forcing consumers to become fully fledged members. Consumers will reach subscription fatigue at some point and choose an aggregator, and if there is no consolidation or content interoperability on the content provider side, then the device providers or network providers might end up playing this role. Aggregation of streaming services into a content marketplace is a no brainer.

Content economics – In 2019, Netflix spent 15+ billion USD on content, it reported around ~20 billion in revenue and a negative 3.3 billion in free cash flow.[6] So, Netflix is right now a great example of a company which digs up a barrel of oil for 10 USD and sells it at 8 USD, except a barrel of oil can only be used once but a piece of content, once created can be monetized multiple times. Netflix's hopes of gaining massive subscriber base continually, to justify investments in creating content, might be jeopardized by the fact that four to five other players in the market are chasing after the same consumers with content that is at least as good. The only way then would be to raise prices, which they have done successfully in the past but as competition ramps up, consumers' willingness to keep paying more for multiple providers will wane. The fact remains, consumers have gotten used to consuming incredible quality of content for extraordinarily little money. In the coming decade, I think some consumers will pay more, some will move to an ad-supported model, many will move to marketplaces for a fully bespoke content offering. But the cost of creating content will also drop with AI, better production technology over-all, and easier findability of quality content. So perhaps we will not need a *Friends* like success to have a cast that earns a million per episode, a big distributor like Warner Bros and a primetime slot on NBC. Perhaps we will be able to achieve the same joy with a lot less due to the changing economics of content creation and consumption.

Ad-supported subscriptions and bundles – The one main difference between music streaming and video streaming these days has been the fact that it is possible to have free or very inexpensive music streaming subscriptions and it's been demonstrated that consumers who want to consume more, and with-out ads, would not mind paying for the service. 45% of Spotify listeners are paid subscribers[7] and Spotify is awfully close to being profitable. This because in-spite of the incredibly challenging margins in the business with increasing scale record labels are starting to accept lower royalties. "Watch my ad and get free or discounted content" has been the mantra of traditional TV channels and the freemium models of music streaming companies and video stream-ing players could start experimenting with this model. But "Buy my product and get free or discounted content" models also exist, especially with telcos where a mobile phone contract gives you streaming subscriptions at discounts. We will see more bundling of this sort in the market where a physical prod-uct brings with it a fixed period subscription to streaming which is in effect consumers paying for content by demonstrating loyalty to another associated brand, Amazon Prime video being a clear example of this.

Ad consumption occasions – Back in the 90s when an ad would interrupt your movie, you would accept that as the unavoidable reality of things and just watch the ad. Then at some point you could change channels, and then stream-ing came about and now suddenly, we treat interruption ads like the curse. God forbid, the 15 second unskippable ads Apple buys on YouTube are pretty but oh so annoying, I do not want to wait 15 seconds to watch my cat video. Ad consumption willingness has changed but it has not gone away altogether, and advertisers should not entirely give up on interruption, because there are opportunities here too. Natural breaks in broadcasts, like between overs in a cricketing test match, or between sets during a tennis game, unskippable ads at the beginning of long form content, in-stream ads somewhat masterfully placed at least 30 minutes apart, overlay ads that don't interfere with viewing quality could all work and will remain. I am not advocating the relentless use of interruption ads, but for those of us who are willing to watch ads for cheaper content subscriptions, there is a way to make ads less intrusive.

Three practical things you should do now

So, we have gone through how the future of TV ads is linked inextricably to the future of content consumption and here too there are many opportunities to create value. To the consumer companies looking at this space I would recommend the following:

Buy connected TV ads. Start working with agencies to make connected TV buys now if you are not doing so already. It might not give you good reach or might not have enough measurability for now but the quicker you learn the better it is. Remember how long it took you to jump on the social media marketing band wagon, you wouldn't want to miss this boat too.

Work with content marketplaces. Identify and start working with the content marketplaces of the future. This could be a streaming service a telco or a device manufacturer so stay in the mix and have the roller-decks ready. These players will be your future gatekeepers vis-à-vis the consumer. Start bundling your products with content, if a family meal at Chick-fil-A could give a week's worth of ads-free TV to Wahad on his Jio content marketplace, he would be more likely to make a dash for that sandwich. Create content and curate content. Find out what type of content works best for your brand's character and invest in making long or short form programs. A good piece of content will give you tons of organic reach and a bargaining chip with media owners in the future.

Be an interruption opportunist. Own the science or get plugged into the science of what kind of interruption ads are still okay. Most of middle class European and American consumers are going to feel the pinch in the coming decade and emerging Asian consumers will not mind saving the extra dollars so ad tolerance might actually increase. Ad supported content streaming is coming for sure and you want to be best placed to have the least intrusive ads when it happens.

A New Kind of Personal Device

Jaden shorts a Merlot

It was a late Sunday morning, that was quite a birthday party yesterday for his sixteen-year-old daughter, thought Jaden. He had promised his wife that he would take her out to a nice boozy brunch in a place she had heard about in Itaewon. He showered, got ready and put on his AR glasses. Hannam-Dong, where he lived in Seoul, and Itaewon were both designated by the government to be in the driverless zone, so he was glad he did not have to drive himself. "Hana, Check the bill for last night", he said out loud and an itemized list appeared which looked okay, he liked to be careful with his hard-earned (and well-inherited) money and he liked his new financial services provider Hana, he felt like she understood him well and was easy to be with, and he felt a kinship although she was just an AI; sort of like the Joaquin Phoenix movie *Her*. His car dropped him off and went off to self-park somewhere, he got a quick notification on the AR that parking would be five coins and he blinked twice to approve.

It was nice spending some time with his wife, and they settled down at a comfortable spot. A menu flashed on his AR and his personal voice assistant Eka immediately pointed out the things she felt he would like, he blinked twice. Eka also recommended that he tell his wife to stay off dessert, her patch implant which was linked to his personal device had received five blood sugar level alerts this last month. "Stay off dessert please love but let's pick a nice wine to make up for it", he said. Eka scanned the wine list for him and recommended a few wines, the L'Apparita 2019 Merlot from the Castillo di Ama winery looked a bit underpriced compared to the others, based on a quick reference of general market prices and menu pricing at the restaurant. Eka suggested that one, which got a double blink from Jaden. He loved a good deal.

The food was good, but the wine was not. On the way back from lunch, Jaden asked Eka to do a quick check on recent reviews on the 2019 Merlot and they were a bit soft, clearly compared to other vintages. He remembered trying the 2009 and 1999 vintages and they too were a bit underwhelming compared to the fantastic wines from all other years mostly. Maybe this was a once every decade kind of situation. He summoned Hana, his financial services provider on his AR, "Can you find me a place where I can short sell a few cases of this Merlot? I think I am on to something that most of the marketplace might not have caught onto yet, good opportunity to make a quick buck". By late evening, Hana had found him a reliable wine exchange that allowed him to short the wine at a very attractive fee and while getting him to double-blink she made a couple of suggestions, "You might be interested in doubling up on your wife's health benefits, I have a very attractive single premium product from one of our partner companies. There is also a short-term opportunity with a partner bank who is willing to pay 50 bps extra interest on a six-month fixed deposit which you can definitely afford right now. And there are three interesting ICOs launching next week by South Asian food tech companies, a sector you have said you're interested in".

"Yeah sure, it takes money to make money, but sometimes it takes a few double-blinks that is all", he thought. What would he do without these important women in his life? Eka, Hana, and of course his wife.

Understanding the evolution of personal devices

Tracing back the history of Smartphones, or personal devices, and what has led us to where we are today, is a bit more complex than say TVs, primarily because there was a convergence of several use cases into one device. So, as we travel back in time we need to look briefly at how mobile phones, personal productivity devices, i.e. PDAs, portable music devices and portable cameras all evolved, and in a couple of decades converged into what we know as the smartphone today. Steve Jobs' 2007 speech introducing the iPhone is one of my all-time favorites and still sends chills down my spine when I hear him say the words: "An iPod, A phone, and An internet communicator". He says it twice and asks, "Are you getting it?". What a pivotal moment in tech history, perhaps the most pivotal of my lifetime.

The first mobile phone service was offered in 1926 to first class passengers on German trains between Berlin and Hamburg. How charming! But the device only started getting personal in the 80s when the world got its first portable mobile phone, the Motorola DynaTAC 8000X, in 1983; it cost USD 4000, very few people ever saw one, and few businesses ever used one. With GSM launching in the early 90s, Nokia entered the game with its Nokia 1011 phone launching in 1992 and now consumers could finally own a phone. The first smartphone launched was in 1994, IBM's Simon, which could send email and faxes, had a touchscreen with a stylus and some productivity stuff like a calendar. The 90s saw more market entrants and the feature phone started appearing at the turn of the millennium with the likes of the Nokia 7110 and the first ever camera phone launching in the year 2000, the Sharp J-SH04. In 2000, Nokia launched the 3310 and it sold 126 million units! In the early 2000s 3G was implemented and Blackberry became popular with the 8100 Pearl. Then in 2007, the iPhone was launched, and everything changed. By 2011, Samsung had become the world's biggest smartphone vendor and by 2015 Huawei and Xiaomi had joined the ranks as leading device providers globally. I am just realizing how difficult it is to run through everything that's happened in this space just in the last fifteen years, fortunately most of you have been alive and have lived it with me, so I don't need to summarize it all.

What has happened is water under the bridge, what is about to happen is likely to be even more disruptive and fragmented. Those of us who will make the right moves today in anticipating the next decade will perhaps build the next trillion-dollar company.

Continued evolution of the smartphone – The form factor of a handheld smartphone will likely be completely replaced by something else in time, but for the next five to seven years at least it will still be around. I feel like the world has done its bit of experimentation on making phones bigger and smaller and thinner and wider and foldable and bendable etc. and there isn't really a lot of value left to achieve in optimizing the shape anymore but there is a long way to go on materials. We will start seeing thinner, stretchable, almost glass like panels without any ports or any buttons, and ever more powerful front and rear facing cameras mounted on the housing. Perhaps we will see hand-held terminals emerging which project the outline of the screen and respond to gestures – something quite akin to the hand terminals shown in Amazon's The Expanse, although that seems a bit far out in the future.

Augmented reality glasses – I would place my bets on this form factor to be the big disruption of the next decade, and I am not alone. Granted that Google glass was a big failure, but it was ahead of its time and the world needed the learning. Every tech company we know is making a big play in this space, most notably Apple. Apple's own project is rumored to have had initial setbacks, but some say the first AR glasses from Apple will hit the market in 2023 and I think we can trust Apple to deliver a product beyond our imagination. Google, Microsoft, and Facebook with its partnership with Ray Ban are all working on devices aimed to hit the market in the early-mid 2020s. With audio sunglasses already available, working well and trending, from the likes of Bose, I think a future where instead of carrying your phone you just slip on a pair of sunnies seems completely likely quite soon.

Personal device clusters – While we continue to focus on the smartphone or AR glasses as the anchor device, we will also see that most consumers will own multiple smart devices, all of which are linked to each other, most likely from the same brand or manufacturer in a sort of a device cluster. So, if you may imagine a Vitruvian man-type of figure surrounded by a plethora of personal devices: A smartphone, a smart watch, a pair of smart glasses, a smart ring, wallet, belt, smart clothing including shoes or any number of trackers installed on the body or implanted in the body. (See Figure 2.3.) Especially in the fields of healthcare and fitness we will see emergence and widespread acceptance of epidermal electronics, which create a wearable "patch" which has skin-like properties or is relatively unnoticeable for the consumer. Beyond the regular metrics like heart rate, calories, blood pressure etc. the ability to measure blood sugar, blood alcohol, heart risk, mood changes, hydration levels etc. and using the data for alerting on medical conditions, medical monitoring or even suggested selling of appropriate products will become a widely accepted use case.

All of this will be synced to the iTunes account or Google account or whichever operating system it might be with your digital identity at the center of it. An important point here is that the device itself will eventually become completely

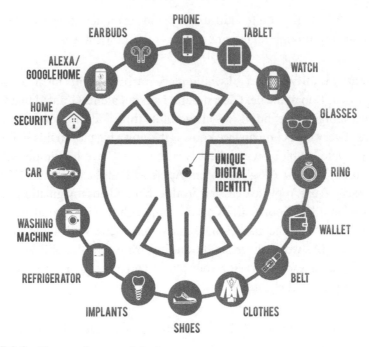

FIGURE 2.3 Cluster of personal devices

commoditized and the hardware very affordable. Perhaps even free, as companies jostle to own the consumer access and to monetize it to service providers. Eventually, for example, all financial service providers will only find an ear with Jaden if they go through Hana and compensate her for it.

Household appliances and smart homes – Although not a personal device per se, smart refrigerators, washing machines, home security systems, vacuum cleaners, hair dryers, toothbrushes, shavers, you name it will all communicate to the future consumers. They will all be linked into the personal device clusters we spoke about earlier and will have the ability to recommend specific products and brands to the consumer. There is already a ton of talk about refrigerators that hold an inventory of what is inside and automatically create a shopping list and we will talk about that a bit more in a later chapter. But consider here the possibility that you are used to buying a certain brand of beer, and the refrigerator actually plays you an ad by recommending to you a new brand when it realizes you are about to run out. Amazon's Alexa, Google home, Apple's Siri and the rest have started off as passive productivity assistants which will speak only when spoken to and do as they are told. But as the installed base of these in-home assistant devices increases so will their ability to discern how and when to best recommend a specific product and brand to you. This could be a huge reach opportunity for companies, akin to having someone listening and sitting inside every consumer's home, ready to make a recommendation when the time is exactly right.

More fragmented but transparent social media – Social media has taken the advertising world by storm in the last decade and especially in the last five to seven years, with most brands shifting enormous sums of money away from TV into Facebook and Google ads. And this has come with huge advantages like targeted reach, lower cost of entry, ability to drive transactions etc. but over the last couple of years a cloud of deep suspicion has started to loom as reliable measurability of effectiveness has not materialized. There seems always to be a massive difference between impressions and views and in simple terms most consumers are not viewing or remembering your ads, especially on the newsfeed. An analogy: Say you were hosting a party and decided to invite your friends, social media reach tells you how many people were sent an invite. It does not tell you how many actually came to the party leave aside how many people actually enjoyed the party. Couple this opacity in measurement with the fact that every year more ad formats and platforms and products are brought to market, add to it the explosion in devices available to serve ads on and it has all the makings of a monster. Running social media will end up being like operating a nuclear power plant – you press some switches and hope things are working well in there.

Fortunately, the transparency debate is front and center today and a number of startups are sprouting up and building services around this, platforms themselves are realizing the need to be more honest about quality of reach and companies are mustering up the right amount of courage to demand they get what they pay for. Over the next few years, we will see much fairer and cleaner social media execution all around even if the actual channel becomes impossibly complex.

Three practical things you should do now

So, just as we are starting to get used to smartphones, and the advertising opportunities it has created over the last five-some years, it is going to change again. And that is inconvenient for some, but it brings a lot of opportunities to create more value. So, while you must be personally excited, if you are anything like me, to buy the first pair of Apple Glasses as soon as they hit the shelves, I'd suggest you consider the following imperatives so your companies can profit from the change as well.

Focus on quality of social media. Start focusing on the viewability of your social media advertising immediately. There are certain types of channels, ad formats, ad creatives and buying models that work for specific marketing objectives and most brands and agencies still learning to do the right thing. When we move to another form factor and the ad types become even more complex, not knowing how to design a digital media mix that works will set you up for being milked by the media owners well into the next decade. Measure what you get and only pay for what you can measure.

Build up owned reach. Start building own reach channels now, however small they might be. It's by no means certain that Facebook, Instagram and Twitter will work on the new devices as well as it does on smart phones and your direct-to-consumer channel, built up with your best consumers could very well integrate beautifully in one or more of the clusters of devices. To power this, collect your own consumer data and build your captive audience, for at least your best consumers. Companies need to assume that their consumers belong to them and the relationships with these consumers which have been built up with years of media spending and equity and habit building can evaporate in an instant when access to the consumer has to go through someone else's device, someone else's application and using someone else's ability to discern who is who on the platform.

Work with device owners. Most brands today do not work directly with device owners because there is no natural intersection, beyond using phones for work. But even those are provided by the telco operators. The device owners will be the ultimate gatekeepers, if Eka and Hana are pre-installed on

Jaden's AR device then that assures them of a place in his mind (and heart). So, start understanding how the device and hardware players can gain from you now and build a relationship, even co-create solutions with them for the multiples of wearables that are around already. Focus especially on the Alexas of the world because they are here and in people's homes already now. I would not be surprised if with falling hardware costs, it even becomes feasible for some brands to give away free devices to top consumers to maintain stickiness and short circuit reach.

A New Way of Building Ad Creatives

Nuno celebrates his 10-yr anniversary

"Gosh, hard to believe it has already been ten years since we got married", thought Nuno as he drove down Avenida Caracas in Bogotá. Not far away from here was Parque Nacional where he first saw his husband, Ed struggling along but still not stopping, at the 2023 Bogotá half marathon. It was his third half marathon then and something just made him want to run next to Ed; he wasn't sure if Ed actually noticed, but later that evening at the finisher's event, Ed came up to him and thanked him for keeping him company. They exchanged numbers, and the rest as they say is history.

As he entered his workplace at the Bogota Philharmonic, where he was second chair in the Violin ensemble, and got into the elevator the screen flickered on and his favorite footballer from Santa Fe looked him in the eye and said, "I've got the perfect gift for you to buy Ed, the new Nike Stable-glide shoes for Overpronators. Remember Nike, the love is yours, we bring the shoes". Interesting thought, he remarked as he headed into another long day of rehearsals. Ed was a marked Overpronator, and he himself was more of a Supinator, that adding another charming element of the Yin and Yang to their relationship. During a break late afternoon, he checked up quickly on the Stable-glide shoe prices and custom design options, looked interesting, he'd consider it he felt.

A couple of years ago they completed a full-length marathon together in Medellin, it was a bit easier there because of the lower elevation and he loved the fact that it, was the two of them together. It was Nike's annual Nike Love marathon, where you sign up with someone you love, and your times are added up together in the end. And there were so many beautiful stories leading up to the event and during the event and after the event, from the older retiree couple, from the husband and his cancer survivor wife and from the two war veteran buddies. He thought Nike was on to something with this idea of people running marathons together. He had also met a lot of great people after that in the local run club in their neighborhood of Zona T. Back home later that evening just as he was getting ready for the Santa Fe game to start, he got a prompt from Nike, "We've put together a short two-minute feature for you, wave to check it out". He waved and what followed was a beautifully shot and put together montage of all the different running routes he and Ed had done, they even found some footage from that very first marathon at the finish line as they both crossed. "Make your tenth anniversary a memorable one. The love is yours; we bring the shoes. Wave if you would like to buy now! Swipe up if you consent to allow us to share this short video with the world and get 10% off". A wave and a swipe and he was set.

A week later, he waited at their favorite restaurant in Chapinero on their anniversary night for Ed to arrive. And just as Ed walked through the restaurant doors, Nuno noticed a familiar gift-wrapped box under his arms which looked very much like the one he had sitting under the table for Ed. He smiled, realizing what Nike had been up to. "Those must be the Nike Cushioned shoes for supinators", he thought; they had been playing both sides all along. Later that evening as they walked down Carrera 7, hand in a hand and looked up at the giant screen above and saw their short video story playing as a Nike Love ad, he realized that he wasn't the only one who had consented.

Understanding the evolution of Ad creatives

A marketer once said to me that our ads need to be such that they are not seen as an inconvenience, but that people want to watch them, and there is a lot of truth in that. Sometimes beyond advertising a product, some ads become iconic in their message and imagery which forever changes how the world perceives a certain lifestyle choice or a certain topic. I am sure each of you have your set of favorites and here I just wanted to remember some of mine and perhaps try to identify the essence of the long-term cultural change these creatives have brought about.

Let us start with the iconic Marlboro Man campaign by Leo Burnett in 1954. That imagery and the associated messaging has shaped the self-perception of male smokers for decades and became such an iconic notion that other art forms including films reinforced it repeatedly. So, a creative literally shaped how consumers felt while they were consuming a product. In 1931, Coca-Cola commissioned illustrator Haddon Sundblom to paint Santa for its Christmas Advertisements and he chose to depict Santa as a happy, generous person with a white beard and a red suit. Prior to this campaign the public's popular perception of Santa was not unified and was not the way he is depicted today. So, a creative in this case has shaped how consumers think of perhaps the most important holiday of the year and the generosity of spirit they associate with it. Next, let's think about the Red Bull Stratos stunt which featured Felix Baumgartner free falling from the stratosphere in 2012, not conceived as an ad per se, but this and several such interventions by Red Bull has cemented the brand's identity towards extreme sports in a way that consumers automatically link energy drinks to peak performance. And energy drinks at least do provide you with energy, cigarettes on the other hand have absolutely nothing to do with masculinity. Think about Budweiser's "Wassup" campaign in 1999, which was probably one of the first commercials to be viewed more often in markets where Budweiser was not available than where it was. The humor took a life of its own and shaggy teenagers still "Wassup" each other the world over, paying tribute to the original idea. The creative crystallized the sentiment of a casual, somewhat rhetorical "hello" which other than the actual hello also meant that the enquirer was a very laid back and approachable person. All this in one expression "Wassup".

And creatives do not always mean images and videos, sometimes it's powerful one-liners like "Just do it" or "A diamond is forever", or iconic music. So, the history of advertising is full of examples of how creatives have shaped behavior and emotions and the entire ad creative industry has over the last decades focused on refining and repeating this magic. But with shorter attention spans and much less ad supported TV how will this creative freedom evolve over the next decade?

Thinking about the broad value chain of how creatives come about we can disaggregate a few steps: There is the germination of the big idea, there's the operationalization of the idea into a ready to go Creative through production, and there is the delivery of the right creatives to the right consumers through media. The clear progress we will see in the coming decade will be in the ease of operationalizing an idea and in the ability to do much better and more efficient delivery to consumers. While AI will play a role in assisting, I do believe that the absurdity of coming up with a breakthrough creative idea which is innovative and impressive will still need the human touch, at least for the near future. There are five key evolutions for us to keep an eye on in this space. (See Figure 2.4.)

Synthetic creatives – I discussed synthetic media briefly in the earlier chapter, it is the ability to generate hyper-realistic images, videos, sounds etc. by a program without actual human intervention. Availability of synthetic media products and agencies will improve in the coming decade, and it will allow advertisers to magnify every single creative relatively inexpensively,

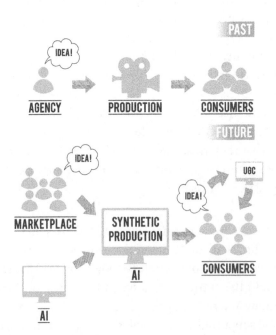

FIGURE 2.4 New creative value chain

by changing just enough of it to suit the specific consumer segment that is being targeted. Think about a single ad creative based on a core creative idea which is then synthetically generated with a person of every ethnicity who speaks the language in the applicable local context. All automated without having to produce a single video or image the traditional way. The cost and effectiveness benefits would be enormous.

AI storytelling – I want to push your thinking here beyond the already exciting world of an AI developing the storyline for a piece of content based on your personal preference. That is great and that runs along similar lines as synthetic media, except a storyline in this case is a sequence of events that the AI synthesizes together to make it more relevant to you. Beyond that, AI will enable characters from the storyline to interact with consumers in a hyper realistic way while at the same time staying unpredictable and true to themselves, sort of like humans. Imagine a Marlboro Man AI or better still a Santa Claus AI as a character in interactive video format who your kids can speak to come Christmas. Maybe your child will discuss with this Santa how she or he has behaved all year round, perhaps have a conversation about the kind of stuff the child likes to do. And then the Santa (or more like Amazon who by then might own all IP related to Santa) makes a recommendation on a toy purchase to the parents who make sure the said toy is bought and delivered. AI will thus bring an innumerable number of characters today confined to the standard issue 15 or 30-second commercial to life and have them participate in your lives.

Dynamic Creative Optimization – DCO as it is called, has emerged in a powerful way with all digital advertising platforms offering it as a product one way or another and if you are an advertiser on the likes of Google and Facebook, you have likely already used it to some extent. The underlying thesis is that by tweaking the way an ad looks to the consumer, you would be able to elicit a much more efficient response. And this could be "I am" type of information or "I do" type of information allowing advertisers to market a different shoe to a Supinator and a different shoe to an Overpronator as an example. But DCO today bases itself on a finite known set of variables which are available in a dataset as attributes so if the segmentation uses age, gender and prior behavior as inputs then all 45-year-old, male, half-marathoners will see the same creative. But there are millions of runners out there, and surely it is not possible to build a wholly predictive model to decide the five parameters that end in a purchase decision with an R-squared of over 90%. This is where AI will come in and will help us dynamically optimize creatives using patterns that are much more difficult to recognize.

Platform-sourced creatives – So with AI and synthetics and targeting it seems like there will be more Science to creatives than there will be Art in the coming decade. I do still believe that the next seven-odd years for sure will rely quite heavily on human genius to come up with the creative idea, the Marlboro men and the Santa Clauses and the Just-do-its. The big change however will come in where these humans are located and how their creative genius is being made available to companies. Like all professional services, creative agencies have built massive global businesses on the back of great talent which is then provided at a margin to corporations in a somewhat opaque and relationship driven marketplace. Sure enough there are always pitches and procurement rules that require at least three bidders etc., but still we are always at the mercy of the few big agencies who assure us that they have indeed the best talent that is out there. But is this true anymore? And even if it were somewhat true today, would it be the case in the next decade? Most of the top creative work could come from small firms or individuals who will be contractable on transparent marketplaces and the traditional agency model might face competition from these marketplaces or even start relying on them. This is not because talent is not choosing to go to large firms, it is because there has always been way more talent in the world than the agency market has managed to give exposure to, digital platforms will make this talent visible.

User-generated content – Or UGC as it's popularly known has been a bit of a hype for the last few years which has died down somewhat. The idea that a company or an individual would create a piece of content, generally at low cost which is then repeated, modified and re-shared over and over again till it gains immense reach is what drives companies to try to create viral content. I would say 99% of the times the attempt to create viral content from companies has been a failure and marketers and agencies always find some "organic reach" number to satisfy leadership while the actual consumer has been pretty much untouched and unmoved by the campaign. I think UGC will make a comeback in a few years because three things will be different with technology: Firstly find-ability of obscure popular content will improve with social listening tools becoming more and more sophisticated in picking up content just as it starts to trend or even before it starts to trend based on AI and pattern recognition. Secondly, with better personal tools on creating high quality media, UGC quality and therefore impact will improve. I think in ten years individuals like you and I will be able to make Marvel quality short films with easy-to-use tools. Finally, companies will be able to use smarter seeding strategies to identify the right micro influencers to re-seed the content to find a scientific best path to virality, if there is indeed one. Consider this – if you were to take the "Baby shark" song and replace it with some other song and incentivize the first 1,000,000 viewers and sharers to view and share it exactly in the same sequence would it still end up with 6.7 billion views? Maybe.

Three practical things you should do now

So, we will see in the creative space as well a lot of movement and opportunities for companies and entrepreneurs to benefit from. As an executive wanting to have skin in the game here, I would recommend the following:

Learn to use dynamic creatives. Start using DCO to the max in all your digital marketing campaigns now. Be it Facebook's dynamic creatives product or YouTube's Directors mix, media owners are bringing more and more functionality and it's up to advertisers like you to try these out to see what works and what doesn't work in the world of DCO for your brand. The optionality and complexity of personalized creatives is just going to explode and if you have not figured out how to use whatever little is out there now, you are unlikely to understand and benefit from what is coming.

Work with creative marketplaces. Start getting creatives off creative marketplaces, at least for your creative needs that are a lot less critical from the overall brand story point of view. Ten years from now you will probably be sourcing most, if not all of your creatives from such marketplaces and the earlier you start and learn, the more efficiency you can drive over the next ten years of evolution. Existing creative agencies will just not be able to make the economics work in putting together the sheer volume of creatives at the frequency at which the digitally connected world demands them. So, the smarter thing to do is to start cultivating options that do work. And while you are at it invest in understanding the path to virality from a data science point of view. Understand which platforms, which micro-influencers, what content types, content length, content attributes, messaging types etc. seem to propagate well and also spend time and money in finding content instead of creating it.

Create own-able characters. Or continue to develop a bench of celebrity endorsers. This sounds like a bit of an odd recommendation but having your favorite football player doing a one-to-one conversation with you will be an unbeatable way to sell stuff and having the rights to your own characters (it's so good to be Disney) or having access to characters will be critical to benefit from this. The trend is current as well, the last couple of years have seen a slew of very innovative campaigns like "Get a WhatsApp call from your favorite idol", it is not personalized and its very rudimentary, but it still works.

So, there you have it, a deeper look at the first frontier. I hope by now you are beginning to appreciate the breadth and depth of impact that digital enablement will have on our companies; we are just about getting started and I feel like we have been through so much opportunity already. In the next chapter we will move away from reach and into the consideration stage. We will look at the much talked about notion of engagement marketing and think through how digital will enable companies to engage consumers.

Notes

1. https://www.marketing-interactive.com/ooh-ads-outperform-other-traditional-formats-new-report-finds
   Global OOH advertising revenues grew annually over the last nine years (2010–2018), with an average growth of +4.1% per year over the period

2. https://vistarmedia.com/
Vistar Media was founded in 2012 by leaders in the digital advertising space, who saw the opportunity to bring the intelligence and efficiency of programmatic technology to the impactful medium of out-of-home

3. https://blogs.oracle.com/oracledatacloud/the-history-and-future-of-television-advertising

4. https://www.emarketer.com/content/tv-will-drop-below-25-of-total-us-ad-spending-by-2020

5. https://liftintent.com/blog/is-connected-tv-the-future-of-advertising/

6. https://variety.com/2020/digital/news/netflix-2020-content-spending-17-billion-1203469237/

7. https://newsroom.spotify.com/company-info/

CHAPTER 3
HOW COMPANIES ENGAGE WITH CONSUMERS

For a few years now, marketers have been touting the move from interruption marketing to engagement marketing. The key message being that instead of making a one-way communication of your brand and product to the consumer and hoping it results in a transaction, you engage a consumer in your brand in a two-way dialogue, and in the process influence them to make that purchase. This made sense to me and I thought of it as a novel and exciting way to think about marketing but, there is a "But". In how many ever conversations, panel discussions, webinars and weblogs I have investigated I am yet to find someone or something that has framed the "How" well enough for it to become straightforward and obvious. Maybe that is because the world is still understanding and coming to terms with the idea of engagement marketing. There was even a global misadventure in the world of social media a few years ago, when brands started to track and optimize for engagement metrics like "Likes" and "Shares" only to find out that there was only a very weak correlation between that kind of engagement and actual purchase. So, I set about thinking this through for myself, trying to maybe lay out one way of looking at engagement marketing, at least from the digital enablement lens so as to offer you readers a way to approach the topic pragmatically.

My fundamental premise is this – underlying all interaction between brands and consumers, there must be a value exchange. You watch ads for free and in exchange get free TV content, you pay money and get a product in exchange, you try a free sample and agree to give the brand a chance for future purchase, you get a fifth cup of coffee for free and agree to have the first four on your own dollar. So, while engagement with consumers makes sense, it would make much more practical sense if it's articulated in the form of the underlying value exchange. It is rare for consumers to engage with brands of their free will without expecting anything in return. Even collectors, who are obsessed with brands and who are amongst the most engaged of consumers, are in it for the sense of community and for the status.

So as brands start broadening this value exchange from mere "ads for content" and "money for product" to a more extensive, multitudinal and frequent exchange they'd create a larger body of engagements with the consumer to eventually, opportunistically drive the primary transaction that earns money. Digital enablement will have a significant role to play in helping companies move towards an engagement model because digital platforms lend themselves extremely well to be the vehicles for such a value exchange. In this section thus, we will talk about the role of digital in evolving how companies engage with consumers by first looking at how companies can harness and recruit a consumer base to call its own and to engage with and then how companies can establish the actual engagement itself through loyalty offerings, additional related digital value propositions and other intangibles.

Harnessing Your Consumer Base

Bart adds a few years to his life

10 am on a crisp summer morning on Long Island and Bart was just driving the short way back from Merrick Golf course towards his newly acquired home on Shore Drive. He and his wife, Jill moved to Long Island six months ago after his retirement and he loved it so far, especially the Golf almost every morning. And it was nice to be within driving distance of his son who had just started living in Manhattan, he still worked for a travel advisory start-up based out of Silicon Valley, but nobody really lived near their company headquarters anymore, which Bart thought was great. He wished he did not have to suffer the bitter cold and crowds of New York when he was in the prime of his professional career at a Bank.

He decided to stop by at the CVS on Merrick Road to pick up a refill of his gut health pills, he was running out. It had been three years now since "the incident" as he and Jill referred to it. He had had a bout of such acute gastroenteritis that he ended up in hospital for three full days. The doctors told him then that unless he changed his diet dramatically, he was at risk of stomach cancer. And then he joined Alka-Seltzer's gut health community "Speedy Gut". The app had some extremely helpful features, where he would just have to take a photograph of everything he ate or drank, and it used photo recognition to understand the gut risk score and make recommendations on whether he should eat it and how much he should eat. It also gave him reminders on when to take his medication and allowed him to learn about his condition through blogs and forum discussions. At CVS as he bought a box of Rennie tabs, the auto-checkout asked him to consent to share his data with the manufacturer, he said "Yes". Later that week, as he was winding down for the day at home, his smart fridge recommended he try out a new probiotic yoghurt product from Danone which tweaks the amount of CFU (Colony forming units), in other words useful bacteria in a yoghurt portion based on your gut health data.

While Bart was going about his day in Long Island, a few things were happening in the background. Bayer, the company that owns Alka Seltzer and owned the engagement platform "Speedy Gut" had recorded Bart's first party data when he signed up for the application. They had been populating this data over time with more knowledge gained about Bart, including his medical history which he consented Bayer to extract from the healthcare provider that gave him his care during "the incident". Every time Bart made a purchase of a Bayer product at the CVS, and consented "Yes", Bayer acquired the data through a second party data agreement with CVS and further enriched their understanding of Bart's purchase behavior. When Danone paid Bayer a fee for acquiring a database of potential probiotic yoghurt consumers as their third-party data and received hundreds of thousands of leads, Bart was included. In reality, Bart was not identifiable, but his fridge was, and Danone merely sent the ad to the fridge. Bart had consented for his anonymized profile to be shared with platinum graded advertisers, graded by an independent body as a clean advertiser, in exchange for a three-month free subscription to Speedy gut.

Bart slept a sound sleep that night and many nights thereafter, happy in the knowledge that he was doing everything he could to not have a repeat of "the incident". He had added a good decade to his life.

Understanding how to build a consumer database

So as we start discussing the importance for companies over the next decade to build an owned consumer dataset, it would help to look at some interesting, and in my opinion successful cases of different companies doing this in their own way, to understand the how and the why of having a consumer data strategy. Companies which are built based on an online subscription model of course have immediate access to consumer data and we will look at a couple of those for inspiration. Much harder to find are "offline" companies who have built successful data acquisition engines, but we will discuss a couple of those as well.

Spotify – Spotify gains access to your personal information when you sign up for the service with your email address and allows you to also enter your gender and date of birth. Spotify keeps track of your devices and recently for the family subscription your location, to make sure a registered family member lives in the same home. The true magic of Spotify, however, comes in how they enrich your consumer profile with your listening behavior and use that to broaden your listening hours and find more people like you to sign up to Spotify. Spotify pays record labels a flat percentage of its revenues and its ability to progressively negotiate this percentage downwards will depend on its ability to demonstrate real distribution muscle to the label by gaining tens of millions of users every year and being able to influence these users to listen to specific music. Spotify will use listening behavioral data from its subscribers to make users discover the type of music they would like. Or keep away music they would dislike by tracking when a track is switched in the first 30 seconds, for example. This not only demonstrates its influence on making songs propagate to the labels but also dramatically improves listening experience and continued subscription. Spotify also uses listening trends to find out what part of its service to best market to potential new subscribers and which artists or songs to "lead with" in driving downloads. The big learning here is that, merely having the contact details of your consumers is not enough and companies need to continue to enrich the database with behavioral information for it to be useful in driving engagement.

Nike – Nike has arguably been the trailblazer in terms of investing into the digital commerce space over the last several years, famously snubbing third party e-commerce platforms to the benefit of its own direct to consumer sales. With an offline store-based model to start with, Nike would have a lot less access to consumer data than a Spotify and their resolution to this was to create a plethora of digital engagement channels from which to acquire consumer data. For starters, Nike now drives almost 30% of its total revenue through its direct retail model either through Nike.com or through the Nike app. In addition, Nike also owns and operates several additional consumer apps and platforms, including, its loyalty program Nike+, its utility apps like Nike Running club and Nike Training club, or its Nike SNKRS app for sneaker-heads to stay current in the exciting world of sneakers. In addition, users can connect their Nike run club app to other fitness apps and wearable devices, like their TomTom watch or their Garmin watch or even their Apple health app which provides an important activity data stream into Nike run club. Nike also has an app called Nike Fit which allows users to take a picture of their feet and recommends a shoe size. So here we see an example of a company focused on providing utility and products directly to consumers and capturing consumer data in the process to turn into insights, targeted offers and propositions to gain continued transactions from consumers. The main learning being that even for companies that are traditionally offline businesses, digital engagement will offer a welcome avenue to start amassing consumer data.

FICO, the OG of third-party data – I have been reflecting on what example to talk about in third party data usage, considering they are generally few and far between and immediately I thought about FICO, the OG (Original Gangster) of third-party data. FICO, short for the Fair Isaac Corporation, is a public company that provides lenders with a credit score called a FICO score with which they can assess whether to sell a credit product, like a loan or a mortgage to a consumer. FICO sources its information from three credit reporting companies, Experian, Equifax and TransUnion that in turn gain information from a variety of sources including the banks and lenders who make credit decisions based on the FICO score in the first place. All three agencies claim to have information on almost a billion or above consumers and are also publicly listed. This third-party data model has been in existence since the sixties and to ensure that companies do not make erroneous decisions on creditworthiness based on incorrect and unfairly shared data the Fair Credit Reporting Act was passed in 1970. In 2003 an amendment to that act also provided that consumers be able to receive one free copy of their credit report from each agency once a year to understand what information is shareable with lenders. In spite of all the lawsuits and criticisms levelled at this system over the years, not to mention the hacking and data leakage scandals, this privately held yet regulated collection, storage and sale of data for purely commercial means has been a large contributor to the ease of giving and receiving credit and has enabled companies to build large and profitable lending businesses. The big learning here is the fact that third party data sold commercially, much as dishonorable as it sounds, can work well when done in a consented and well-regulated fashion.

Three practical things you should do now

Over the next decade we will see companies all over, attempting to build up their consumer database, loyal consumers, new consumers, prospective consumers etc. Retailers and companies who have a direct relationship with consumers will have a much easier time with that than brands that do not have a significant role in the actual transaction itself, which could include most consumer products, particularly FMCG. To make this build happen over time companies need to be patient and act along a few important directions recommended below.

Collect First- and Second-party data – Start building a direct channel to engage with your consumers and start accumulating consumer data through this channel. (See Figure 3.1.) This could either be a direct sales channel like Nike.com or it could be an additional utility like Nike running club, or a loyalty program or even something specific like the Nike SNKRS app that is not necessarily transaction related. Make it mandatory for consumers to share their data with you if they want to take advantage of promotions or participate in campaigns and competitions. Even offline events could serve as an easy

FIGURE 3.1 First, second- and third-party consumer data

channel to gain consumer data, ask consumers to sign-up on a tablet at the activation location. First party data collection is a game of accumulation and with patience and over time, with consistent execution you will start hitting interesting numbers.

Convincing your partners, be it retailers or media channels or other collaborators to share consumer data with you will be a long arduous process but it definitely will not happen if you do not ask for it. Start making consumer data sharing a regular ask in all joint business planning and contract renegotiation discussions. Make promotion spend contingent on having the underlying consumer data shared back with you. Most importantly, understand the value of having the consumer data by benchmarking it to the cost of purchasing third party data or your internal customer lifetime value calculations and be ready to compensate partners for the data being shared back with you.

Buy third party data – Buy, buy, buy. I do not know why conventional wisdom is to look down upon third party data as low quality and almost a cop out but that is just not true. There are some incredible sources of high-quality third-party data which are regularly refreshed and companies looking to get a leg up in this space should start allocating funds to buy data every year. Start with small audiences on multiple providers to get an understanding of what is out there and the efficiencies the data provides in reaching and engaging consumers. I think over the next decade as data security concerns start getting allayed there will be a lot of more publicly available data and we will see third party data quantity and quality rival that from the walled gardens like Google and Facebook.

Enrich your data and manage consent – While you are stacking up individual data records, focus as well on getting as much "I do" type of data added to your database as possible. In general, I would say if you have not updated a record in a month you have probably lost that consumer. Think of the consumer data from a monthly active user (MAU) point of view – if you have not engaged the consumer, whose record you are carrying, in a month then that specific person is not really your consumer anymore. Activating the database could take the form of reaching the consumers through some message and tracking receipt, offering some promotion and tracking redemption or transactions or understanding if the consumer used any other use case on offer. Every interaction would leave a data trail which you should capture into the database – somewhat like Spotify does for listening behavior for each consumer.

Last, but not the least, have your legal teams do a comprehensive review of data privacy regulations in all your markets and develop appropriate guidelines for the organization on the Dos and Don'ts, but do impress upon your legal team that the idea is to adhere to the law and not to over-regulate the company above and beyond what is legally required. A simple rule of thumb has always been that "consent is king", but as data acquisition happens from multiple sources at different points in time, and as in many cases it is bought or transferred in bulk, the nature of consent received for each data record itself needs to be recorded. Most consumer databases provide comprehensive consent management features or if not, there are several consent management platforms available in the marketplace which you would be well advised to study and make full use of. This would help keep a clean record on data usage, which will not only help your corporation avoid fines from regulators but also demonstrate to consumers that their data is indeed safe with you and their trust is placed well in your hands.

So, there you have it, step one of engaging your consumers, harnessing their data and ensuring through at least monthly interactions that they are indeed your consumers. A final word of advice, consumer data acquisition is a long-term play, both from the point of view of how long it takes to acquire the data and how long it would take to realize the gains from this acquired data. You will need to demonstrate patience and the willingness to invest in the build over the next three to five years without seeing immediate returns on that investment. The alternative is to wake up in a world five years from now where you are the only company who does not have any consumer access and you would likely not have a company anymore either.

The Future of Loyalty Programs

Because Odin pledged allegiance to The Syndicate

It'd been a couple of months since Odin's epic beach vacation in Sri Lanka and he was just amazed at how quickly it had got to the point again where he was in dire need of another vacation, and this in spite of the fact that his company had moved last year to a four-day week. He is starting to gather that vacations for him were not just about escaping work but also about escaping himself and his own expectations about how he ought to be living his life. Somehow when he was not in Berlin, all bets were off, he even allowed himself to eat a couple of real steaks instead of the plant-based meats that he had wholeheartedly adopted. But vacation or not, he at least had that one thing, that one place to go to when he felt the need. He had The Syndicate.

Odin pushed himself out of bed and biked over, half asleep, to his gym which was a couple of blocks down from where he lived. He had a discounted membership with early access to some extremely popular spinning sessions because he was part of The Syndicate. Syndicate members kept a low profile, so he did not know how many of the spinners today were from The Syndicate. Not knowing was part of the allure. As he was Uber-ing his way to work later that day, he marveled at the new Syndicate skin on his Uber-app, it was all in dark mode and used Syndicate lingo, so a ride was called a Mission and the destination was called the Rendezvous, very slick.

He had lunch later that day with a colleague and just as he was about to pay, his colleague caught a glimpse of his Syndicate full metal credit card, people had not used cards for a while now, let alone plastic. Colleague: "What the hell is that?", Odin, completely overreacting: "It's nothing, drop it, I don't want to talk about it". You do not talk about The Syndicate. Odin was very much looking forward to The Syndicate's annual meetup next month. A full day of special access events and activities and a lot of fun. Most importantly, finally the ability to talk openly about being in The Syndicate and to be around people like him. It really made him feel like he belonged, being a third-generation descendant of Russian migrants in East Germany meant he had always had identity issues to deal with and this was really his crew, his people.

As Odin got settled late night into his worn-out Gaming chair, put on his VR gear, he psyched himself up to start thinking less like Odin and more like his in-game Avatar. This is where he felt like he could be himself, the real Odin, not having to decide his fate, because that was decided by The Syndicate. Not having to think with "Zweifel", as the Germans called it, about his objective. The Syndicate told him who needs to be killed and he did what the Syndicate said, simple as that. He took a sip of his favorite energy drink, took a deep breath and jumped off the burning building, guns blazing into another three-hour session of Assassins Creed – The Syndicate Redux.

Understanding modern-day loyalty programs

Over the course of the next three topics, we will examine the different type of value exchanges underlying the build of a great digitally enabled engagement platform and we will start here with the notion of loyalty. Let us look at a few successful loyalty programs and archetypes of today and learn from them.

Starbucks loyalty – Of all the single brand, single product loyalty programs out there, and there are ever fewer for reasons we will discuss later, the Starbucks loyalty program is a stand-out for not only having survived but for having re-invented itself to add real value to consumers and the Starbucks company itself. The Starbucks program offers a few very relevant consumer benefits: An app which allows consumers to pre-order, pay and skip the queue to pick up, an e-Wallet to top up and pay for in-store orders seamlessly, free drinks and merchandise through points, free coffees on your birthday and special event invitations, ability to sync music from the Starbucks store with your Spotify playlist, sending gift cards to friends, locating stores etc. In short, by identifying and digitally enabling a variety of use cases that are linked to a user's Starbucks experience and making it easier and more valuable for the consumer to participate in this experience, Starbucks has managed to engage and keep the consumers loyal to the brand. What helps Starbucks is the fact that most consumers build a daily consumption habit and, in that context, having an owned app and loading it up with a variety of experiences makes it worth the consumer's while to maintain it on their smartphones. Starbucks of course gains valuable consumer data in the process which helps it get sharper on the personalization it offers to each consumer to keep them coming back every day.

Amazon Prime and Alibaba's 88VIP – No discussion on loyalty programs today can be complete without touching on Amazon Prime and its oriental equivalent 88VIP by Alibaba, both with their similarities but also slightly different underlying philosophies. Amazon Prime is a paid subscription ser-vice which, for USD 119 per year gives members access to valuable benefits on Amazon's entire family of use cases including: Free delivery on certain shipping options, Exclusive deals on Amazon.com and at Wholefoods, Prime Video, Music, Gaming and Reading and others. At last count Amazon Prime had 150 million members.[1] While Amazon makes significant membership revenues from the program, the cost of the benefits awarded far exceeds this revenue. But the paid nature of the program creates a mental stickiness in the consumers' minds towards Amazon's owned ecosystem of use cases. Alibaba's 88VIP also does the same, in the sense of providing access to discounts for members but also linking into video-streaming (Youku), food delivery (Ele.me), music streaming (Xiami), movie ticketing (Taopiaopiao) etc. The one fundamental difference between Prime and 88VIP is that 88VIP membership can be paid for or earned by consumers if they dial-up their engagement with the Alibaba platform by writing reviews, interacting with other consumers and using a variety of use cases. So a value exchange of loyalty to a consortium of use cases in return for bundled discounts from the consortium clearly works well. In this case the use cases in the consortium are all owned by the players but that does not need to be the case. Another learning is that consumers need to feel like they have earned the right to receive the benefits either by paying in cash or through actions. The stickiness that comes with the sense of belonging outweighs the potential demerits of having a paid program, as Amazon and Alibaba have quite profitably figured out.

Airline and credit card loyalty – Now let us look at the original loyalty program experts starting with Credit Cards. I would generalize, that the only reason most consumers use credit cards these days instead of using a direct debit instrument is the loyalty benefits they offer, and most of the card points are used towards airline miles. So, in a way, card issuers have become very dependent on their relationship with Airline miles. On the other hand, Airlines too have become completely dependent on their mileage programs for their survival, particularly on card issuers buying these miles in bulk and handing them to consumers. Information here is hard to come by, but a recent valuation exercise in the US saw that American Airlines' AAdvantage program and United's MileagePlus program are valued higher than the Airlines themselves! The loyalty program entity of the airline makes a profit by selling miles to card companies at twice the price at which it buys a redemption seat from the airline – thus 50% margin. Card issuers don't mind as long as they are able to continue to drive consumer acquisition – more consumers equals more credit revolvers equals more interest income. And as long as they are able to drive card usage – more transactions equals more interchange income. Difficult to average out the multitude of programs across markets but card companies will pay ~1–2% in miles benefits, make upwards of 10% in interest rate on revolvers and 1.75%+ on interchange rate on transactions. Phew! So, the bottom line is this: Banks have tied up with Airlines to make consumers use and pay for a product they don't necessarily need (credit cards) to inadvertently pay a rightful price for a product they do need (air travel). The big learning here is the utility of putting two symbiotic use cases together to create a somewhat esoteric bundle in the consumers' minds where everyone wins.

Three practical things you should do now

Clearly from the examples above, the future of engaging through loyalty will rest on the ability to create consortia. For those of us lucky enough to have use cases that are relevant daily, like Starbucks or for those who have a massive ecosystem of use cases on offer like Alibaba or Amazon this task will be easier. Unfortunately, most of us are like the card issuers or airlines and we need each other. So, the next decade in loyalty programs will belong to the best collaborators and here is a quick review of the things you would need to think through.

Design the right consortium of use case owners – Pick the right partners to join up with along two clear dimensions, use cases that make sense to bundle together and companies which have a similar state of willingness and tech ability to make things happen. I spent some time a few years ago building up a consortium of partners that included e-commerce, Video streaming, Ride hailing, and the package was directed to early adopters of digital use cases. We stood the program up in a few months and it worked incredibly well for everyone because we were somehow in the same boat, working with similar tools and understood each other well. But the anchor was a clearly defined consumer segment which we agreed would find utility in all our use cases.

The program works because of the simple notion that the cost of acquiring a consumer (CAC) to a consortium of use cases will be lower than the added-up cost of acquiring the same consumer separately into each individual use case.

The consumer acquisition benefits in themselves should make the consortium worth it for all partners and you would need to be able to demonstrate that for each participant. But consumers will also only stick to the program if the partners continue to offer benefits to consumers that make it worth their while. (See Figure 3.2.)

Make the consumer experience seamless – At the heart of the consortium will lie the shared consumer database, and the fact that it is shared would mean consumers will need to consent to all partners. I personally think it makes most sense to adopt an all-or-nothing approach to partners by not allowing

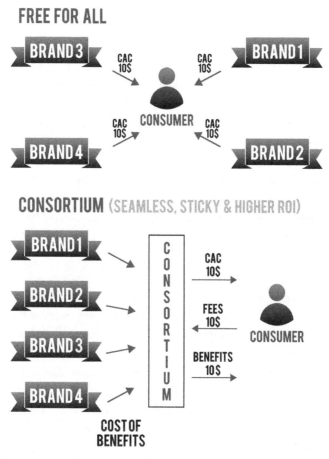

FIGURE 3.2 Benefits of a loyalty consortium

consumers to opt in or out of any individual partner. This keeps the consortium simple and encourages companies to only add partners to the program that add value to the relationship. This also avoids overly complex consent management for the consumers. The actual act of recording usage on each use case would happen on individual platforms and you'd need to connect your consumer database to each individual partner through APIs to ensure "I do" type consumer data flows into the unified database in real time or in near time. Much as complex as it sounds there are ways to decouple this entirely by allowing each partner to develop their own loyalty points and establishing a "points exchange rate" at the back end or using a payment provider as an integrator and funding cash into an e-Wallet sub-account which can only be spent on partner use cases.

True benefit will only accrue when the experience is seamless, meaning the user signs in just once and the discounts accrue to the user automatically every time she or he makes a purchase. Seamless experience is only possible with full real-time connectivity through APIs. Payment providers can play a valuable role here because most manufacturers and brands have no way of creating a reliable record of purchase. Another alternative is to place unique identifiers on each pack and allowing consumers to self-record purchase after consumption. The difficulty here is in verifying that consumption has happened by placing e.g., scannable codes inside the packaging. You would need to build out and continuously improve upon the end-to-end user experience for purchase, consumption record and redemption flow for each partner in each retail channel.

Run it as a separate entity – Setting the consortium up as a separate entity and a separate brand has several benefits. Partners are more willing to join a consortium if it is seen as being independent of one major anchor brand. It is a lot easier to work through cross-charging and transfer pricing implications if the construct is structured as a separate vehicle. Consumer data can belong to the entity and consortium partners can enter into data sharing agreements with that one entity instead of with each other. There are several other benefits in creating an entity which can run this as a business transparently by itself, but by far the most important is the focus on "making ends meet" that this would bring to the idea. If the entity if not able to make a profit by virtue of ensuring that the CAC advantage and the CLV advantage of consorting outweighs the cost of running the entity then clearly the consortium has not made sense, is not adding value and changes need to be made.

So, there it is, a few pointers on where to start as you embark upon building your consortia and driving engagement through loyalty. As we move into the next topic my final piece of advice would be to understand that in this new world you need to give to be able to get. I have seen companies being irrationally protective about consumer data especially with non-competing companies because of absolutely no reason at all. Open your books and your minds and you will see it is the right thing to do.

Providing Additional Value Through Digital Products

Wahad makes a Jjajjangmyeon

It has been six months now since Wahad and his wife decided that he would become a full-time SAHD, Stay at Home Dad. His wife got a big promotion at work and they had to move to another part of town, that meant a new school and a new life altogether for the daughters and it was best for him to stay home and take care of them and manage the household. As he sent the women in his life off, one at a time, to their respective school buses and Ubers with their packed lunches and snacks, it was 9 am and he slumped into the living room couch and opened up his "The Dad app".

First things first, he went straight to the kid's fashion section and started reading up on what 12-yr-olds were wearing these days. There were some useful resources here like a guide on what size to buy, the girls were always growing out of stuff and it was just so difficult to master the art of buying clothes that were somewhat oversized but not too large. He was able to pick out dresses and then render an image of how his daughters would look wearing the clothes, then ask his wife to have a quick look-see before he ordered. He bought a couple of matching dresses; they would look pretty wearing those during Eid he thought. Next up, he scrolled to the sports section of the app. Here he found a full inventory of sports and the boys and girls leagues and match schedules for each sport. He made a note of the Hockey game schedule for both his daughters and noted down practice sessions in his calendar. It was great to have this facility, there was so much enthusiasm in India around sports and it was nice that this community was helping people connect to each other and have their children play together in a safe and well-equipped environment.

There, now that he had done some shopping and planning for the girls, it was time for him to focus on himself. His wife had been pointing out a bit too often these days that his hairline was receding somewhat faster than before. He was always dismissive of this focus on his looks, but truth be told, he was starting to wonder if he should do something about it. He went into the "Self-care" section of the app and there was an entire sub-section dedicated to Hair care. He found a shampoo and hair tonic bundle and after having read some reviews from some other dads he decided it was time to start looking into the hair loss issue more intently. Now he needed to figure out what to make for dinner, he wanted to surprise the wife with something different today. She had been getting very deep into a lot of Korean dramas these days and he had tried and failed to sit through a couple of episodes of melodrama and over-acting. But she loved it and his daughters were also very much into K-pop, which he liked as well and very much enjoyed dancing to just to embarrass them. So, he had noticed how irrational Koreans in the dramas were about their love for Jjajjangmyeon and he decided to give it a shot. The Dad app gave him an easy to make recipe, with chicken of course, and he was able to order all ingredients with one click for a one-hour delivery, how convenient.

Somewhere in a data center far far away, the following companies registered consumer engagement that day: H&M in their kids fashion platform, Decathlon in their local sporting leagues platform, L'Oréal in their Men's care platform and Nestle in their cooking platform.

Understanding how companies build digital products

While we spent time earlier in this chapter looking at awarding loyalty benefits to drive consumers to engage with your brand, we will now look at examples of companies that create engagement by providing value to the consumer that goes beyond the product itself. We will look at a couple of successful examples and some great attempts at doing this.

Redbull – As far as engagement marketing goes, you would be hard pressed to find a brand that does it better than Redbull and I only have tons of respect for everything they do. So, what is it exactly? And how has it come to this point where even before you open that can of Redbull, just the act of picking it off the shelf gets the adrenaline flowing? Redbull has essentially taken that notion of energy and adrenaline and created so many opportunities for the consumer to interact with their brand in a context that is full of adrenaline that the association is now completely habitual. There are a few things Redbull does: starting with sponsoring extreme sports like skateboarding, skydiving, BMX etc. Redbull has a major presence in motorsport sponsorships and there is perhaps no form of motorsport left in the world for a consumer to enjoy where he or she does not interact with the Redbull brand. Beyond sponsorships, Redbull also owns several sports teams including most famously Red Bull Racing and Scuderia AlphaTauri in Formula One, Football teams in Australia, US, Brazil and even in ESports. Among Redbull's digitally enabled platforms belongs Redbull TV and if you have not experienced it yet, you should. Redbull provides hours and hours of incredible and free to view content, films, shorts, documentaries and live casts related to Formula One, Skating, Biking, Dance, Gaming, Outdoors, Adventure etc. The quality of the content is incredible and inspiring and makes you want to make a run for the next convenience store and buy that can of Redbull. Redbull TV can be streamed through the Redbull app. In addition to the Redbull TV app, Redbull also has a few gaming apps available for download, including Dirt Biking and Snowboarding. So with this wide assortment of engagement opportunities with the consumer which are so accurately tied to the core values of the brand, it is no surprise that Redbull holds a commanding share of the energy drinks market which few competitors have managed to make a dent into.

Under Armour – It's with mixed feelings that I am sharing this specific example because while the acquisition and usage of digital use cases was a great plus, there are so many other things that didn't quite go right for Under Armour that has landed it in the perilous position that it is in today. But let us rewind a few years when Under Armour was still cool for teen consumers, and Tom Brady and Gisele Bundchen were endorsing the brand which was giving Nike and Adidas a run for their money. In 2015 Under Armour bought MyFitnessPal for USD 475 million adding to its previous purchases of MapMyFitness and Endomondo.[2] The idea was to make headway into connected fitness, by on the one hand providing value to consumers as they worked on personal fitness and on the other hand gaining consumer insights from the fitness apps and connecting them to real product introductions in the market. The interesting point here is this, these apps and the connected fitness business unit continue to earn subscription revenues and provide actual operating income for the company, even as the actual apparel business suffers scandals, performance issues and is generally being out-competed by rivals. So, the big learning here is two-fold, an engagement platform side-gig can and should be run like an independent business and can actually make money. But recent events suggest that much as successful as this side business might be, the core business still needs to continue to deliver for the company to stay relevant.

H&M, Zara, L'Oréal, IKEA – These companies and many others have created interesting attempts at adding value to consumers by providing related and relevant use cases, and while I'm sure they'll admit the journey is just starting it's interesting to see how a lot of companies are approaching this space. H&M has launched platforms like the Perfect Fit app which allows customers to create their own digital avatar and have it try clothes on, or the image search embedded in the H&M app which allows customers to take a picture of a billboard or off social media and search for similar clothes by H&M. Zara has introduced Augmented Reality inside their stores where shoppers can use their phones to see models wear specific clothes. L'Oréal bought a Canadian startup Modi-Face in 2018[3] which allows consumers to try on hair color or foundation tones on themselves before making a purchase. For their professional brand L'Oréal also enabled one-on-one consultation with an expert who then used AR technology to place specific make up products on the consumers face in a video chat. IKEA is working on a feature that would allow consumer's to visualize how a piece of furniture would look like in their home by turning simple room photos into a 3D visualization of the room and allowing consumers to select and swap out specific items. IKEA also bought an online marketplace for Handymen called TaskRabbit in September 2017,[4] which provides among other things, furniture assembly. Many examples and several forays, and over the next decade we will see companies being bolder and bolder as they break out of the focus on products and start creating use cases which can be independently monetized with consumers.

Michelin and Guinness – One of my favorite examples on engagement is the Michelin guide more for its history than its current form. Michelin, the tire company, started the guide in 1900 when there were very few cars on the road and therefore limited demand for tires. The idea was to get people out and about and indirectly spur car and tire demand. Over the years, the guide has achieved iconic status and the link to tire sales has waned, but it is still an interesting case. The *Guinness Book of World Records* has even more interesting origins. Sir Hugh Beaver, the top man at Guinness Breweries got into an argument in a bar about the fastest game bird in Europe and realized that a book which would list the answers to such debates that pop up in pubs the world over might be handy to have. Guinness does not own the record book anymore; it has exchanged hands a few times and is now owned by Ripley entertainment. No learning here, just some interesting trivia and if you really were to want to take something away then take away the fact that there are popular examples out there of corporations building out well renowned side-gigs which have become household names and have taken a life of their own.

Three practical things you should do now

Building a digital product isn't easy and in many ways it's like doing a startup within your company without any funding worries and with a ready consumer base. And while an entire book probably needs to be written, and you'll find many already have been written on this topic, I wanted to put down some thought starters here for you to start addressing this build immediately.

Think of the core idea – Thinking about what use case you would offer to consumers seems like the obvious place to start. In general an idea could be linked to the consumer's purchase journey – as is the case with the H&M, IKEA or

L'Oréal examples, or linked to the brand identity and brand attributes – like the whole suite of use cases that Redbull operates or even linked to your products functionality – in a way belonging to an extended family of use cases like the Under Armour connected fitness concept.

Map out the consumer journey – Be prepared to spend media dollars to drive consumers to the platform, be it through dedicated marketing efforts or through your existing media support for brands. Allow consumers to transact while they are using your platform. While in the beginning this would feel like you're trying to support two business models at the same time, over time your investment needs in engaging consumers through ads will be lower as the platform itself gains organic reach and engagement. (See Figure 3.3.)

Create a sustainable business model – Think about ways to monetize the platform so it makes its own revenue and profit. This will help you to push the

BUILD A PLATFORM TO ALLOW CONSUMERS TO...

AWARENESS ...FIND AND UNDERSTAND YOUR PRODUCTS

CONSIDERATION ...COMPARE TO OTHER SIMILAR PRODUCTS

PURCHASE ...BUY ANY PRODUCTS

USAGE ...ENHANCE THEIR EXPERIENCE WHILE USING YOUR PRODUCTS

RE-PURCHASE ...SUBSCRIBE TO YOUR PRODUCTS

ADVOCACY ...SHARE THEIR EXPERIENCE WHILE USING YOUR PRODUCTS

FIGURE 3.3 Providing value along the consumer journey

concept to a point where it really starts adding value to the consumer – if it is not worth paying for, it is not creating value.

The final bit of advice here is to think less incremental and more disruptive and to get on with ideas, much as ridiculous as they sound. The future belongs to platforms and not just to brands and very few platforms are built with full knowledge and confidence of how things will turn out. As legend has it, YouTube was initially conceived as a dating site along the lines of hotornot .com, little did the founders know that five years later they would be serving 2 billion videos a day. Think about all the ideas you have had which you decided not to act upon just five years ago because they were too out there or somewhat disconnected to your core business. You might have passed on a YouTube.

Engaging Through the Intangibles

Jaden's daily facial care ritual

Porcelain skin, they used that terminology to describe the flawless, glowing and tight skin on your face in Korea. Historically reserved for women, but over the last decade men too, including Jaden, had taken on that aspiration to have porcelain skin. Jaden was making his way to an event, staring out the window and reflecting on his skincare journey that started maybe 15 years ago. He had just hit 40 and his wife told him that how he treats his skin every day will decide how old he looks ten years from now. It was a bit like managing his stock portfolio, by being active and diligent every day he had eked out an awesome return over ten years.

So, like he would do with a stock, he first off started to educate himself and he found a very professionally written and clever series of blogs and ted talks about men's skincare by Kiehls. It went into the science of age-ing and unpacked the utility of the different products on the market and introduced him to the ten-step skincare routine Oil cleanser, Foaming cleanser, Exfoliant, Essence, Serum, Mask, Eye cream, Moisturizer and SPF. And of course, the daytime and nighttime or the summer and winter variants of it. The weblog became his go to place for getting educated on the topic and he liked how it was entirely male focused. He remembered one of those rare times that he participated in a raffle hosted by Kiehls, but only because they were giving away a Harley Davidson bike! He did not win it of course, and he knew how improbable it would be, but he was anxiously looking forward to the winner being announced. They did send him a bunch of free samples though and that was good enough payback for scanning a QR code on a pack. Speaking of Harleys, Kiehls' "Bike Journeys" concept was hitting its fourth season and this time they were going to do the Hanoi to Ho Chi Minh city route. Twenty bikers (with porcelain skin), riding over ten days, exploring along the way and becoming friends – that made for a great show and he was looking forward to it. Maybe next time he will apply to be part of the biking crew, although he would probably need to learn how to ride a Harley.

He arrived at his destination, it was a Kiehls Brotherhood event, with a couple of new product launches, unveiling a new custom designed Harley to put in their Gangnam showroom and a meet and greet for their top 100 consumers with the ragingly popular K-pop girl group 2MUCH2BEAR. That selfie with the group is going to give him endless bragging rights with his friends. It was a packed event, perhaps a thousand men all on invitation only. You had to have had an annual spend on Kiehls of over USD 1000 to be invited into the Kiehls Brotherhood and this was his third year in a row. He was keen on making some business contacts here, it seemed like the kind of place a real estate fund manager would attend, and he was keen on selling some co-working space backed REITs today. "It was going to be a great evening," he thought, as he entered the main room with shining lights glistening off a thousand porcelain faces.

Understanding engagement through intangibles

Earlier in this chapter we looked at driving consumer engagement through value exchange in the form of loyalty benefits and additional use cases. It's time now to look at the third leg of a value exchange where we gain the consumers' engagement by providing them intangible benefits in return. While there are many such intangibles, the ones that I think will feature most prominently in the future are Education, Gamification, Content, Status and Community.

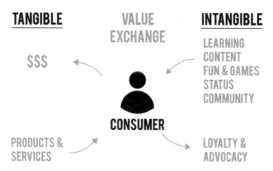

FIGURE 3.4 The intangibles exchange

Let us look at examples of how companies have acted along these intangibles. (See Figure 3.4.)

How TransferWise educates – TransferWise is a hugely successful startup in the international remittance space, started a decade ago and now does 5 USD billion of monthly transfers across the world.[5] The core idea is to match the incoming and outgoing for all currencies and to only make a "net" transfer, in the process saving international remittance fees. The other angle is to provide the service and the associated savings to consumers in a simple to use, transparent and easy to understand interface. Over the years TransferWise has built a strong consumer base by educating consumers on the intricacies of the international remittance space through some key actions. For starters, TransferWise provides an extremely easy to use comparison tool on its platform that allows consumers to understand within a few minutes how the service would benefit them. The onsite or in-app experience also does a great job explaining how and why the service can offer this benefit. TransferWise relies heavily on word-of-mouth with an incredibly significant share of users coming to the platform through recommendations from friends. The company measures the word-of-mouth quality through NPS scores but also focuses on steering the quality of messaging by ensuring consumers not only recommend the rational benefit of saving on fees but also get behind the emotional mission of not allowing large financial institutions to use opacity to overcharge users. So, consumers educate each other on the product but also help drive an emotional connection to using the service. TransferWise publishes a lot of high-quality articles on the topic of international remittance in multiple languages and countries every year. These articles feed into its search marketing strategy, get shared and drive education in a big way. TransferWise also has its own blog where it shares content related to personal finance, living abroad and, of course, remittances. The company keeps its interruption marketing or advertising messages very functional or mission-driven and invariably you will read about not just the fact that the service is cheaper but also why it is so. Finally, TransferWise's social media team clearly spends a lot of careful time answering one-on-one queries on Facebook etc., from prospective consumers. In fact, the word of mouth is so strong here that you routinely see existing consumers "sell" the service to new consumers on a Facebook chat under a TransferWise ad.

How Alibaba gamifies – Gamification is gambling for the most part, I just wanted to get that straight up front. Over the years, the idea of gamification has started to get a bit blurred as companies try to include any form of engagement under the gamification umbrella but for the purpose of this chapter gamification means gambling. And as far as gamification goes, I think Chinese tech players, especially in the e-commerce space, are a decade ahead of the rest of the world, and there is a lot to learn from it. Alibaba is, of course, one of the masters at this and its 11/11 Singles day sales of 38 USD billion in one day in 2019 are testament to its ability to use engagement and translate it into transactions. Over the years there have been many different games allowing consumers to have the chance to win disproportionate value compared to the investment made, with the one critical difference with actual gambling being that there is absolutely no downside, beyond time wasted of course. Broadly, Alibaba has used a few archetypes of games to drive sales. In its simplest form are games where an individual plays to earn a coupon and in the process of playing that game engages with a brand. This has taken the form of a brand trivia game, where consumers answer questions about brands, or a Pokémon Go type AR game which has consumers walk into retail stores and chase a cat to earn a coupon. A much more passive gamification happens with the relatively simple raffle or spin-the-wheel type of games where consumers are randomly chosen and awarded without having to perform any action, but you see much less of these as Alibaba is clearly big on expecting engagement in return for coupons. Then there is a slew of games that pit groups of people against each other such as the group gifting game where users gift red packets to each other in a group. Groups compete against each other with the winning group with the largest amount contributed getting more value to spend. In the Hong Bao stacking game in last year's 11/11 the group with the highest stack took all the earnings. And finally, there are the loot boxes, mystery boxes with a fixed price which could include, and always will, products that far exceed the actual price paid by the consumer. The consumer thinks she or he is winning disproportionately, and brands get to drive up basket size and encourage trial purchases.

How Coke creates content – Coke Studio Pakistan debuted in 2008 and has had 12 successful Seasons ever since its conception and is a rare and interesting example of a consumer brand having achieved significant engagement by creating and sharing top quality content. Pakistan and South Asia in general has a rich history of folk music and large sections of the populace have a deep appreciation for original local music forms like Sufi, Qawwali, Ghazal, Bhangra etc. Over the last couple of decades with the advent of cable TV in the early nineties and then streaming music in the last decade South Asian youth have had incredible exposure to western Pop and Rock music. Coke as a brand has associated itself with music since long with the intention of drawing a parallel between the optimism and unifying qualities of music with the values of the Coca-Cola brand. Coke Studio took the two music genres of folk and western music and worked with local artists in Pakistan to create some unforgettable music that was not only great to listen to but also represented Coca-Cola's values of building bridges between people, culture and genres. The Pakistan edition of Coke Studio also found great success across the border in India where it took on an additional meaning, set against the backdrop of two populations which were very much alike but have spent the last 70 years at loggerheads. In India, Coke itself was banished in 1977 in a time of fervent nationalization but re-entered in 1993. The brand's ability to weave itself into local music was also symbolic of the brand's ability to weave itself into the local fabric of the consumers. Over the years the series has produced some of the most viewed songs on YouTube, created incredible amounts of organic reach for the Coca-Cola brand but more than anything else engaged millions of consumers in South Asia, immersing them in an experience that allows them to sample what it means to drink a Coke, even before they actually drink one. Beyond music Coca-Cola has also been a regular supporter and sponsor for the FIFA World Cup and the Olympics; in these instances instead of taking on responsibility to create original content, the company has chosen to associate itself with these mega events to remind consumers as they experience these events, the happiness stemming from the sporting camaraderie and the awesome experience of watching a game together is something that consumers can also get to in some measure by just cracking open a cold can of Coke.

How Singapore airlines builds status – There are very few companies that do status as well as airlines do and very few airlines that do it as well as Singapore Airlines does. I remember when I first moved to Singapore around a decade ago and started flying "SQ" as it's stylishly referred to. As a potential SQ flyer you go through five progressive levels of self-actualization, and you have to believe me when I say that something as seemingly trivial as airline status affects people's self-esteem in good measure, especially in this part of the world. So, the first level, so to say, is for you to emerge out of the low-cost wilderness of Air Asia, Jetstar or Singapore airlines' own Scoot airline and pay twice as much for a flight ticket on SQ. The only functional benefit being that, instead of having to buy a pathetic meal you get a pathetic meal for free, and the status of not having to fly budget. Next, you become a Krisflyer member by just signing up so you can start earning miles and there is pretty much no real functional benefit to speak of at this stage other than some insignificant member privileges. Next up, once you rack up 25k miles comes Krisflyer Silver and the benefits you get with that status upgrade are absolutely nothing. You earn miles a bit faster than you did when you were just a mere member. Then at 50k miles comes Krisflyer Gold, and it unlocks that most sought-after facility of the airport lounge so you can have mediocre free food in a comfortable setting rather than indulge in the amazing eating options most airports offer. But that's not it, while you're sipping a machine dispensed cappuccino in the lounge, you'd notice that there's another fancier lounge with better food, showers and free toothbrushes reserved for business and first-class passengers and PPS club members. PPS club membership comes to those who earn 25k miles in business class instead of economy and at this point, on top of the status and nicer lounge, you unlock a bunch of cool things like discounts at duty free shops and priority in booking. But you would be mistaken if you think you have reached the zenith of status because for mega-spenders on business class there is the PPS Club Solitaire which gives you curbside check-in and priority immigration. An incredible ladder and people can go to amazing lengths to attain and protect their airline status, providing the airlines with much needed engagement and providing us tons of lessons to learn from.

How CrossFit creates a community – You have probably heard about Cross-Fit several times and perhaps too many times. In Brad Pitt's *Fight Club*, they say that the first rule of *Fight Club* is to never talk about *Fight Club*, well it is the other way around for CrossFit. The first rule of CrossFit? Always talk about CrossFit. But for all the criticism of the workout style and the recent scandals that the founder has faced, which I don't want to get into, the one thing that amazes me is the strong sense of community the brand builds in their gyms and across gyms. Four things we need to understand to learn from CrossFit's community building. Firstly, the business model is based on starting thousands of communities worldwide. CrossFit gets a fee from every gym that chooses to be affiliated and gyms build communities of members, so the global CrossFit community has upwards of 150k individual gyms each with its own group of diehard CrossFitters. Secondly, the hour-long session, which is called a WOD, workout of the day, is followed by everyone who is in the gym that day and scored individually or in groups. People workout together and egg each other on by supporting and competing and most gym goers end up becoming friends outside the gym. It was very heartening to see people having WOD sessions on Zoom when gyms were shut during the COVID lockdown. Thirdly CrossFit trains instructors along three levels requiring progressively higher teaching experience but reportedly also allows for the trainers to innovate inside the workout regimen, so the product itself, in this case the workout regimen is community sourced and developed as we go along. And finally come the CrossFit games, which allow for anyone to participate and compete along a pre-defined workout and through various mechanisms qualify for the global games. It is sort of like the Olympics but with hundreds of thousands of gym-goers competing all at once over a period of time. Talk about community building! Assuming it survives the rocky patch its founder has decided to put it through, I see a bright future for the CrossFit brand and whichever company ends up owning it.

Three practical things you should do now

Engagement is not an either–or but more of an and. Providing loyalty benefits, additional digital products and intangible value can and perhaps should all figure into your broad engagement strategy. As for the intangibles, here is a way to think about those.

Understand which intangible value ad fits your brand – A retail bank that offers different statuses makes a lot of sense and that happens all the time, if the same bank starts offering some gamification maybe it might go against the brand identity the bank is trying to project. But outside a few exceptions, most brands and companies could apply any of the intangible engagement devices rightfully and it is just a matter of picking the one to two which most closely reflect the brand's values.

Pick one thing at a time and do it well – Educating consumers, the Transfer-Wise way needs a multi-pronged approach with onsite assets, PR and blogs, word-of-mouth and advertising copies. Gamification needs to be multifaceted and constantly refreshed, be it single person or group games or be it contingent on consumer action or pure chance. The content you create needs to be good enough that people know your brand because of the content and not the other way around. The statuses you award need to identify and play on the consumers need to constantly separate themselves from each other to keep them hungry for more. And the communities you build should be tight enough to create real relationships. You do any of the above and I am sure you will see lasting engagement with your brand and your company.

Make sure you have people running this full-time – Companies need to be serious about this type of engagement and resource these efforts well. A full-time community manager for example, who monitors, seeds and listens to conversations within a community play is critical to keep the engagement going. For companies making a big play in content of course it is important to have sizeable teams focused on just that. Even on Gamification, monitoring the win rate, engagement rate, fraud etc. are important aspects of making things work and you will need people to take care of that.

So, there it is, the second frontier which talks about the evolution in How companies will engage with consumers and what role digital enablement will play in it. We spoke about harnessing consumers and engaging them through loyalty benefits, added value use cases and finally intangibles. In the next chapter we will explore different aspects of how the actual purchase will happen in the future. See you there.

Notes

1. https://www.wsj.com/articles/amazons-late-prime-day-now-in-october-set-to-fuel-record-end-to-year-11601269260
2. https://www.wsj.com/articles/under-armour-to-acquire-myfitnesspal-for-475-million-1423086478
3. https://www.wsj.com/articles/loreal-applies-digital-makeover-to-sales-efforts-11605046234
4. https://www.wsj.com/articles/ikea-to-acquire-online-freelancer-marketplace-taskrabbit-1506618421
5. https://transferwise.com/sg

CHAPTER 4
HOW CONSUMERS TRANSACT

What do Albert Einstein, Frederic Chopin, Charles Darwin, Mahatma Gandhi and Rosa Parks have in common? Well, for starters they are all dead. But it is not just that, they were all also self-proclaimed and marked introverts who actually could not be bothered with dealing with real people. I bet they would have loved online shopping and all the amazing opportunities e-commerce offers to completely dehumanize the commercial experience.

In the previous two chapters, we looked at the changes we can expect in how companies reach consumers and how companies engage with consumers as they get closer to making a sale or a transaction. In this chapter we will look at the transaction itself and imagine how this will change over the next decade. It is hard to pinpoint exactly where in the consumer's journey reach ends and gives way to engagement and where engagement ends and gives way to transaction. In fact in reality the process is much more cyclic and haphazard rather than being entirely linear, but for the purpose of holding a narrative and understanding how things work, it makes sense to break these chapters down as if they were individual process steps. So, if you are all up in arms right now about the consumer journey not being linear anymore etc., please calm down, I have heard you.

I have broken down this specific chapter into four parts based on the nature of the transaction or the purchase and its location. We will start off by looking at "At home" transactions where e-commerce will play a big role, but in a much more evolved way. We will then look at purchases made "On the go" or out and about and reflect on how digital enablement will change that purchase journey. Next, we will look at what I like to call "Browse" purchases, where consumers tend to want to do some final bits of research and trial before the actual transaction. Finally, we will study what I like to call "Consult" purchases where consumers need actual consultation either before the purchase is made or where the consultation itself is the product being sold. As before, we will look at some technologies, some early case examples, stretch our imagination and think about imperatives for us to start acting on now.

The Future of at Home e-Commerce

Nuno prepares for fight night

It was UFC 500, one of the most sought-after fight nights in Ultimate fighting championship history, and Nuno was excited about hosting his friends for a watch party at home. Over the last decade, UFC had grown massively in popularity all over the world, and with a local hero from Bogotá fighting in the middleweight category Nuno was sure the entire city was going to be tuned in. Nuno had always loved martial arts and he loved the UFC, just the right combination of sport, skill, drama, name-calling, adrenaline and once the fighters were in the Octagon, it amazed him that they absolutely pummeled each other but respectfully stopped short of killing each other, with restraint shown pretty much when it was most necessary. So much of the world's problems would be solved if people were just a bit more restrained with each other.

First things first he had to stock up on beer, so he Googled "Carton of Black Whale wheat beer" and Google's search threw up the best available prices for 30 min, two-hour, same day, next day and next week deliveries. He picked the same day slot, paid with Google Pay without leaving the search page. He noticed that it was going to be sent to him from the closest Ara store, picked up by a part time delivery person but none of that mattered to him, he just needed it to be delivered on time as promised. For food he was going to order empanadas from the new neighborhood kitchen "La tia curiosa", which was in fact a 20-year-old college dropout guy who made some interesting types of empanadas. He liked the truffle versions and had ordered a batch of 24 four days ago, for delivery today. He asked Google, "When will I receive my Empanadas?" "Nuno, your empanadas will be delivered by Donny at 5 pm today. Donny will also bring you your Carton of Black Whale wheat beer".

Fast forward to midnight, and the last of the guys left. It was a great evening and Nuno took a quick look at his Google checkout account to see how much he spent on the whole evening. He sent a split-bill request to everyone for the pay-per-view charges on the UFC fight, the food and drinks were on him of course. His checkout insights page reminded him that he had been spending a bit more than he ought to on alcohol last month and he could save 20% if he ordered in advance instead of wanting it same day every time. It recommended he buy another carton of beer right then because based on the last six months of history he would most likely need it. Just as he was about to buy, he got a notification from his fridge, "Running out of eggs and milk, press here to add to cart". A few clicks and he was done for the day.

It sure was good to never run out of things, and even better to know that he was always getting the best pricing on everything he bought. Time to look forward to UFC 501!

Understanding the evolution of at home e-commerce

E-commerce, as we know it, has been around for over two decades and if you would consider tele-shopping as a form of remote commerce then even longer than that. While companies and categories continue to come to terms with e-commerce in its current form, the way e-commerce works will also evolve over the coming decade. Underlying this change, in my point of view, will be an aggregation of, for lack of a better word, sub-channels and a disaggregation of services. Let us delve into this concept for a bit before we investigate the details.

E-commerce sub-channels today are differentiated from each other based on the nature of products bought – Buy an iPhone on Amazon vs. buy groceries on Amazon Fresh vs. engage a handyman on TaskRabbit vs. order a meal on UberEATS etc. All these sub-channels exist in separate apps and are built with all necessary services in the app itself. The user today must download and maintain a plethora of marketplaces on his smartphone to be able to access these when needed. This will change over the next decade as marketplaces will emerge that aggregate across several sub-channels to deliver an easy to access and unified shopping experience to the consumer. This will be even more relevant once the form factor for the personal device starts shifting away from the smartphone towards something else.

Broadly, the four key services that each e-commerce sub-channel needs are: a searchable product catalogue along with useful product information, access to inventory of whatever product or service the platform is selling, ability to have that product or service delivered to the consumer and ability to process and receive payments. Most sub-channels today build their own service stack or have a one-to-one service contract with a specific service provider to deliver these services which the platform then forwards to the consumer. Going ahead platforms will potentially be completely decoupled from the service providers and will enlist a provider for a specific order on a lowest cost basis. In the below topics, I will go through each of these services one at a time and help explain how the above evolution would work. (See Figure 4.1.)

Findability – Not sure if this is really a word in the English language, but a core value creation lever in e-commerce is the fact that the platform allows

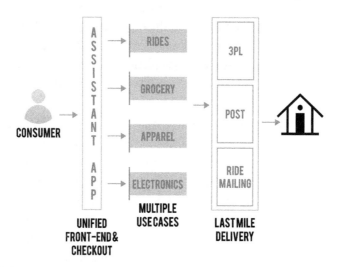

FIGURE 4.1 Disaggregation of e-commerce services

the consumer to find and access a much wider and larger variety of products. This has many different important elements in it including Search, Product information, Comparison, Reviews and lately Engagement. A significant portion of e-commerce sales are from regions where traditional retail options are not able to provide access to the same products, so findability is an important component. Consumers need to be able to search for whatever they want and more importantly search results need to be smartly sourced and displayed, so the consumers find what they want among the search results. This is pretty much exactly what Google does which is why I believe Google will have a big role to play in aggregating e-commerce through its search platform which you already see in the form of sponsored catalogue adds or through the Google shopping platform. Consumers today click on a product displayed on Google and then finish their purchase on the actual e-commerce platform. In the future, they would likely never leave the Google environment.

But regardless of if it's Google or Amazon or someone else entirely, aggregators will emerge which will allow you to search for any product or service you'd like in one unified interface, and present all possible options to you to make a decision based on. For each option, the platform will source and render important product information for you to study. The aggregators will also display different service level options for you to make a decision on where to buy from – just as Nuno, in our example above, was shown how much the same crate of beer would cost him for different delivery times including immediate, same day, next day and next week deliveries. The aggregator will also display product and seller reviews much like a marketplace platform does today so the best performing products and sellers will get better visibility and will be more findable.

Distributed inventory and manufacturing – The all-important convenience factor that e-commerce brings to the consumer comes at a cost and more often than not e-commerce platforms and brands have not been able to pass this shipping cost on to consumers as they have engaged in multi-year-long, and in some case decades-long consumer acquisition campaigns through free shipping. To start with, this behavior of not requiring consumers to pay for convenience will change in the next decade and there will be an expectation that users shell out at least part of the shipping fees, with the rest being subsidized by savings in the value chain from not having to own and operate physical storefronts. Retailers will start focusing quite heavily on ensuring last mile delivery costs to consumers are as low as possible by making sure products are available to ship as close as possible to the consumer's actual location. Brands and retailers will use several different models including own warehouses, own stores acting as warehouses, setting up owned forward deployed warehouses, renting warehouse space with third parties etc. to ensure inventory of fast-moving goods is widely penetrated into the marketplace.

Likewise, some elements of manufacturing and last bits of customization will also happen much closer to the consumer to make sure that the last mile distance is as low as possible. A simple example of this is in the food preparation space, and the now infamous Luckin coffee[1] in China was a great case of how this model can find incredible success with consumers. Cloud kitchens, central kitchens or dark kitchens, whichever way you'd like to refer to it are all examples of distributed manufacturing and we will see this strategy being implemented more often in other consumer goods especially when it pertains to products that merely need to be mixed and filled before delivery.

Delivery and consolidation platforms – e-Commerce players have traditionally used a mix of own fleet and third-party logistic providers in executing the last mile delivery. In addition, the last few years have seen the emergence of startups specializing in performing last mile deliveries for e-commerce and ride hailing companies that are looking to monetize underutilized ride capacity have also broken into making e-commerce deliveries. Public postal services too are making a significant number of deliveries for e-commerce players. But despite all the new capacity being added to the last mile delivery sector, I believe there will not be enough capacity available to affordably deliver products to people's homes. Two major events will happen sometime over the next decade which will greatly help this conundrum. Firstly, autonomous deliveries will finally become a reality, be it through drones or through self-driving cars although this might take another five to seven years to make a difference in earnest.

The other event will be the establishment of open platform last mile delivery marketplaces where individuals and companies can offer to participate and make deliveries part time. In a way Uber and other ride hailing services were designed to be that way, offering up a way for car owners to monetize their asset (the car) and their time, in ferrying people around by participating in a platform just by downloading an app. Most ride-hailing companies have turned into more glamorous and tech enabled taxi companies, and that is fine because there seems to have been a market for that too. On last mile imagine this, you're doing a quick shopping run, and while you're at it, your e-commerce aggregator sends you a message telling you that if you were to pick up an extra bag of groceries for your neighbor and drop them off on their doorstep, you'd get a 5 USD cashback on your groceries. I think a lot of flexible capacity on last mile deliveries will enter the market through such platforms which will be a Godsend for consumers and retailers.

Standalone checkout – The e-commerce checkout page is where you review your basket of purchases, enter your payment details and finally make your purchase. This is a critical step in the process because, beyond summarizing information to the consumer, it requires the platform to make a real time assessment of if the consumer can in fact pay for the product and capture the payment details or the payment itself. Most e-commerce platforms work with a variety of payment providers to give consumers as much optionality in paying for products as possible. I think consumers will become amazingly comfortable and accustomed to "tokenizing" their payment details with third party checkout providers like PayPal or Stripe or Google Pay or Apple Pay. So regardless of the actual payment instrument you are using or the payment institution that is guaranteeing that you are good for the money you owe, you would be represented by a payment or checkout provider. I think device manufacturers (Apple Pay) and findability and search platform owners (Google Pay) have a huge advantage here because they don't need to convince the user to download their payment application, its already pre-installed or payment information is already saved in some context.

To illustrate it a bit better, when you do a route search on Google Maps you get shown what an Uber ride would cost you for that route. You can click and open the Uber app if you have it and then continue your experience and payment there. But you can also book the ride entirely through Google Maps and pay for it through your credit card saved on Uber or a new one added on Google Pay. You never have to leave the Google or Android environment.

Of course, Uber still needs you to have an Uber account first and because they still make the same money on the ride, creating this ease in booking is a big competitive advantage. Being able to run a scaled business that makes money will be much more important that being able to spin some unbelievable narrative around wanting to be a Super-app which needs your consumers to be in your native environment all the time. Uber seems to have understood this well. But on the other hand, Google will also need to start sharing consumer data with use cases that it embeds inside its platform and this will be important for the findability piece we discussed above as well.

Appliance ordering – Not exactly an e-commerce service, but I think this will be an important trend for us to consider. We discussed in an earlier section of the book how your appliances will have the ability to suggest e-commerce orders to you. Amazon's now discontinued Dash button was a forerunner for this concept. Amazon now expects Alexa to take on the burden of suggesting to you what products you need or should buy. Beyond actively recommending specific products and brands to you, your appliances would also construct shopping lists for you. Smart fridges for instance are already available in the market but have exceptionally low penetration because they are expensive, and the supporting infrastructure and consumer behavior has not caught up yet. This will change, and your smart appliances will link into your findability platform or your checkout platform. While I don't think an appliance will directly order stuff for you without you knowing, it's very likely that your fridge will throw up a recommended list for you to merely approve and add to your basket. This is something that has a lot of brands worried because it gives the device manufacturer like Amazon or operating platform like Google the control over recommending specific brands. But to be fair this has been happening for years through online marketing on Facebook and Google, paid search on e-commerce and through shelf fees in retail. It is just a new form of shopper marketing that brands will need to get their head around and get comfortable paying for.

Three practical things you should do now

So that was an overview of where I think "At home e-commerce" is headed – there are a lot of moving parts here, but directionally the theme around aggregation of sub-channels and dis-aggregation of services will likely hold true. So as a brand trying to benefit from this trend I would recommend three key strategies:

- Ensure you have as wide a channel strategy as possible so you allow the e-commerce marketplace for your products to take shape, but be rational and only follow pricing and promotional logic that makes sense in the long-term.

- Focus on creating a unified view of your inventory across the marketplace, this might take you five years depending on your level of distribution so start now. You must know in real time, accurately, how much of your finished goods are sitting exactly where.

- Finally, find ways to collaborate now with device makers, potential e-commerce aggregators (Google), payment and checkout players and last mile logistics players to think through how they can play a role in your route to market immediately now. Your experience and relationship with them will give you a basis to build from when the market is ready for the future.

The Future of On-the-Go Commerce

Bart's day out in New York

The date was set, Bart was going to turn 60 in a couple of weeks and his son had decided to take him on a night out in the city. Just the two of them, being men about town. Bart thought back at all those evenings when Jill was out traveling or out with her friends when he would take his son, then just a kid, out for pizza and ice cream. Bart would down a few beers while the kiddo gulped down what seemed like gallons of Coke. Later in life, they both had a shared love for Single Malt whiskeys and that had been their annual thing to do, head out to a whiskey bar and just hang out together. As the day arrived, Bart decided to head to the city earlier; it had been a while since he had just hung around by himself and this was as good an opportunity as any.

Bart got off at Eighth Avenue – Fourteenth street around 11 am and decided it was just the right time to have a laid-back brunch by himself, here in the Meatpacking district. He had read up extensively on the French bistro

"Le Cadoret", with its outside seating and especially the Croque Monsieur Truffe. Walking over was a breeze, he had his reservation, and he knew exactly what to order and most importantly what not to order. A welcome change from back in the days when you would need to walk to five places before getting a spot in NYC. After a hearty but lazy brunch he decided to walk over to Chelsea market for a bit of a browse and made a beeline for the Wine store he had read about. Holding up the augmented reality function in his wine connoisseur app, he was able to see ratings, reviews, price comparisons and recommendations for every wine on the shelf. He picked a Rioja, two Merlots and a case of Cabernet for Jill – scanned the code and paid for the wines through his phone. The shop would deliver it to his place in Long Island over the weekend and he did not have to interact with anyone throughout his time in the store.

It looked like it would rain, and he realized he did not have an umbrella. Fortunately, there seemed to be a Super-vend across the street, he popped over and bought an umbrella, a bag of M&Ms, some fresh squeezed orange juice, some Renny pills and a cardigan – because why not. The vending machine recognized his face and automatically charged him. Later in the evening he met up with his son and they headed to a steakhouse which this time his son had picked. This specific restaurant prided itself on doing things the old-fashioned way. There was a paper menu, and a waiter to take your order. You were not able to specify the exact macro-nutrient composition of your made-to-order artificial meat steak, this was real meat. There were no robots scurrying around, just people bringing your food out to you. What is more you actually had to ask for the bill, and they brought you an actual paper bill in a leather-bound folder. They only accepted cash here, but since there were hardly any ATMs around and most people didn't have cash, they charged your payment account and gave you some cash when you came in, so you could have the "cash experience".

He was about to fork out the dough, thinking it was literally the first time all day that he had to reach for his wallet, which these days only carried photos of his family. But just as he was about to, he realized he did not have to as he heard those words that would make any father endlessly proud, "Don't worry dad, I've got it covered".

Understanding the evolution of on-the-go commerce

A big part of consumption for our consumers happens, and will continue to happen, outside their homes. Companies term it on premise, away from home, on-the-go, dine in, imminent consumption or whatever one might want to call it. I am clubbing all these transactions and purchases together as "On-the-go commerce". I guess broadly you can say that this is shopping that happens outside the home for consumption outside the home, and generally the shopping event is from a timeline point of view close to the consumption event. The on-the-go experience of the future needs to optimize for time, and seamlessness will be the key underlying principle of this evolution making the shopping as automated and de-humanized as possible. In restaurants the dehumanization will take shape with almost everything becoming self-serviced. In some cases, instead of us going to the store, the store might come to us, wherever we might be. And finally, and perhaps most interestingly we will end up with a virtual rendition of our cities and augmented reality will give the on-the-go experience an incredible new dimension. Let us look at all these elements a bit deeper.

Future of vending machines – Come to think of it, a dehumanized form of on-the-go retail has been around for decades, the good old vending machine and smart vending will emerge in a big way in the future with a few interesting trends that will give it shape. First and foremost, cashless vending machines will become the norm, especially when the consumers' payment account is tokenized and stored with the machine operator, a mere facial recognition will be enough to process the payment and there will be no more need to rummage for coins, or have banknotes spit right back at you or to insert a credit card in a piece of equipment in a subterranean parking lot in the middle of the night. Inward facing cameras will keep inventory checks real time and replenishment routes will be fully optimized based on actual and expected sales. Vending machines will have a much broader variety of items, as a much more precise management of supply, to be in line with demand, would make it possible to keep obsolete inventory to the minimum even on special products. (See Figure 4.2.)

Vending machines will be connected to the devices around them, display reach adverts on digital OOH screens as discussed in the earlier chapter,

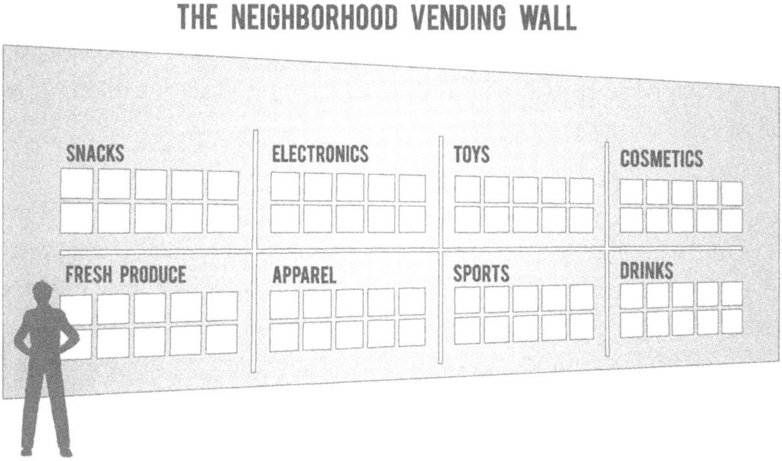

THE NEIGHBORHOOD VENDING WALL

FIGURE 4.2 The neighborhood vending wall

modifying the marketing messages and copy according to the person who is in proximity. Machines will display assortment and pricing based on the purchase history of the consumer standing in front of the machine and push out promotions to consumers in its proximity. What is interesting to note is that most of these functions already exist and you would likely find videos on YouTube of smart vending machines in Japan. What needs innovation is the underlying economics of owning a machine and putting it up in the right place and stocking it with the right inventory. With major advances in better stocking, location mapping, consumer differentiated pricing and additional opportunities to monetize the asset through OOH screens and in consumer engagement, we could see a new business model on vending emerge in a big way the world over.

The automated store experience – The convenience store experience will become more and more automated and seamless. Amazon launched its Amazon Go concept store in Seattle which was opened to the public in early 2018. I visited the store last year and it's quite a fun experience, after of course having to download Amazon, signing in, after having to recall my password, store my credit card etc. so I could scan and enter the store to start with. Basically, the store is packed with cameras and computer vision analysis that understands what you pick up and put into your basket so when you leave the store, it just charges your card stored on your Amazon account and sends you an invoice. Truly seamless but feels a bit excessive, to be honest, and that is perhaps the reason why the concept is not exactly exploding on the scene as yet.

Much more likely is the possibility of allowing users to scan as they go with their own smartphones, a technology that already exists and is in application in several supermarkets and convenience stores around the world. Having scanned whatever items you put into your basket, you pay with your tokenized card on your phone and walk out of the store. In a way, this is technology that takes the vending machine idea and converts the entire store into a giant vending box for the consumer to step in and find an item and leave. The added advantage of this model is that it allows retailers to create added value in the shopping experience on the device the consumer is scanning items with, including pushing promos, giving out nutrition information, encouraging upsizing and bundling and bringing in gamification in store. One advantage of this is personnel cost savings for the retailer, which has been a cause of some protests in the US against Amazon abolishing cashier jobs, but I think the much bigger advantage is in the time convenience it creates for the consumer by not needing her or him to queue up at the checkout.

A store that comes to you – I remember distinctly, when I was a kid, my mom would call up the grocery store and tell them to send over a few pantry top-up items. What was often a nephew of the store owner, would then be promptly dispatched on a bicycle to deliver our items within 20 minutes flat. And often my mom would tell the store owner to ask the young nephew to pick up some laundry along the way. Companies like Dunzo in India, the digitally enabled errand boy, took this concept and put it on a digital marketplace. In places like India where labor cost is not an immediate problem and there are tens of thousands of entrepreneurs willing to enter the gig economy to make a quick buck, we will see reliable ways to make sure your items come to you within minutes instead of you having to go to a convenience store.

We will also see a digitally enabled version of the traditional ice-cream trucks or milk trucks or the modern-day ultra-hipster food trucks. Instead of the ringing melodic and somewhat sinister music, you would receive an alert on your smartphone that the truck is nearby. In fact, in some categories milk-runs are making a comeback again with the added advantage of using big data analytics to understand which routes to take and which specific locations to keep the truck in. A few years ago, there was even an experiment in using this concept to create mobile ATMs, in the form of people who were carrying cash, who would be willing to give you some of it once you linked your phones and you had made a bank transfer to said person's account. Not surprisingly, the idea did not work as it was a glaring invitation for criminals directing them exactly to those people who were carrying cash around. Still, the idea of using an app to get a person to bring you something within minutes will have great appeal in the future.

The future dining experience – We discussed in the consumer trends in an earlier chapter how people will spend more time outside and potentially consume many more meals outside as well. Digital will play a big role in the future dining experience from end to end. Starting with influencing where people eat, food blogs and influencers already play a huge role in helping consumers decide and this will continue. As the sheer quantum of reviews increases, platforms will emerge which make much better sense of reviews left over time on multiple platforms and help consumers pick and shortlist. Any kind of reservation, pre-order, pre-payment etc., essentially use cases that reduce the time between arriving at a restaurant and starting the meal will continue to find massive usage and perhaps there is indeed a future where you'd really hardly ever have to wait for a table and all restaurants would always just be at optimal capacity. One can only hope.

The in-restaurant experience will be completely digitized as well with digital menus, tailored in real time to your profile and preferences if these are known. We will see automation in the kitchen and in the more menial tasks like carrying dishes out and plates back into the kitchen. The higher end you go the more human the service will be of course, but most quick service restaurants will start having fewer and fewer human tasks over time. COVID has given a shot in the arm to table apps, which allow consumers to place orders on tablets at the dining table, and these will become commonplace especially with the falling hardware costs. Payment, as we discussed earlier in this chapter, will be completely seamless based on digital wallets operated with a swipe of a hand or with facial recognition. Even post-meal, consumers will be encouraged to engage with the restaurant by leaving a review and recommendation or taking a picture and posting it somewhere for which he or she might receive a discount on a subsequent purchase.

A virtual rendition of the real world – Finally, I would like you to consider and imagine this, the entire real world, complete with streets and homes and shops and parks and offices, all of it captured and rendered in the virtual world. Sort of like Google Maps but with an extremely high density of information. I think this is inevitable and while it will take time, insane amounts of computing and storage power, and a lot of regulation to work through, it could happen faster than you think. A Maps-like application, loaded onto a consumer's personal device, maybe smart glasses would tag and enrich real world locations with valuable commercially relevant information. You could be walking down the street and restaurant ratings and product prices and promos would pop up as you walk down. You would be informed of where your friends might already be dining so you can join them or avoid them depending on how you feel. I could go on and this feels almost like science fiction, but it is all within the realms of possibility and as the technology starts becoming more commonplace, valuable use cases will no doubt emerge for companies and consumers to benefit from.

Three practical things you should do now

And that is where, according to me, On-the-Go commerce is headed. So, for companies touched by this, what should we be doing right away? Again, the top three things:

- Firstly, if you own vending assets start thinking about how to digitize these and monetize these to create a new business model for the future; if you think your products don't lend themselves well to vending, think again. Imagine how the consumer would experience your products on an Amazon Go shelf, visit the store if you need to, and understand if your packaging and visual identity needs to change. Think about the ice cream cart business model, is this something you could bring into your category if it were possible to run a business profitably?

- Second, if you are in the foodservice business, as a restaurant or a product owner, start off by creating an end-to-end digital consumer journey now and really invest behind technology. I think the pace at which the dining experience will be digitized will be unprecedented, especially post-COVID and you would not want to be left behind.

- And finally, work with Maps, and literally put your stores and products on the map. This will represent your first foray into virtual reality, and you will need the basics in place when the related use cases emerge, and consumers start adopting them.

The Future of Browse Purchases

Odin celebrates singles tag

November 11 was here, one of Odin's favorite days of the year and he was looking forward to a day of celebration of being single with lots of food, drinks and of course discounts. He also had a date in the evening today, perhaps this was his opportunity to not be single anymore, but quite honestly, he loved being by himself and doubted if that would change at all anytime soon. "Onwards with the day", he thought, as he headed to Wittenbergplatz towards KaDeWe, short for Kaufhaus des Westens.

At KaDeWe, a few years ago they remodeled the sixth floor into a high-tech supermarket, where he went first, figuring he would get some grocery shopping out of the way. He normally ordered online but for KaDeWe he made an exception, perhaps paid a bit more but he just loved going there and spending a good couple of hours. In the fresh foods section, which was endless, he felt like he was engaged in the entire life story of every vegetable and every piece of meat – he scanned a few packs of ham and some vine tomatoes for his salad tomorrow. In the dry goods section, there were few products on the shelf, but he walked through massive floor to ceiling screens which changed the products and prices that were displayed as he walked through. He scanned away as he walked through. After a quick lobster roll snack on the seventh floor, he headed down to the first floor to the shoes section. He had been eyeing a pair of Air Jordan mids for a while and wanted to try them on once before he bought them. They seemed to keep coming back in fashion every decade or so. As he entered the Nike section, straight away he was directed to the Air Jordans aisle; they knew he was researching. He tried on a couple of sizes and settled on a size 9, received an offer, buy immediately now and get 5% off! So, he did.

From there he headed on to the fourth floor to look at some coffee machines, his Nespresso machine was a decade old and he was ready for something new. The new Nespresso professional series was looking great and the storefront on the fourth floor was designed like a giant machine that you walk into and see how the machine operated from the inside. The water, brewing ratio, grind size, contact time, brewing time, brewing temperature, brewing turbulence etc. There was so much that went into making that perfect cup, and they walked him through the whole process, and he felt very well-educated. He even brewed a couple of cups himself trying the coffee out. Scanned and bought, and now it was time for his date, which was at a gas station. Gas stations had really re-invented themselves over the last few years since driverless cars, electric cars and public transportation drove down fossil fuel car ownership to a point where gas stations started becoming a bit redundant. He walked over to the "Shell stop" at Martin Luther Strasse where he was meant to see his date. The idea here was to "Refuel yourself", Shell had taken the approach to turn their gas stations into mini-Spas where consumers could come and rest for a few hours, get a spa treatment, work out in the gym, sit and read in the reading room, and of course have a quick meal.

Odin saw his date and was glad she looked prettier in person than she did on the dating platform he used. Oh, and she was part of the Syndicate! Maybe he would not need to celebrate Singles Tag next year after all.

Key elements of the evolution

I define "Browse commerce" as purchases where the consumer feels the need to interact with the actual product he is buying, in person, before making the purchase decision. The product might eventually, and most likely still be delivered but shopping in this case will become more about decision making and education and less about the actual checkout, payment and delivery. With the focus firmly on experiencing the product, I will walk through a few different retail concepts under this topic including the future of the supermarket, the future of apparel retail, future of appliance and furniture retail and how people make big ticket purchases like cars. Finally, I will also spend some time reflecting on potential new and yet unheard-of retail concepts. As we walk through these different models, I will discuss what the end state could look like and what role brand owners and product manufacturers could play in that end state.

The future supermarket – I am sure most of you have heard of, if not visited, the Hema Fresh supermarkets in China, and the future of supermarkets is very well on display here. Over the next decade this concept will spread everywhere and get dialed up even more so along a few dimensions. For starters, consumers will visit supermarkets not for convenience but for the experience, as convenience shoppers will prefer to stay at home and order. Supermarkets will have to completely remodel their layouts and offerings to make it a fun destination for shoppers to shop in, this will mean fewer larger locations. Most consumers will maybe do a monthly visit to a supermarket instead of the weekly visit and will use this opportunity to find and try new products in person. (See Figure 4.3.) Brands will have the opportunity to drive a lot more experiential marketing onsite, including sampling and new product introductions in the new supermarkets. Fresh foods will take up a much larger share of the retail space. In spite of consumers ordering a majority of their stock-up online, I think there is some sort of an animal instinct in us that makes us want to touch and feel and smell fresh produce as we plan to eat it and supermarkets will pivot in a way to include almost a modernized wet market inside.

Supermarkets will also just be fun to be in, with better lighting, music and in-store design but tons of gamification. Augmented reality will allow users to understand the story behind each product, allow users to compare price and nutrition information. Shelves for dry goods would be completely digitized and will change depending on the consumer that is standing in the aisle. Imagine a personal care shelf that completely transforms itself when a man is standing in front of it instead of a woman. This will also happen with pricing and retailers would be able to differentiate on-shelf pricing based on the

THE FUTURE SHOPPING CALENDAR

FIGURE 4.3 The future shopping calendar

consumer lifetime value, so if a first-time user is standing in front of the aisle, the prices might drop to drive recruitment. Supermarkets will allow users to dine in, very much like Hema does today where you can pick your live crab and have it cooked for you right there and then. Checkouts will be seamless as we discussed earlier and of course you would never have to carry your own bags home; they would just be delivered to you.

The future of apparel retail – e-Commerce in fashion retail has been exploding over the past few years and it has taken its toll on store retail for sure. This was further exacerbated by COVID19, but there will still be a role for physical stores to play in the future and we will talk about that here. Consumers will perform most of their research on apparel at home, either actively in the brand or retail platforms, or passively led into it by influencers so the role of window shopping might be diminished to an extent. The need to try out clothes has always been the primary reason why e-commerce has had a difficult time breaking into fashion, but most fashion retailers have extremely easy and free return policies which will continue in the future. Fashion retailers will benefit from co-locating stores in larger shopping destinations, so consumers drop by as a part of a larger shopping trip that includes a visit to a supermarket and a restaurant. Once in the store, the consumers will find that digital enablement makes it easy to find items, try items and compare items. As consumers arrive at an outlet, they would be able to sync their online browsing journey with the store, so they are immediately directed towards the most relevant assortment. Consumers will have access to AR and smart mirrors which will allow for trying clothes out without changing into them. AR will allow you to compare several outfits side by side without having to change into one and then having to remember the one before. Stores will also serve as locations for consumers to do customization of clothes in real time, you would be able to design your shoes in store and then have them manufactured right there for you to pick up immediately.

For introducing new brands, styles and products, we will see several companies using pop-up stores in high frequency areas which are then wound down once enough awareness is reached to rely on an e-commerce-based model for actual orders. Other interesting formats would emerge including a rental proposition or a subscription box type of proposition where you are sent a box of clothes every month based on the prevalent styles. But these will be e-commerce based.

The future of appliances and durables – Consumer electronics, home appliances, kitchen appliances, furniture and other durables which are heavier but also need more research due to the larger ticket size will see an even stronger differentiation within the shopper journey, with online research followed by offline experience followed again by online or offline purchase and home delivery. Large appliances and furniture have been delivered in any case since decades, and consumer electronics and small appliances have seen major inroads made by e-commerce over the last few years. Education and experience remain key for brands to drive consideration and the importance of flagship stores for this will continue to remain. Roughly half of all smartphones, for example, are sold online now but Apple's flagship offline stores are still the rage combining the right amount of shopping, product education and product experience. As product features proliferate fast, consumers will need to be able to learn and experience the devices they will buy and brands will use retail space to differentiate themselves in the consumers' minds in terms of how the usage of a specific product will impact their lives.

In case of furniture, IKEA's entire model has been based on creating an experiential space allowing consumers to see how the furniture looks in action. Furniture manufacturers will try to add digital rendering to maximize the number of items they can put on display and minimize the steps the consumers need to take in the checkout, while IKEA is great for browsing, it is still painful to checkout. Easy checkout could also take the form of furniture and storefronts distributed across the city and even displayed in-use. Imagine taking a picture of a chair you like in a restaurant and finding it online immediately and buying it then and there to have it delivered to your home in a couple of days. Perhaps in the future IKEA would not need massive stores everywhere if everywhere in the city could literally be a store.

The really big purchases – Some pivotal asset purchases like cars, mortgages, high end furniture etc. will of course continue to have a large in-store component but a significant amount of research will happen online, albeit in a curated and brand owned environment. Brands will need to focus on making sure the entire end-to-end consumer journey is tracked and controlled and appears seamless from online to offline as it is time to make the sale. With the amount of emotional attachment a car buyer has with the brand, a lot of car stores will need to convert into brand experience destinations instead of dealerships. The pre-purchase research would lead consumers into scheduling test drives, scheduling experience visits and learning about the brand history, understanding the technology included in the car etc. The post visit journey could include customization, continued responses to queries, facilitating the payment and financing options, getting introduced to the brand loyalist community etc. Brands will keep consumers in the loop as their product is being put together through the supply chain further enhancing the relationship with the consumer through the buying process.

A new kind of store – I believe over the next ten years we will for sure see new retail models emerge, a bit like the spa at the gas station which was entirely a figment of my imagination. This has happened before, with store concepts like Don Quijote from Japan with its unique assortment and late opening hours, now expanding across the world. Especially as the physical movement habits of consumers change over time, in the long-term I think people will spend much more time outdoors and they'll be doing things outdoors that they do not do today, the relevance of real estate assets will shift. Shared workplaces, neighborhood manufacturing areas, old people communities etc. would need different retail models but consequently maybe large parking lots, business districts, gas stations might not be as necessary and will throw up new retail space to make use of. Case in point is the mill land in the heart of Mumbai which with the closure of cloth mills decades ago is now finding use in huge destination retail venues.

Three practical things you should do now

So "Browse commerce" as I term it will see a lot of changes as above, with a big focus on brand experiences in a modified and digitally enabled environment. As brand owners and manufacturers, the three things you should start doing to benefit from this change are as follows:

- Firstly, think about what experience you could design surrounding your product, for consumers to come participate in, in the future retail destinations. When the bulk of your consumers start ordering your products online, you will need to be able to build your brand on location through a flagship experience.

- Second, if you are in the durables business, think about what education journey you need to send you consumer on and tweak your store experience towards that. Equip your store merchandisers with the right technology to up the game on in store education.

- Finally, work with photo recognition technology providers to allow consumers to photograph and search for your products and link the searches to e-commerce pages. Above everything else think of your stores as an important link in the consumer's journey as she or he decides on your products and makes the eventual transaction somewhere else and prepare to reconfigure.

The Future of Consultation

Wahad's big weekend of fixing stuff

"Wahad, when are you going to get the shower fixed?" "Wahad, why is the TV picture warped?" "Wahad, you should get that mole checked." "Wahad, have you signed the girls up for their piano lessons?" Wahad this and Wahad that, he was being chased all the time by his wife to do things around the house. For a former bike repairman, he knew shockingly little about how anything else worked and never really got around to fixing anything. When he did attempt to fix something, he was surprised at how easy it was and how little time it took and found himself wondering why he did not just do it the first time around. This weekend, he decided it was going to be different and he was determined to clear his backlog of tasks so his wife would leave him alone for a few months until the backlog filled up again.

"Alexa, the TV picture is warped, how can I fix it?" Wahad asked and Alexa asked him to tell her what kind of TV it was. Then she carefully guided him through the different things that she had "heard" that tend to go wrong most often with a TV of that make. They landed soon on the exact nature of the problem, turned out Alexa knew about such issues happening to other TVs of the make and also knew how to have it solved. She dictated step-by-step instructions to Wahad, who did exactly as he was told and lo and behold! Fifteen minutes later the TV was fixed. "Alexa, I need to have a mole checked" he said, and Alexa once again asked him a couple of clarifying questions. Based on his description of the mole, she recommended he go to a cosmetic dermatologist instead of a medical dermatologist. She asked for his insurance details and based on his policy found him a few recommended dermatologists and checked if he would be okay with an appointment with the ones on the list. Once he had confirmed, she set up a video appointment in a few hours and when it was time, she dialed him in. Wahad had a quick 20-minute consultation, and the dermatologist took a good look at the mole and decided it would be best if Wahad went in the week after for an in-person check.

"Alexa, the shower head is broken and needs fixing" Wahad asked and Alexa immediately looked for a plumber appointment on the same handyman platform that Wahad used to work on, making sure she only selected amongst plumbers with at least a four-star rating. Alexa also placed an order on Amazon for a new shower head in anticipation of the plumber's visit. Three out of four done within half a day. As for the piano lessons he had already set those up last week and this Sunday was the first of ten sessions. The Piano teacher was conducting this lesson simultaneously for five students remotely which made it much more affordable. The girls saw some videos and followed the notes as they were played, the teacher herself "did the rounds", and entered a one-to-one coaching mode several times during the hour-long session. He was glad about being able to provide his daughters these lessons, coming from a poor bike repairman's family in rural India, he could never have imagined his daughters could have a private piano tutor.

Later that evening after dinner, Wahad proudly proclaimed to his wife "TV, Showerhead, Mole and Piano done". His wife cheekily told him what a great trophy husband he was and gave him a warm hug. "Alexa, turn off the lights", he said and mouthed a "Thank you" to her, wondering if Alexa could read lips.

Key elements of the evolution

The final type of purchase I want to discuss is Consult purchases. By this, I do not mean consultation offered to purchase a product but purchases where the consultation itself is a product. This could be advisory, or it could be a service in general and this world will also see a lot of changes. The fundamental issue with humans providing consultation and service is the fact that scalability depends entirely on adding more humans on the supply side. Digital enablement will play a big role here in unlocking additional capacity and in matching supply and demand in a more effective way. As we get into the details of the different consultation models, we will differentiate along different consultation pathways, starting with fully automated consultation, remote assisted consultation and finally in-person consultations. We will also look at the future of services marketplaces which will be an important element in the coming decade. These consultations could span several types, including Travel agents, Doctors, Pharmacists, Household repairs, Real estate, Teaching, Banking, Investment, Accounting and tax, Lawyers, Designers etc. As we go through these models, I will present a few real-life examples of companies and startups that are attempting to disrupt this space by offering digital consultations.

Completely automated consultation – This is consultation where there might be an illusion of a human involved but it is in reality completely automated. This is possible in cases where there is only a finite and discernible set of solutions to offer from to the consumers based on the consumer's specific question or problem. It of course already exists and a great example of this is airline and hotel bookings. At any point in time with all the world's supply being available to be picked from, a program can with relative accuracy provide you with the best booking and best route for the best price or duration or any other constraint you might have. Two important changes will happen to fully automated consultation in the coming decade. First, the consultation experience will become more and more human like. Chatbots on utility websites with predictable names like "Jamie" and "Ben" can today already have a somewhat human like conversation and provide predictable answers to predictable questions. Back in 2018, Sundar Pichai did an incredible demonstration of Google's voice assistant making a haircut appointment and even though the variables are completely finite e.g., type of service needed and time slot asked for, the fact that there was a hyper-realistic human voice making a phone call made it altogether impressive. So, in the future you will book your flights in a conversation with Google home or Alexa or Siri or whoever.

The second change will be in the form of AI driven automated advisory for topics for which it is not possible to discern a fully finite solution but quite possible to make an educated guess. For example, asking for a restaurant recommendation which is tailored to your tastes – the difference between "Alexa, what's the best rated sushi place in town?" and "Alexa, what sushi place in town do you think I'd like best?". This, for instance, will become relevant for use cases like Robo Advisors. Robo Advisors are automated investment platforms which invest on your behalf without having a human investment professional and charge much lower fees as a result of it. Contrary to the name, however, today's Robo Advisors do not actually advise, they merely execute on your instructions. They are not built to take risks on behalf of the consumers and are not equipped to recognize complex patterns, take educated guesses and consider market experience to benefit from risk taking. With the advent of AI, perhaps this will be possible, and we would see full automation in solving problems for which there is no mathematical optimum easily calculable.

Digital assisted remote consultation – Two words, Zoom meetings. I guess before COVID I'd have had to spend some time explaining and elaborating on this specific type of transaction but I'm guessing we have all had our share of Teachers, Lawyers, Accountants and Doctors on Zoom calls so most people will get what this is about. Beyond an improvement in video quality and the emergence of better scheduling systems etc., I do not think there is a lot of technology advancement needed to spark this off. But there are still some ways to go in a couple of areas before the world starts benefitting in earnest from remote consultation. For starters, in almost all sectors where this is applicable, we need to understand what kind of consultation works well remotely and what does not. For example, Telehealth is on an exponential growth trajectory since COVID, especially for non-essential healthcare but collective experience is now telling us that in a patient's healthcare journey, the very first consultation is best done in person and follow up consultations can in most cases be done remotely. Primarily because diagnosis is much easier in person, of course, but follow up is also much easier if both the doctor and the patient have some information on the condition to base ongoing checks on.

Next, the pricing models for online consultation need to be established as does a trust and reputation basis for choosing the provider. Would you pay a lawyer who consults you on the phone the same rate for his time? From the lawyer's point of view the opportunity cost could be an in-person meeting but from the consumer's point of view it is a lower service level. Perhaps the lawyer would not have taken a remote session if he had a more lucrative in person job to perform. Once enough supply and demand build up on a platform, prices will hopefully be set by the marketplace and some sort of rating and review system will bring in the quality gauge to go along with the pricing.

And finally, regulators will as usual, have to play catch-up and establish frameworks around how consumers are protected both from bad consultation but also how confidentiality laws would apply and how insurance companies cover these consultations for tele-medicine specifically. But the benefits are obvious, for consumers by creating access to services and driving affordability, for consultants by allowing for another channel to monetize time and for public services like healthcare by reducing the burden on physical facilities.

In person consultation – Of course, in the end there is probably no other way to get the best possible consultation experience than to meet the service provider in person. But here too, digital enablement will play a role in the future. Over the years, bank branches have, of course, changed from being intimidating bureaus to colorful and glitzy shopfronts and there are fewer and fewer of them every year. While most administrative tasks and transaction banking tasks are performed remotely by consumers, for some pivotal personal financial decisions having an in-person meeting will continue to be an important option as it inspires a feeling of trust, reliability and secrecy that is critical to financial matters. Banks around the world are changing the look and feel of branches to be more like a co-working space and a cafe and a lounge put together. And while that goes a long way in brightening up the overall branch banking experience, most banks today could still do a better job of educating consumers in the products they have to offer. A little bit like the coffee machine experience that Odin went through in the previous topic, we will see banks create much more immersive sales experiences in their physical branches to be able to bring relatively complicated products to consumers in an easy-to-understand way. And this trend of using an array of digital tools to perform a consultation would breathe a lot of efficiency into other topics like law, taxation and even healthcare.

Imagine being able to do a literal walk through of your body to understand exactly where the Sciatic nerve is getting pinched in your lower back to be able to understand why a specific set of exercises will help. Or imagine a piano teacher who brings along an exoskeleton glove which guides the student to imitate the way the teacher's fingers move along the keyboard. Or imagine the personal fitness instructor who is able to use a plethora of wearables and data feeds from your body, during your workout to push you just to the limit and make sure that that is done as safely as possible.

Services marketplaces – Freelancer marketplaces have been around for quite some time now and most of you might have used one for some odd job here and there. They have been somewhat in the background, quietly growing their user base but not really gathering much attention. The gig economy, and along with it such marketplaces are here to stay. But these too will see some evolution in the coming decade. The breadth of services available on marketplaces will continue to expand and include more and more complex services so instead of someone to fix your shower you might hire an interior designer. As the value of the services offered starts increasing and demand increases, platforms will need to differentiate against each other based on the bench of freelancers they have on offer. And we will see marketplaces investing more resources on finding, developing and keeping talent on the marketplace even to the extent of providing support systems to individual freelancers such as co-working spaces or equipment. Platforms will also start investing in creating collaboration between freelancers and allowing jobs to be shared and allowing for communities to be built. In a later chapter, I will discuss how the gig economy and such marketplaces could form a major part of the employment structure in our society and when a marketplace affiliation replaces a corporate affiliation, people will expect the same sense of belonging from the platforms they work on that they receive today from their companies. We will explore this topic further in that chapter later.

Three practical things you should do now

And that's where consultation commerce could end up in the next decade. For companies in this space the pathway is clear and here are my top three recommendations:

- Most important of all is to start experimenting, partnering and working with voice assistants even if it is for a small pilot today. Start offering remote consultation as a product if that suits your category but do understand that this is not meant to be an inbound call center. If you cannot charge for it, then it is not a product.

- If you offer in person consultation, think about how you can use AR, rich media and immersive environments for better story-telling and education – digital enablement does not merely mean giant TV screens in the lobby, a co-working space and a high end coffee machine.

- And finally, tap into freelance marketplaces as consumers but also as providers. For underutilized capacity inside your company, this could be a great learning experience and a way to monetize the company's capabilities with non-competing clients.

In this chapter we looked at the actual point of sale or the actual purchase. We reflected on transactions executed from home and how these will evolve over time. We delved into On-the-go commerce including dining out and vending among other things. We then looked at the future department store and the idea of browse commerce before finishing with consultation commerce just above. That is a lot of disruption all packed into almost 40 pages and each topic could deserve a chapter of its own. But we have more frontiers to cover, and we are halfway there! Next up, in the fourth frontier we will look at how companies design products and brands.

Note

1. https://www.wsj.com/articles/behind-the-fall-of-chinas-luckin-coffee-a-network-of-fake-buyers-and-a-fictitious-employee-11590682336

CHAPTER 5
HOW COMPANIES CREATE PRODUCTS AND BRANDS

"If I had asked people what they wanted, they would have said faster horses", said the opening page of another consulting presentation attributing the quote to Henry Ford. This was the nth time that I was seeing this quote and something about it just did not sit right with me, so I looked it up and sure enough – there is absolutely no evidence that Henry Ford actually said this. But even if he did, does it make sense to not listen to your consumers? What the consultant did not reveal was how the Ford story eventually turned out. Ford was able to piece together contemporary ideas like the assembly line process and give consumers what they wanted, an affordable car. Sure, he sacrificed design flexibility, but he was going for affordability and something tells me he knew precisely that that was indeed what consumers wanted. Within a little over ten years Model T sales went up from 10,000 to a million. Now this is where it gets juicy. Ford forgot to listen to the consumer and General Motors introduced "A car for every Purse and Purpose" in the 1920s and Ford, adamantly pursuing the Model T saw its market share halved in five years before finally relenting, shutting down its factories and reconfiguring everything to start producing the Model A. So next time you see someone quote that piece of wisdom, smirk internally to yourself because now you know.

There is no alternative to listening to your consumers, and visionaries who have shaped consumer needs managed to do so because they understood what the consumer wanted, not despite what the consumer wanted. In this frontier we will explore how digital will play a role in helping us understand what consumers want, much better than we do today. We will look at how companies can respond to this by delivering to the consumers exactly what they want in a personalized product, and especially how digital will help make that model economically scalable and feasible. Having looked at product attributes, we will then turn our attention to brands, understand why brands matter and how digital can help drive up or negate the importance of brands to the consumer. Finally, we will look at the future of localization where value creation happens much closer to the consumer and propositions are designed in the community.

The Future of Consumer Research

The latte that Jaden made

Oreo flavored latte sounded like a great idea. Jaden had stepped out of his office for a quick mid-morning cup of coffee at the local Starbucks. Reading up on the new beverage being introduced on the digital menu board, he was intrigued. He loved Oreos and he loved lattes and it just made sense for the two to be put together somehow. He got himself a Grande and remembered seeing some cafes in Paris serving these last year. In fact, he also saw them in Melbourne early this year. As he was sitting back at his desk and loving the new flavor, he didn't know that that very product idea was a result of Starbucks using photo recognition and image analysis to look at what consumers were eating and taking pictures of, at their pre-identified list of 100 opinion leader cafes worldwide. These photos uploaded by consumers on social media, along with any tweets and mentions, were fed into a model that served up potential new product ideas for Starbucks to take and bring to the masses. What Jaden also did not know was that Starbucks had developed five different concepts of fusing an Oreo cookie with a coffee, including using an Oreo flavored syrup and what they called was an Oreo dunk. And these concepts were tested using different price levels for different cities worldwide, using an AI model which simulated the purchase intent consumers would demonstrate for each of the options, for different prices and a potential consumer response. The model suggested the flavored latte as the clear winner for Seoul at the 8000 Won price point and that ended with the latte making its way to Jaden.

Over the next few weeks, Jaden bought the Oreo latte every single day and it became part of his daily ritual. He met his friends over a coffee once and posted some pictures on social media as well. His robot concierge, Hana, asked him if he was willing to allow Starbucks to access his phone usage over a few different apps in return for a weekly free coffee and of course he said "Yes", he loved a good deal remember? Somewhere in the background, Starbucks aggregated Jaden's latte buying behavior and started connecting it to other desserts and snacks he bought. It was clear that he loved Oreos, he bought them every week in his weekly grocery order, but they saw that he also bought Maltesers. Every single week. A consumer insights program put together these two events and tried to find other "Jadens" in the marketplace, only to realize that not only was there a strong correlation between latte purchases and confectionary purchases but certain types of confectionary, the biscuity type, featured quite heavily. A few concepts were created, and AI tested, and the Malteser crunch latte was born.

It was now three months since Jaden's first Oreo latte and as he went down to Starbucks, he was shocked to hear that the product was not available anymore. Just as disappointment was about to kick in, he noticed there was a new latte in town. "Maltesers! Definitely going to have that one", Jaden exclaimed to himself. "It's almost like they put this idea together just for me", he thought as he took a warm satisfying sip. Little did he know that they actually did put that idea together just for him. For all practical purposes it was a latte that Jaden made.

Understanding the evolution of consumer research

The next decade will bring evolution in the way consumer research is collected and in the way it is analyzed. As we explore this topic, we will start off by delving into the trends surrounding consumer insight collection and we will look at four pathways. We will look at advanced media processing tools which will distill useful insight from the public domain by looking at text and photographs and voice and finding data embedded within. We will then look at passive metering as a vehicle for gaining direct consumer insight. Audience and consumer data sharing, which we touched on in an earlier chapter is also relevant here and we will look at that from an insights point of view. Based on these renewed sources of insight we will delve into Artificial Intelligence and understand how this will apply to consumer insight generation. Finally, we will look at how company performance data and consumer insights data start merging over time.

Media processing tools – Everyday, consumers the world over leave a trail of information in the digital world as they go about their lives, and our ability to access and analyze this data trail to generate useful insights continues to improve. Once better computing power, technology and products break on to the scene, this source of insight will become an important element for companies to base decisions on. A couple of years ago, I met a startup founder in China who had developed a smart system of scanning windmill blades using a camera fitted on a drone to detect cracks, which he demonstrated could be used to have a robot roam around in supermarket aisles, taking hundreds of pictures to create a complete shelf intelligence study including assortment, pricing etc., and send it to brands in an easy to use tool. So, this exists today.

Companies have been using Google Trends data for the past few years as an added source of insight, essentially asking, "What are people searching for?". Scraping of websites to glean useful information also exists and several products have broken onto the marketplace that give real time e-commerce execution insights to companies and retailers. Web-scraping and search trends will continue to be useful as companies figure out where and how to use the insights provided by these. Computer vision will be the next big thing after web scraping. Video and image files will be read to understand consumer behavior – for example, how do consumers move about in a store? How do they interact with a shelf? Walmart is already said to use computer vision to detect browning of bananas automatically instead of sending a store employee to check. Millions of images analyzed every day for consumption trends and locations will add another layer of richness to understanding what matters to consumers, taking social listening to the next level. Audio analysis to detect satisfaction or distress among consumers will allow for more segmented service delivery for automated consult type of transactions.

Passive metering – Quite frankly, it surprises me that the use of passive metering has not quite been as widespread as it should be. Perhaps this has to do with the obvious privacy concerns that would arise. Passive metering is essentially asking for a consumer's permission to load a program on their phone which would record passively what the device is being used for. It is kind of like a TV meter installed on a phone, and consumers are compensated for their participation in the program. This works much better than a consumer panel, because it is an actual record of consumer behavior and not self-reported or questionnaire based post-analysis. I think over the next several years, as reliable providers, useful insights and a regulatory framework crystallize, passive metering could completely replace panels, especially as offline purchases are also paid for using personal devices. Digital consumer panels will also become more mainstream, I just read a Wall Street Journal article the other day and I paid for it by answering a five-question consumer survey about a Chinese smartphone brand. That felt awesome and I think what I said was useful to the brand. Products that allow for getting quick feedback on concepts using an incentivized and simple mechanic like a left or right swipe (ode to Tinder) already exist and will start becoming the mainstay of how research is conducted, for example Unilever's Idea swipe app.[1] Passive metering is also able to convert your phone into a listening device, subject to your permission of course, and can listen for your ads or your product mentions to understand offline media effectiveness better. And in the future your smart glasses could also track which OOH media you are looking at.

Allowing your device to share your location and your wearable to share even more information, depending on the type of wearable, is another way to participate in passive metering. During the COVID pandemic, traffic data shared by Google insights on if people were returning to work or going out for recreation was a big input into recovery planning for most companies.

Move from aggregates to individuals – Insights are best served in aggregates as decisions are made in aggregates. This is unlikely to change in the future, although when we talk about personalization later in the chapter, we will see the importance of disaggregation. Today's aggregate data is based on surveys or second party scan sales data that is sourced by an intermediary like Nielsen, and then put together and fed to companies. In terms of usage and behavioral insights most companies access a household panel, by the likes of Kantar, the results of which are adjusted to suit the whole population and decisions are then made based on these aggregates. As companies start building out their own consumer databases in earnest, there will come a tipping point when

FROM   **TO**

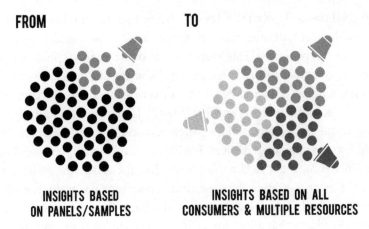

INSIGHTS BASED
ON PANELS/SAMPLES   INSIGHTS BASED ON ALL
CONSUMERS & MULTIPLE RESOURCES

FIGURE 5.1   From partial to complete insight

there will be more individual data in the hands of the company, and aggregates will be based on audience analysis on their own consumer data platform. (See Figure 5.1.) This might sound like wishful thinking but imagine this, your consumer database has an inventory of all current and prospective consumers and necessary "I am" type of demographic information. You have the ability to populate second party data feeds directly into your consumer database so you'd have access to transaction data on all your consumers, you'd be able to map media audiences on to the same consumer data (subject to the walled gardens allowing this) to get a view of reach and media consumption. You could have a passive meter running on a section of the audience which gives you enough insight to build analyses. I think this is a reality that brands will need to start working towards, and while this seems like a long-term effort, as mentioned several times in the book, there is no alternative to having your own consumer data.

Artificial intelligence and predictive analytics – The topics we have discussed so far all contribute towards making an insane amount of real time and granular data available to companies. So, what do we do with all this data? Advanced analytics or big data analytics products already on the market can put together and cut and slice this information and present the data to you, but it is still just a summary, albeit a readable summary and not just some data feed. I think we will likely spend the next half a decade on having our data accessed, cleaned and summarized for us and that is a big deal already. The second half of the next decade will belong to AI.

We spoke about AI in the previous section, when we discussed the Go game with Lee Sedol and if you remember, AI comes in handy when pattern recognition is so complex that there isn't enough computing power to come to a definitive answer. So, to that end, we will see AI applied to a variety of business problems that are essentially trying to predict an outcome. How will a specific pricing move impact product sales? How will a competitor response impact product sales? How much can we expect to sell of a new product? What is the likelihood of achieving OTIF targets? When will a machine likely break down? You get the gist. But one important thing I want to bring up here – AI can predict outcomes which have some underlying causality, however complex, and here it can analyze many input parameters to give you a prediction. What AI cannot do is predict events that are almost entirely based on chance. Can AI predict the weather? Potentially if there is a large amount of data on all the different parameters that cause weather for the AI to learn. In a way, there is cause and effect in everything that happens in the world, but most events are an outcome of such a complex cocktail of inputs that no AI can predict those.

Convergence of insights and performance management – Consumer insights, is in many ways, like holding up a lens to the consumer and exposing what is seen to the organization to make decisions based on. But the insights function can also act as a mirror especially because the analysis and insight generation capabilities are the same irrespective of if you are looking at external data or internal data. I think over the coming decade the knowledge and insights function and the performance management function in an organization will converge into a unified function that sources and crunches data and presents insights to managers. I love the holding the mirror analogy because I think it implies that the performance analysis is done by someone on the other side and the independence in showing things as they are will be critical to companies. I am imagining a function that is called the "Single source of truth" function.

The difficulty is this – data scientists today have little idea of what matters to business leaders and business leaders today have even less idea about what type of data science is available to use. Insights leaders in most companies are primarily experts in managing consumer research agencies and making excel models and consumer research agencies are just not innovating fast enough and not attracting the right data scientists of which there are too few around anyway. The next few years will need to see a major uptake in data scientist supply and better definition of landing roles for these folks in companies.

Three practical things you should do now

So, there is the future of consumer insights and as usual, I have got my top three imperatives:

- Start working with companies that provide rich media processing and passive metering now to build a business case on how this would be beneficial to your company. There are several providers in the market and most of them do not have a massive inventory of success stories yet, so it is up to us to take a chance on them.

- Focus on building up your consumer database, we spoke about this when we talked about engagement and this is also relevant here and includes first, second and third-party data. And as you build your database, establish routines to drive insights from the data you have.

- Finally reorganize your insights function to be about data science, performance management and any other insights and measurement tasks you have in the organization. Within five years your insights team should look more like a group of data scientists and less like a group of research agency account managers.

Future of Personalization

Nuno likes everything Nuno style

Seven am in Bogotá, and Nuno wakes up and stumbles into the bathroom where he squeezes a dollop out of his Colgate Nuno toothpaste, minty of course with blue gel granules with a cinnamon flavor. He thinks maybe next time he ought to add some Himalayan salt to it when he makes his online order. He never quite understood why people are not more particular about the flavor of their toothpaste; they spend hundreds of dollars on a bottle of wine that they empty in one sitting but not think anything of shoving standard issue toothpaste in their mouths twice a day! Not him, he does his toothpaste Nuno style. Down in his kitchen he is about to fire up his De'Longhi coffee machine, he recently downloaded the Colombian artist series, a coffee program that dispenses coffees the way famous Colombian artists liked to drink theirs. He was not happy with the Fernando Botero, too acidic, so he decided to brew a Gabriel Garcia Marquez instead, it would probably be mellower he thought. Coffee and Art, that is a good mix and another example of doing things Nuno style.

As he got ready for work, all his clothes were monogrammed of course with his initials. His Uniqlo Khakis, his GAP shirt, his H&M cardigan all off the shelf but monogrammed. It was so easily done; he did not understand why anyone even wore generic stuff anymore. Not him, he did things Nuno style. His shoes were even more special, brown suede boat shoes with tassels. He designed those himself after having searched everywhere for the right look, slimmer, not too pointy but not too square, no garish metal clips, tassels that were interesting to look at but not too much and with super comfortable in-soles. Zara allowed you to do an entire end to end shoe design and what is more they were ready for pickup within a day. He had a lot of friends asking him where he got the shoes and he grudgingly gave away his design code to a couple of colleagues from the percussion group at the orchestra. At least he received a 5% cashback for everyone who used his design, the Nuno style.

His lunch was a salad from the local salad bar, he had pre-constructed his salad for each day of the week based on his nutritionist's advice and his own personal taste, and it was put together exactly the way he wanted. His beverage, too, was dispensed with a specific amount of carbonation, twice as much caffeine and a hint of cinnamon. Ed thought it tasted horrible, but he loved it. It was Nuno style. Later that day, Nuno dropped by his bank branch to discuss a mortgage for a house he and Ed had seen and were considering buying. His relationship manager was waiting for him with the home loans team who all seemed to know everything about him. They even asked him about how he enjoyed UFC

500, and told him that if he did close the mortgage with the bank within the next 30 days, they would buy him tickets to go watch UFC 501. That pretty much almost sealed the deal in his mind, Nuno style.

Later that night as he lay in bed and it was time to doze off, he felt the warmth of the weighted blanket. It was not how he would have liked it, Ed liked to crank the temperature way down to 21 degrees and he was more of a 26 degrees kind of a guy. He had yet to meet a married couple where both partners liked the bedroom temperature to be the same, perhaps there was some science to it. Well, he guessed this was one thing which was not like the others, was not quite Nuno style.

Understanding the evolution towards personalization

Allowing consumers to get exactly what they want, the way they want, of course sounds like a great idea. But the issue with such personalization has always been the ability to do it affordably at scale. This is where digital enablement comes in as it unlocks personalization for consumers by creating transparency in options, guiding a consumer through the personalization journey and allowing big data analytics to power the personalization effort and manage its implications on the company's supply chain and economics. We will discuss the ways in which digital enablement will drive personalization and enable collaboration between brands and companies in allowing consumers to create all kinds of bundles and product combinations. We will also talk about how digital enablement would help think about economics at an individual consumer level and allow for experiences to be tailored at the individual consumer level. Finally, we will look at how consumers could be rewarded for the role they play in devising their own personal product and service preferences.

Hyper-personalization of products – Personalization is neither new, nor impossible to achieve and consumers have been receiving products made exactly to order for a while. Be it the Subway sandwich which is assembled along your wishes or a haircut that you receive exactly the way you want it to be, most of the times. The obvious issue with that is that this type of personalization is quite labor intensive as it needs a real person to help

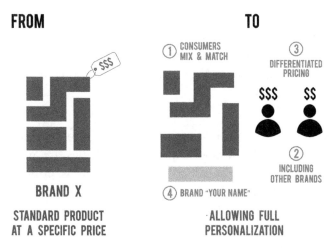

FIGURE 5.2 Full personalization for consumers

put together your personal product for you. Digital enablement will let us allow consumers to personalize their products themselves and companies to service this personalized demand profitably. (See Figure 5.2.) The must-have here is the ability to deconstruct your product into its sub-components so there are degrees of freedom for the consumer to play with. The analogy I love to give here is of LEGO. You can buy a set of pieces and make your own thing, or you can buy the Eiffel Tower set and build an Eiffel Tower. The Eiffel Tower set will have some special pieces and some common ones, and you could make whatever you want with those. Once the sub-components are put forth, a digital platform can help create an engaging way for consumers to remotely "mix" their product along constraints set by the company. Imagine for example a "mix your own cereal" platform and while it has not found mainstream appeal yet, there are some niche ones out there. You have an online environment where you can mix your choice of granola, oatmeal, rice crispies, muesli, freeze dried fruits, nuts, seeds, superfoods etc. and see how your mix affects the price per kilo and the calories and nutrients per serving. If it is too much you can always default to the pre-mixed "Eiffel Tower" granola.

On the brand or manufacturer side, you would have the ability to disallow certain combinations, set appropriate pricing and control the available ingredients aka the Lego pieces. Most importantly however, as a platform of this sort gains traction and scale, brands will be able to anticipate demand for ingredients much better and much more in advance so the cost of fulfilment could become lower and more acceptable as most consumers default to certain mixes. Brands can also use these consumer mixes as potential inputs into developing new recipes.

Extreme collaboration – Bundling of products across brands has been around forever as well, however most often bundles are made between products belonging to the same manufacturer. This is primarily because creating cross-company bundles is both operationally difficult and financially difficult to reconcile. Digital commerce will make extreme collaboration between companies possible in a few ways.

Firstly, big data analytics on purchase patterns and affinity products will reveal intersecting trends on what products consumers tend to buy together. So instead of bundling a face wash with a deodorant, you might realize that canned soups go as well with deodorants and create that bundle, although this one was just me randomly thinking of products. Secondly, the actual bundling of two physical items together, which has traditionally been a painful process can happen virtually on the e-commerce platform and if necessary, then also physically as the products are picked and packed before delivery. Thirdly, the attribution of the discount to the bundle constituent items becomes a lot easier if they are being sold online as special SKUs can be created and then deleted relatively easily for the specific purpose of bundling. And finally, the reasons and the story behind the bundle can be explained in a more compelling narrative online so the consumer can make sense of why the items have been clubbed together. A great example of this happened during the COVID lockdown where several brands came together within a few days and put together a "Home survival" product bundle with minimal additional operational effort on most e-commerce platforms. One can only imagine how difficult it would have been and how long it would have taken to build this up in a bricks-and-mortar setting.

Personalized experiences – Beyond physical products, we will also see companies making their services as personalized as possible. Spotify and Netflix do this at scale already today, by keeping track of consumer's content consumption behavior online and recommending additional content based on that. Stitchfix, an online clothing retailer has created an entire business model around personalized service where a user, after providing some initial information, is matched to other existing consumer profiles and immediately provided with a personalized wardrobe recommendation. Stitchfix also employs many style consultants who give continued fashion advice and provide recommendations to users based on their profiles.

So digital enablement will on the one hand gather consumer behavioral data to build personalization based on that, but also allow service providers to find specific patterns and deploy personalization at scale along these patterns of consumer preference. Another excellent example of personalized service provided at scale is Grammarly, a digital writing tool which helps correct spelling, grammar, style etc. Grammarly sends fully personalized weekly emails to millions of users telling them how their writing performance has been over the week, and how they can improve. With all this however, we are merely scratching the surface when it comes to service personalization and this will change much to the joy of consumers over the next decade. Imagine for example, walking into a McDonalds store and being greeted by name, imagine the cashier remembers your last five meals and can give you a loyalty discount without you asking for it. Imagine they know a thing or two about your interests and strike up a brief conversation about your favorite sports team and imagine your favorite song comes on in a few minutes just as you sit down for your meal.

Personalized product economics – Pricing is probably one of the most under-used levers in revenue management and most brands leave a lot of money on the table due to difficulties in carrying out price differentiation in the marketplace and ensuring pricing compliance from retailers, especially in the fragmented trade. As companies build up consumer data and transaction data and get visibility on the lifetime value and continued purchase behavior of consumers, we will have the ability of differentiating pricing by consumer. This could be in the form of vouchers or cash backs or dynamic pricing displays if those are available. In the end state we will measure profitability not on a per-transaction or a product or category basis but on a per-consumer basis. After all, companies build products and services to serve consumers and if each consumer is a profitable consumer the company itself will be profitable.

So, if a consumer in front of the shelf is a potential recruit or a lapsed consumer, he will be offered a lower price than a regular consumer. A consumer who has loyally continued to buy a brand's products will receive discounts and loyalty benefits within the allowance that his consumer level P&L allows the company to disburse to him. The pricing and margin economics thus could become completely personalized to each consumer making the marketplace more efficient overall, so everyone wins.

Consumers monetizing personalized products – Another interesting phenomenon that will emerge in the next decade is the ability for users to be able to monetize their personalized products by allowing others access to them. A bit like how Nuno's own shoe design earned him a 5% cashback. We can find examples today that go in that general direction. Late last year, for example, Vans launched an interactive shoe customization contest where three winners were awarded cash prizes, trips to Vans HQ but most importantly Vans would produce and sell their shoes. Etsy, the handmade items e-commerce website has seen huge success and has been an opportunity for consumers to monetize their personal creations. YouTube encourages consumers to create original content which content creators can monetize if they achieve certain levels of viewership. These are not exactly the same as an average consumer chancing upon a great personal creation and then being afforded a platform to sell it further, but I see a lot of potential in that. From an economics point of view this could also allow brands to charge a premium on personalized products which the consumer would pay and then expect to recover in part from monetization opportunities.

Three practical things you should do now

With these elements in mind, here are the three things brands ought to start focusing on right now:

- Start by thinking about what a Lego looks like for your category and your product and conceive a pilot to offer consumers an opportunity to explore personalization on a small scale. It would be important to get a read of whether personalization matters at all to consumers and how complex it would be for your company to offer it up.

- Start creating virtual bundles on e-commerce platforms immediately, assuming you are available on e-commerce platforms. Try to understand how to map out affiliated products and services and try out different collaborations to see what makes sense.

- Finally, start your journey on differentiated pricing by creating visibility on new customers and repeat customers and building up a consumer lifetime value model. It might take you a while to get this right, long enough for on shelf price or e-commerce price differentiation to emerge as a feasible lever but starting now will give you the right learning to get there.

Continued Relevance of Brands

Bart's second love

Golf, golf, golf. What was it about the game, Jill always wondered, that made Bart obsessed with it? "Golf… is the infallible test. The man who can go onto a patch of rough alone, with the knowledge that only God is watching him, and play his ball where it lies, is the man who will serve you faithfully and well", said P. G. Wodehouse, one of Bart's favorite writers. It was such a big part of his life, he even moved to where he lived in Long Island just to be close to the golf course (and his son of course). And within that universe, he was firmly aligned to Titleist, his son is an avid supporter of PXG and has been trying to convince him to buy into it but something about a golf brand with the word "Xtreme" in its name just puts Bart off, after all it's not just about the functionality.

So, what is it about Titleist? he gets asked often. Well, for starters he loves the focus and history on quality and accuracy, a legacy that is apparent in its very founding. Phillip "Skipper" Young started the company when he realized that most of the golf balls he was playing with were made poorly and the core was not well-centered, which reduced shot accuracy, and so he set about making the "dead center" Titleist golf ball. That story was important to Bart. Then there is the reputation with the so many Masters winners of the past and present using Titleist drivers, putters and of course balls. That makes him feel like he is part of a bigger community that extends from the enthusiasts, all the way to the best professionals in the world.

Part of the reason why he has stayed within the Titleist brand is also the fact that they have provided great functionality to him. The Scotty Cameron putter has really improved his performance and he does not feel so tense any more when putting, he is not sure he could use anything else. He has also gained a lot over the years from the "Team Titleist" community, he has participated in product tests, he has been able to connect with likeminded golfers, has taken lessons from pros and of course has benefited from tons of promotions. And last but not the least, he believes in what the brand stands for. A couple of times over the last decade he has seen how Titleist immediately withdrew association with pro golfers who made right wing statements or had some ethical breach. He was also impressed by the mettle the Titleist team showed as they took the fight to Callaway and later to Costco. If you do not take a stand on important issues relating to fairness how could you be involved in sport, where fairness is the very foundation of healthy competition? Golf is truly his second love and Bart does not feel like he will ever break-up with Titleist.

Understanding the evolution of brands

Before we go into the details of how brands will stay relevant in the future and what role digital enablement could play in that, let's look briefly at the history of branding in general, to understand why we have brands in the first place. Branding as such first started sometime in the stone age where our ancestors must have started burning a mark into their livestock to demonstrate ownership. The evolution from then was to move from denoting ownership to denoting source where first pottery, done a few thousand years ago, then stones used in the pyramids and eventually medieval products were marked to denote where they originated from. Enter the industrial revolution and as mass distribution became possible, companies needed to overcome the fact that their products were not locally well known and therefore not trusted. They achieved this by printing brands and logos on the primary and secondary packaging and this led into trademark regulation to ensure these brands were protected. Advertising then ushered in the golden age of branding up until the late 90s, allowing companies to build stories and an identity for their brands using massive reach muscle as the differentiation. But things have been somewhat up in the air since then, with consumers understanding the fact that lack of fame and scale does not necessarily mean lack of quality and functionality. So, we have had local brands emerging strongly, private label brands making a dent and even the concept of "Brandless" taking shape over the years. So now what?

I think brands will still have relevance for the foreseeable future for a variety of reasons, but the relative weight of those reasons will change and brands that are able to make that shift will manage to survive. There are several attributes of brand relevance, but there are five that for me are the most important, and we will look at how digital enablement influences these over the next decade. They are trust and quality, status and community, functionality and value, depth and breadth of habit, and finally an ethical stance (See Figure 5.3.) Let us walk through these.

Trust and quality – Consumers have traditionally relied on well-known brands to feel secure about the quality and consistency of the product or the experience delivered, and about the fact that claims made by the brand will actually be true. This I think is the most basic of utilities that brands bring, and consumers have always been willing to pay a premium for this. We will see a lot of disruption in this space over the next decade as consumers start relying on other ways of deciding on whether they should place their trust in a specific product or service. Take for example hotel accommodation and

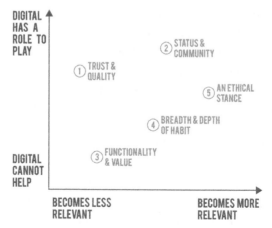

FIGURE 5.3 Changing reasons for brands to exist

the TripAdvisor example we discussed in Chapter 1. While there might have been a time when a Hilton or a Marriott meant something and as a discerning traveler you would keep to the big-name brands for the assurance of consistent service, that is already not the case. TripAdvisor and its associated rating and review system has made it possible for small and midsized hotel chains to be evaluated on a level playing field. The same holds true for Music, where instead of relying on big-branded record labels and well-known artists as the only source of great music, user rated platforms like Spotify have made independent labels and musicians as well equipped to succeed as big labels. Likewise, e-commerce platforms have given local and niche personal care products the opportunity to be seen and evaluated alongside major global beauty brands.

So, having a well renowned brand name, which is kept well renowned by relentless advertising, is not any more the only way of establishing trust and the promise of quality. Companies do not need to stop advertising but will need to play the new game as well. You already see managers of big-name hotels answering queries and taking feedback on TripAdvisor, you see record labels trying to compensate Spotify better every year to have their bench of artists get better visibility, you see large personal care companies ensuring their sub-brands compete strongly with niche personal care brands on e-commerce such as L'Oréal's La Roche-Posay.

Status and community – Consumers have used brands to up their own self-esteem and show off to others that using a certain brand means they are of a certain social status or belong to a certain niche community. This utility of brands has not changed, and if anything, the desire to differentiate oneself is far higher now and will continue to increase over the coming decade. So, there is a lot of value here and digital has also a role to play in this. It is a lot easier today, than it was a couple of decades ago to create a status brand and to formulate a niche community. Take Supreme for example, the skateboarding and hip-hop culture associated hype brand. Doesn't have a lot of locations, hardly does much advertising but by being connected in the right communities, projecting a certain lifestyle, making very small production batches and picking just the right celebrities to wear their clothing in public, Supreme has made sure the products exchange hands at exorbitant prices in the secondary market, and teenagers the world over are willing to give an arm and a leg for a tattered used hoodie. I don't need to explain Apple, and the sheer number of people who camp overnight to get their hands on every newly released iPhone which by now, from a functionality point of view is no longer the leader in the market, and less so if you bring price in the equation. Take Lululemon as another example of a brand which sells primarily yoga pants, but with the right guerilla marketing, building communities, merchandising their stores the right way, having beautiful store personnel, they've created a sense that there's really two types of yoga pants in the world. Lulus or not-Lulus.

So, providing consumers with a sense of status and a sense of belonging to a niche community is something that is super relevant and at the same time something that small brands can do as well as big brands. The important thing here is going to be how well large brands use digital to execute their community builds and the hype aspect going ahead e.g., Nike's SNKRS community build and how well current status brands can maintain the status e.g., Lululemon's attempt at staying current and exciting with their purchase of Mirror.[2]

Functionality and value – Consumers expect large brands to continue to innovate and improve their products and continue to improve their lives as result of it. The fact that I buy a well-known brand repeatedly means I am convinced that with every subsequent version, the brand will make my life easier and better. I think going ahead this will become an important differentiator between successful and failed brands. Most major share gains in the marketplace can be attributed to just having a better product that provides more value. The luxury car segment in Europe for example; I had the privilege early in my career of spending some time in a German car manufacturer and I have never seen such commitment to product excellence in every possible way. Sure, the three brands Mercedes-Benz, BMW and Audi trade users and places between them in the Luxury (S-Class, A8, 7 Series), Executive (E-Class, A6, 5 Series) and the Large (C-Class, A4, 3 Series) segments but they have consistently taken the top three spots in those segments since a very long time, the exception being the Passat in the large segment which like Audi is owned by Volkswagen. Or take Dyson for example with its vacuum cleaners, bladeless fans, hair dryers etc., which despite the higher prices, deliver much better functionality and consumers expect more from the same appliance compared to another brand. Or take Shake Shack or In and Out burgers, the quality of the meal is consistently good and way above the sort of burgers you would get in other fast-food restaurants, which justifies the price and the consumer loyalty.

So, in an environment where there is absolute transparency on the features and benefits in the consideration building phase, companies which work hard to build the best product features for their consumers will win and this includes digital enabled features. Brands that do not innovate and bring in digital led experiences, engagement and purchase into the consumer's journey will have disappointed expectations and will lose loyalty.

Breadth and depth of habit – Consumers are creatures of habit, we are biologically wired to build habits and keep them intact. Our brains spend a lot more energy when they must understand and process something that has never been experienced and more energy means more food which means more hunting, and which means more exposure to predators. We are just trying to develop habits, so we do not get eaten and the emotion of comfort and warmth that we experience with familiarity is in fact linked to that. Great brands have over the years established themselves so firmly in a consumer's day that this habit is going to continue fueling consumption. Or is it? On the other hand, we hear the traditional adage that habits can be built in 21 days, so there is that. Here is my thesis; habits are important, but they can change and with the amount of exposure to brands and lifestyles that we have today, all brands are at risk of constant disintermediation. The idea of Netflix and Chill did not exist a decade ago, and now, allowing Netflix to lull you to sleep is one of the most widespread habits around. How about bubble tea if you are in Asia or Kombucha in all hipster neighborhoods in our big cities. Did not really exist a decade ago and it is hard to spot a young adult without some Boba in their hand these days. Yoga pants, we talked about earlier, somehow made it from seldom seen on Jane Fonda videos in the 80s to completely acceptable outfit for almost any social engagement.

Brands will need to figure out how to stay habitual for the consumers and this both in terms of frequency and occasions or touch points. It is also important to understand that consumers see brands and not companies and most consumers have no idea which companies make which brands. I guess, another way of putting forth what I am saying is that we will see many more umbrella brands with several underlying and connected products and propositions emerge. Digital will have a role to play here as well, in connecting all these underlying propositions together, establishing a single view of the consumer and providing digital enabled use cases. For example, we could see Redbull like brand strategies emerge where beyond the beverage, the brand has created a space of itself in consumers' lives through sporting events and content and I am sure there is more to come from Redbull.

An ethical stance – What an apt time for me to write this, while the world and particularly the US being torn in an increasingly polarized debate over issues that make you wonder if you're still in the 2020s. Consumers will expect brands to take a stance on key issues and clean up their act. The rise of cancel culture might mean the end of the road is already here for a lot of brands and companies but for those that emerge, digital tools will serve as a way to understand consumer sentiment through better social listening and also to walk the talk in terms of doing something about key topics. Say for instance a plastics recycling education campaign launched digitally, or a marketplace for carbon credits for frequent flyers or simple digital marketplaces for consumers to donate to frontline workers in the fight against the recent pandemic. Digital gives an easy and immediate way for companies to make true on their promise on important ethical and social issues, and I sure hope to see a lot more of that happen over the next decade.

Three practical things you should do now

So that is where I think brands are heading over the next decade. Will we still have brands? Yes, absolutely, but the promise of quality and status will not be enough grounds for brands to exist, there needs to be more. Once again, here are the top three things we must do:

- Invest heavily in shaping opinion about your brand on open platforms and marketplaces and media so consumers understand that you deserve a quality premium, a status premium, and have an ethical voice that syncs with the consumer's preference.

- Second, do not take your products' attributes for granted and keep working at providing additional functionality to consumers because they expect it from their favorite brand. A faltering core product proposition will bring you down even if you have built an amazing portfolio of side business, case in point is UnderArmour's loss of share in spite of MapMyRun etc.

- And finally extend your brand to more occasions and more touch points, think about what the brand represents and bring those propositions under your umbrella. This might mean your company will look different in five years than it does today, but isn't this what transformation is all about?

The Future Localized Franchise

Odin supports his community

Berlin Mitte, quite literally the middle of Berlin was what Odin called home since almost a decade now, and he loved every bit of it. Tiergarten, Branden-burg Gate, Checkpoint Charlie, Potsdamer Platz, Unter den Linden, Fernse-hturm, all the museums, all the history. He was so proud and lucky to be living in this part of Berlin and he was determined to make sure it retained its charac-ter and its charm. There were weekends when he did not feel the need to leave the neighborhood at all, and this was shaping up to be one of those weekends of just being in the middle of things.

He realized he was running out of dishwashing soap and shampoo and fig-ured he would do a quick run to the neighborhood Spaetkauf, the traditional convenience stores in Berlin, commonly referred to as "Spaeti". There was a time a few years ago when they were fast running out of business, especially in the face of stiff competition from Aldi who started rolling out new CVS stores at record pace as consumers moved online, and started using offline visits merely for small top up purchases. But a bunch of Spaeti owners got together in the community and set up sort of a group that collaborated and stayed relevant together. This Spaetkauf did not look much like the original one though. As he got there, Odin headed to the refill stations and filled up his bottle of Sunlight pro dishwasher and Sunsilk shampoo. Unilever had set up refill stations all over the city, especially in the Spaetis back when the war on plastic was in full effect. He also remembered he needed a new casing for his gaming controller which he had completely worn out, he made a quick online order and deployed the design he wanted to the 3D printer sitting inside the Spaeti. While he sat and had a coffee, his casing was printed and ready to be taken away. "Where did we get all these spares from before 3D printers became widely available?", he wondered as he headed onward into the middle of the middle, Mitte.

He stopped by at the Doener Kebab joint a couple of blocks down to get some McChicken nuggets. This specific location had just received a McDonalds license and it was working out quite well for them. They received the frozen nuggets on order, the oil for frying, had to use the fryer bought also from McDonalds and the right packaging which was all easy enough for the Kebab joint. Apparently, they also got their Ayran buttermilk drink, from McDonald's horeca ingredients supply business. On his way back, he decided to pay a quick visit to the bank branch, to meet his investment advisor about an ICO that his company was considering sometime soon. Deutsche Bank and Commerzbank, the two biggest competitors in Germany had started collaborating on their branch platforms since a few years ago. They both used each other's bank branches which were now unbranded, hot-branching like hot-desking. They had also opened branch usage to utilities, ecommerce pickups and some other players and he had heard that the hot-branching platform was making money for both banks. Who would have thought!

Back home, Odin felt happy that things were alright in Mitte, the Spaeti stayed, the Doener kebab place stayed, the bank branch stayed. The community was intact.

Understanding the evolution from being centralized to being distributed

Our world as it is, has been through progressive waves of centralization since prehistory. As humans emerged from Africa and progressively spread through Europe into Asia and through the Bering strait into North America and then South America (pre-Clovis settlement supporters please calm down, this is not a history book) they followed true decentralization of authority and enterprise. Just cover as much ground as one can. As hunting gave way to farming, humans settled in one place. Farming being much more productive on a "calories produced per calorie spent" basis, allowed people to specialize, gave rise to production, and art, and eventually government. And so, centralization started as power to govern how you lived was concentrated in a chief. Then there was religion and the power to govern what happened to you after you died was concentrated in the priests and the imams. Then came the Industrial Revolution and brought in another wave of centralization, this time for economies of scale and resource arbitrage. I think almost nothing I own has been made in the city I live in. And right now, we are at an inflection point again, perhaps the first one since the Ice Age.

We will see decentralization in how products and brands are put together and offered to consumers over the coming decade in many forms, which we will talk about here. For starters, we will see influencers create their own micro-brands and their own micro-products. We will see local retail communities emerge and fight back against big global conglomerates. We will see local production spread out into neighborhoods and even production at home in the consumer's household. Local and neighborhood businesses will thrive, and global giant companies will power this local movement through their platforms. (See Figure 5.4.) How novel and wholesome, let's dive into it.

FROM GLOBAL

1. GLOBALLY RENOWNED BRANDS
2. GLOBALLY DEVELOPED PRODUCTS / PROPOSITIONS
3. GLOBALLY SPREAD OUT MANUFACTURING
4. GLOBALLY MANAGED DISTRIBUTION

TO GLOCAL

LOCAL BRANDS BUILT ON GLOBAL MARKETING PLATFORMS

LOCAL RECIPES CREATED WITH GLOBAL TECHNOLOGY

LOCALLY MANUFACTURED ALONG GLOBAL SPECS

LOCALLY DISTRIBUTED UNDER GLOBAL GUIDELINES

FIGURE 5.4 Localization of propositions

Influencer brands and products – We have discussed a few times so far the impact of influencers and I think this will continue. We learn by imitating and imitation is essentially what drives the influence model, so I do not expect it to change. What will change is the authenticity around influencers, or more like the lack of it. The rush to make a quick buck by making up a fake representation of yourself online and monetizing it has shaken people's belief in the influencer model and I think it will get a lot worse before it starts getting better. And it will get better because platforms will emerge that testify to the authenticity of influencers and the bad ones will be weeded out.

Influencers will decentralize the consumer journey in many ways. For starters consumers will become aware of products and start considering in earnest only when their anchor influencers demonstrate trial and usage, not in today's paid influencer model but with some degree of authenticity. Eventually you might see influencers create their own brands entirely self-created or a curated "playlist" of brands. Imagine this, you walk to a Slurpee machine in a convenience store and ask it to dispense to you a Slurpee just like say Dwayne Johnson drinks his. The Rock's Slurpee. Influencers will pre-program and mix their product ideas and consumers can buy the bundle and compensate the influencer for allowing them to use their pre-mix. So, you could have a morning breakfast with eggs à la Kanye West and Cereal à la Kim Kardashian, or you could get your post workout Gatorade à la Tom Brady.

At home and near home manufacturing – Companies will attempt to enable manufacturing or assembly of products to be as close to the consumer as possible. This has a dual advantage in that the cost of shipping and last mile will be avoided, and personalization will happen almost at the point of consumption allowing companies to dramatically lower SKU complexity. There have been several business models in the making around this concept. Take for example the Nespresso machine, where in addition to the several other things that made it a big success, the fact that with milk, water, the machine, and a variety of capsules the consumer could put together a large number of different coffees by himself at home. Or take the example of IKEA, which ensured that simple product design, clarity of instructions and portable packaging of parts enabled them to shave off the task and cost of transportation and assembly from their prices.

As far as 3D printing is concerned, and I might turn out to be very wrong here, I think personal ownership of 3D printers might not have a lot of utility beyond craft and hobbies. But a neighborhood 3D printing facility could be especially useful to print spares, or more so to print fashion accessories from the likes of H&M and Zara. Add to that stations to refill products, stations for package-less products, e-commerce delivery spots and e-commerce return spots and dark kitchens for restaurant brands and you'd almost imagine a neighborhood utility center which is part warehouse, part factory and part utility space. With a Starbucks, of course, because those will still be everywhere.

Hyperlocal companies – Small businesses will definitely have a slump for a bit, especially now dealing with the after-effects of the COVID pandemic but over time the cost of doing business will go down as more platforms are available for businesses to make use of. Local brands will get wings and will propagate a lot easier across cities and states and even countries. We are already seeing massive importation from different markets for sales on e-commerce. During my time in the Alibaba ecosystem, the CEO used to talk about wanting to be able to ship products from China within a day to anywhere in Southeast Asia. Couple the commercial freedom of being able to sell anywhere in the world with the marketing freedom of being able to reach anyone anywhere in the world and you have a truly borderless business model. Especially in the services sector this started long ago with business process outsourcing and we will move to personal process outsourcing soon as well.

I grew up in a beautiful town called Nashik in the West of India. Amongst many others, one thing my city was known for was grapes. In that idyllic and wholesome setting, a returnee from the US decided to experiment with winemaking and few years later started a winery starting a local trend which made the city the wine capital of India in a decade. Just last week, my wife noticed that our local e-commerce platform thousands of miles away had wines from that vineyard, available and selling. And the fact that a young wine from that Tier 2 city in India can make its way here is a true testament to how the "glocal" marketplace will continue to evolve.

Local retail communities – Mom and Pop retail will most definitely shrink, but I do not think it will entirely disappear. Digital platforms will offer the same scale advantages to small stores that a large convenience store chain or a fast-food chain inherently has. Aggregators will emerge and have already emerged in China for example that will go on and modernize thousands of mom-and-pop shops and digitize them, to the extent that they can compete directly with large convenience store chains. Perhaps there will also be a consumer trend at work here which focuses on supporting local entrepreneurs.

The other major advantage that mom-and-pop shops have is their almost endless flexibility in accepting lower returns on their asset. In a regular corporation, if a specific store does not deliver on the growth targets or delivers a profit margin far lower than anticipated, there will be consequences for the store manager. In a mom-and-pop environment, the owner entrepreneur will accept a far lower return if it comes to that, by selling at a much lower profit and this flexibility will in the end mean the shop survives. This very reason has been responsible for massive growth in marketplace e-commerce, where independent merchants sell to consumers, compared to retail e-commerce, where the platform buys from brands and sells to consumers. Individual merchants and wholesalers can make economics work like no corporation ever can which is why they have thrived.

Global and large company platforms – Many large companies will realize, in time, that their key value add is not merely building a quality product under a reliable brand, but they also have the opportunity to convert their capabilities, built out over years, into platforms to monetize them. Take the McDonalds example from Odin's day, again just my imagination. And why would a corporation that is hard pressed for growth and does not have the capital to build store assets not convert its brand identity, recipes and supply network into a platform, and micro-franchise it out to millions of individuals? Or the banks who have branch assets, the possession of which is in no way a competitive advantage anymore, could choose to sell them off or find ways to collaborate and monetize those and create new revenue streams.

This is not new, and companies are used to monetizing their key asset of consumer relationships under the guise of cross-selling products in a "use my consumer to make more money" scheme. And in the same vein I think we will see platform business models emerging from every single asset a company can find including: real estate space, machinery and equipment, shelf space, warehousing space, spare human resources, agency relationships, supply contracts, playbooks and approaches, cash flow etc., you name it and corporations will start making money off it.

Three practical things you should do now

So as a company looking at the coming decade how do you localize your franchise? Here are my top three takeaways:

- For one, invest smartly in authentic influencers, which has two implications, understand how to measure effectiveness of influencer relationships and make sure you focus on authenticity.

- Secondly, start looking into localized manufacturing or assembly of your products even on an experimental basis. It probably will not make financial sense yet, but it will be "in the money" once consumer sentiment and acceptance have turned enough.

- And finally build a platform strategy, take every idle asset you have in your company and think about how you can sweat it. Then sweat it and build it out more until you finally end up with a real business model to profit from.

So, there you have it, this is how companies will put together brands and products for their consumers in the future. We started off by looking at how companies will gain consumer insight differently, we then moved to think about the amazing benefits of hyper-personalization. We thought through the future of brands and their continued relevance, and we ended with a focus on how localization and decentralization in products and propositions will become an important notion for companies to be mindful of. In the next frontier we will step further back in the supply chain and look at how companies will manufacture and distribute products in the future.

Notes

1. https://www.marketingweek.com/unilever-develops-tinder-for-ideas-to-speed-up-the-pace-of-decision-making/
2. https://www.wsj.com/articles/lululemon-to-buy-at-home-fitness-company-mirror-for-500-million-11593465981

CHAPTER 6
HOW COMPANIES MANUFACTURE AND DISTRIBUTE PRODUCTS

It was sometime in 2005, and I was hard at work inside a German luxury car factory in the South of Germany. It was a pivotal time for the brand, they were about to introduce their first SUV and it looked amazing. I was quietly hammering away at my Excel model at my desk – I had one job and one job only, to get the doors to Bratislava. The chassis was being made in the north of Germany and loaded onto a train which reached the assembly line in Slovakia. The body was being pressed into shape at the factory in Bratislava and the doors here in Baden Württemberg. My job was to plan the exact production schedule for the batch of SUV doors so we could load those on a train that left the factory for Bratislava so they arrive there just in time for them to be sent to the assembly line. And my God, that killed me.

Rewind a few years, this time it was 2003 and I was in Mumbai writing my graduation thesis and the topic was "A Critique of Taguchi's methods for total quality control". The two main notions of the many that Taguchi proposed over his career, were that of "Loss to society" and "Design of experiments". The loss to society concept, in a nutshell, meant that companies should not quantify the impact of lower quality production just locally on the company's P&L, but think about the broader loss to society. In his design of experiments work he proposed a way to run test production runs along different combinations of input parameters and then the use of statistical methods to decide on the best possible levels for all inputs, almost like a pre-cursor to AI. I tried hard to dispel both these methods but the more I thought about them, the more I realized that the underlying principle was sound, the world just had not caught up to it.

A few years later I was back at thesis writing, this time sitting in the then newly built public library in Berlin, the topic was "Kollaborative Planung in der Autoindustrie", it means in English exactly what it sounds like in German. The idea was simple, if suppliers and OEMs setup joint teams and share data and plan their production end to end as if it were one company, the efficiency benefits would far exceed the perceived value lost in contract negotiations where you would have given away valuable insight in your own company's operations. Back then, some 12–15 years ago it was still very uncommon for companies to open up and establish enough trust to work together.

Three separate incidents and all three of them a pre-cursor to the sort of decisions and activities companies will continue to make. But more importantly there is comfort that finally, we will have in the coming decade, the technological wherewithal to operationalize our ideas around a more connected, efficient and better utilized supply chain.

In this frontier we will look at four topics: Starting in the factory we will look at how manufacturing will look like in the future, we will then exit the factory and look at warehousing and logistics and how that might evolve. Following that, we will delve into the different routes to market and examine how distribution will look like with a focus especially on fragmented trade. And finally, we will look at reverse logistics as a critical component for recycling and returning waste. Let us dive in.

The Factory of the Future

Wahad's slow cooker gets put together

"Haleem! Korma! Nihari! Paya!", the girls shouted out in unison, when Wahad asked them what they wanted to eat at Eid. Ramadan was in its second week now, and they were all fasting. They had just passed what he liked to call the hunger cliff, around the 8th day or so when the body just got used to not eating, and suddenly the month long fast did not seem like such a big deal anymore. But he wanted to start planning the Eid feast for his family and he wanted to get it exactly right this time because his wife's family was going to be visiting. They always had their doubts about their successful daughter marrying this son of a bicycle repairman and if not with his career, or the lack of it, he could at least impress them with his culinary skills. Wahad decided, it was finally time for him to get that slow cooker, a slow cooked Nihari would just do the trick he figured and he went onto his favorite e-commerce platform and placed his order, triggering a curious sequence of events that would end up in him getting his slow cooker within a couple of days. Here goes.

The slow cooker broadly consisted of six main parts – there was the glass lid, the aluminum outer casing which was custom painted according to a pattern Wahad uploaded, a ceramic inner pot, the temperature control unit, the power unit and finally a few plastic parts like handles etc. It was quite an easy piece of equipment to put together and did not cost a lot to make or to buy.

First off the aluminum shell, that was pressed not far away from Mumbai, the press shop had a direct link to an online press job marketplace which put up jobs in real time, either bulk jobs that were made to spec or spot jobs that were made to order. Press shops the world over could take up jobs and commit to a delivery time and a price. Considering Wahad had picked a pretty standard size, the shell was pressed as a part of a larger batch. The accepting press shop consolidated a few batches together that were destined for the same paint shop and had it ready to ship within a couple of hours. Likewise, the paint shop was part of a marketplace as well, but it was a very local operation and had a preferential agreement with the press shop, so it was able to deliver the custom paint job for a much lower cost. The paint shop itself was completely unmanned, a robotic arm, read the family portrait that Wahad wanted printed on the slow cooker and coated and spray painted the shell.

The temperature control unit and the power unit were all pre-shipped out from the UK, the darling of the world these days when it came to low cost labor and cheap production. Brexit had made the economy extremely competitive indeed and everyone had jobs, they just did not pay very well. The ceramic shell was however where the real magic lay, the brand owner in this case had a patented layering technology that allowed for recycled materials to be compressed and layered in the right form. Those were pre-shipped out of Germany and together with the temp unit, the power unit, and the painted aluminum shell everything arrived at a neighborhood manufacturing lot a couple of hundred meters down from where Wahad lived. The plastic parts were 3D printed and a technician assembled and packed the slow cooker within ten minutes, tested it and it was ready to go! The day after he made the order, Wahad received a collection request and he simply stopped by and picked up his custom slow cooker himself. Industry 4.0 had helped him get his mother-in-law on his side.

Understanding the evolution in manufacturing

Industry 4.0 has been a buzzword now for half a decade and as usual there is a swarm of consultants out there, all well versed in the terminologies, ready to deploy reportedly tried and tested approaches. They will talk about sensors and automation and data and blockchain and augmented reality and a bunch of other fascinating stuff. But I thought perhaps it might make sense to step away from the technicalities for just a bit and to think about what the underlying principles are. Often, any kind of innovative use case applied in the factory gets classified under the Industry 4.0 umbrella and while it is most likely useful, it misses the point in the long term. I will discuss Industry 4.0 as it relates to manufacturing specifically along four key principles: Decentralization, Interfacing, Self-regulation and Virtualization. (See Figure 6.1.) And then I will try to explore what role, if at all, humans will still play in a fully 4.0 Industrialized context.

Decentralization into services – Over the next decade, we will see the beginnings of a massive decentralization of manufacturing tasks broken down into specific services. There are a few implications to consider here. For starters, what this means is that there will be no central production planning authority per se which decides the scheduling of a piece of work in all its steps, instead each constituent manufacturing step will run independently as a service provider taking up jobs as they come along and optimizing for itself. This would only work if there is enough installed capacity in the marketplace for the jobs that are actually relevant and as companies hit capacity and scheduling

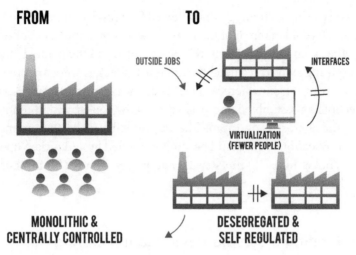

FROM

TO

OUTSIDE JOBS

INTERFACES

VIRTUALIZATION
(FEWER PEOPLE)

**MONOLITHIC &
CENTRALLY CONTROLLED**

**DESEGREGATED &
SELF REGULATED**

FIGURE 6.1 Industry 4.0 in the factory

constraints, they will invest the right amount of capital in installing additional capacity. Similarly, idle capacity or unproductive capacity will not be able to receive jobs and will shut down.

Secondly, manufacturing might not be centralized in one location and perhaps the era of mega factories is over, as connectivity and remote operations can make sure parts are produced to the same specs regardless of where they are produced. Especially the further along the product is in its assembly, we might see the last stages of the assembly happen as close to the consumer as possible, with the ultimate in late-stage manufacturing being actual 3D printing or consumer own assembly at home, the IKEA way. Third, the establishment of transparent task marketplaces will make this decentralization possible. These marketplaces could, at times, be private internal marketplaces or, at times, open marketplaces with active bidding for jobs. Enterprises which take up these jobs will have their performance on quality and reliability available for the "customer" to make the right job allocation based on. The big advantage of this would be a much better asset utilization, production lines that sit idle because captive demand is exhausted can start performing jobs for third parties. Finally, the ability for a specific unit to be completely decentralized in deciding its own schedule will create the right incentives for asset owners to focus on quality, effectiveness and expertise. This in turn will provide more cost efficient, robust and longer-lasting products, lowering the cost to society – Taguchi would be happy.

Establishment of interfaces – With widespread and almost complete automation in most if not all steps of the manufacturing process, machines will communicate directly with each other. This will happen across the value chain and perhaps there is a version of the world where, as there are changes to expected consumer demand, say for a specific product, because a certain set of influencers have made it go viral, that information could be relayed through the distribution, back to the assembly and through to the component manufacturing and the raw material supply instantaneously, and allow the owners of the different decentralized services in the value chain to adapt their activities accordingly. Similarly, changes in raw material prices or availability or quality could potentially be rather quickly reported up through the chain all the way to the point of sale and the brand to convert into a valuable consumer benefit.

I cannot help but draw an analogy here between the modularity drive within software development, that we discussed in the first chapter where we talked about applications being broken into services connecting with APIs. The same thing will happen here, albeit in the physical world. Technologies such as IoT and 5G connectivity will have a big role to play here to enable machine to machine communication but as will AI as it relates to demand forecasting in especially complex multivariate consumer markets and raw material markets. Such end-to-end alignment across the value chain will save millions of dollars in obsolete inventory at all stages of the supply chain and the ultimate benefactors of this will hopefully be the consumers.

Self-regulation and flexible roles – As these decentralized units connect with their supplier and customer units through direct interfaces, they will also self-regulate their operations to maintain quality of output and make changes in their configuration to do a wider variety of tasks. Machines will monitor their own output and adapt in real time to changes in quality to maintain consistency but, more importantly, sharing of information across manufacturing steps in real time could also allow for subsequent steps in the process to be configured so as to compensate for off spec output. The ability of automated systems to reconfigure themselves in real time will also allow the same manufacturing step to simultaneously adapt to and produce to a variety of different specifications with minimal setup time. This will reduce the need to have multiple lines and reduce overall downtime for the manufacturing units.

Virtualization – When you start imagining this complex network of mini-factories, some centralized, some down in neighborhoods, spread out geographically at various stages of the value chain, a critical element for all of this to function well will be absolute transparency and easy visibility on the manufacturing activity. In this future factory setup, every machine, every inventory regardless of how big, complex or small and simple will be represented in a virtual world. This through a network of IoT sensors, and smart RFID tags constantly updating the status of activities and location of products along the supply chain. This information will then be represented in the virtual world and serve two main objectives, provide factory workers, with the right wearable device, all possible necessary information at a glance and provide an easy control tower for the manufacturer to have full visibility and ability to drill down into the smallest details of the operations to make sure things are proceeding as planned. Exception management and especially root cause analysis will become a lot easier than having to trace through a sequence of production activities distributed across several companies and owners.

The human element – So where will the human be in all of this? Will everything we buy, and use be put together in these smart connected supply chains, maxed out on automation? Beyond the fear-mongering, I do believe there will be a loss of factory jobs and even planning jobs as automation takes over, there is no escaping that and attempts at preserving jobs to the detriment of tech advancement could result in a loss of competitiveness. But there are market forces at work here too and let us think back at the very first chapter of the book where we talked about value creation. The fact that a robot is replacing a person on the shop floor essentially means the job that the person was doing has stopped adding incremental value, over and above what the robot is adding. Or in other words, buyers and consumers do not think it is worth paying a human extra for a piece of work that a robot is able to do with perhaps better quality for a lot less.

I see three possible outcomes as a result of this. For starters, there will be areas where brands will be able to convince consumers that there is indeed some value in having human manufactured or human serviced products. The entire hand-crafted space, for maybe more of an emotional attachment or sometimes from a feeling of social responsibility, will continue to thrive and smart companies will maintain some traditional manufacturing to benefit from this premium. Secondly, people will move into other value-adding jobs although this will be easier said than done. A change of vocation even across generations takes courage and motivation and we spoke earlier about the human tendency to stick to recognizable patterns to save energy. So, some people will make it but not all, resulting in unemployment and popular discontent which is the third possibility. In this popular discontent scenario, which is the most obvious mid-term outcome, we will see governments being voted to power who will slow down the advancement of Industry 4.0 maybe by a decade or more. But markets where that happens will continue to lose competitiveness globally against those markets where the society is able to collectively move itself to a completely different vocational model. This is difficult, but literally the only way to continue to create value otherwise there is a real risk of reverting our workforce back into jobs, where they are producing goods for other markets and earning salaries so small, that they aren't even able to afford the stuff they make with their own hands. Perhaps this is how the hunters felt when farming started taking shape in pre-historic times and it is time for us to make a mega-transition again.

Three practical things you should do now

So, you are a manufacturing leader, and you are keen on getting onto the Industry 4.0 bandwagon or perhaps you have already started and are wondering where it is all going. Here is my simple advice to you:

- Think about the principles underlying Industry 4.0 and not just the technologies that enable them. I mean sure, using Blockchain to get better supply chain traceability sounds fancy but what is it really achieving? If decentralization, then how exactly does it help and is there another way of achieving that? Build a principle-based Industry 4.0 agenda and not just a technology-based agenda. Ask yourself how you can deconstruct your manufacturing into services and not just how you can install more sensors.

- Start building that control tower to gain full transparency on the end-to-end supply chain. As you start with an ambitious vision you will realize how incredibly dispersed all your manufacturing data is and how difficult it is to get it all together in one place. So important to acknowledge that building that data thread is a multi-year journey and there is no better time to start than now.

Open your enterprise up to third party manufacturers wherever possible in a big way. Access to and knowledge of how to best utilize a third-party manufacturing network will be a big value driver in the future in addition to in house manufacturing where there is a clear technological and competitive advantage. The successful companies of the future won't be the ones that make our products but the ones who know how best to get our products made.

Future Logistics

Jaden's unmanned Duvel

"Jaden, your carton of beer is here! And it came from Belgium?", asked his wife, completely confused. Why anyone would order anything from outside the country, leave aside from a different continent, was a mystery to her. But Jaden was a mystery to her often and she had realized the key to their happy marriage was to live and let live. Jaden rushed to his carton like a kid during Christmas and opened to reveal his 12-pack of Duvel. Duvel was a pale ale with a whopping 8.5% alcohol and beyond its formidable reputation, what Jaden liked about it was that it was still privately held by a family in Belgium and brewed only there. And Jaden was a sucker for an origin story, and high alcohol content beers.

The brewery, near Antwerp, was by now completely automated as most breweries were. The tasting was still left to actual humans, although the AI had by now easily surpassed the actual tasters on market impact metrics. The crate of beer was put together in the factory and transported to the warehouse where it was stacked by robots and registered on the warehouse management system. An outbound export container was planned a couple of weeks before Jaden ordered, there had been a recent "incident" in Seoul where the famous Korean rapper "XtrimPayN" was seen chugging a Duvel and orders had gone through the roof. An unmanned truck picked up a couple of pallets and drove them to the Antwerp port. An unmanned port transport vehicle took the container to the ship and loaded it on. The ship too was unmanned, almost, it still had a security crew, an engineering team and a couple of officers but most of the time they did pretty much nothing onboard. The ship brought the container to Busan, where an unmanned truck picked up the pallets and transported them to a warehouse in Seoul. That very night, Jaden had made the order and he had asked for a weekend delivery.

A couple of days in the warehouse, and then exactly four hours before the pre-agreed delivery time the carton was taken off the pallet and shoved into a refrigeration unit, once again by a robot where it cooled down. Forty-five minutes before the delivery time, Eka did a quick check with Jaden, "Are you okay to receive a delivery in 45 minutes?", and Jaden blinked twice. The carton was taken out of the refrigeration unit and laid out by a robot on an outbound pickup pad where a swarm of drones were waiting quietly in queue. The next one in line swooped down and picked up the carton before lifting off again. As the drone left the premises, Park Jongmin the security guy, sitting on a reclining chair did a click with the counter in his hand, knowing fully well that his was probably the most useless job in the world right now, counting drones for no reason. And exactly 30 minutes later Jaden's wife took in the delivery.

It did not end there of course, 12 bottles and six hangovers later, an unmanned garbage collection truck emptied Jaden's glass waste bin into its belly and took it back to the local recycling plant – which by the way was also unmanned.

Understanding the evolution

The ideas around Industry 4.0 and the principles that we discussed in the earlier topic are as valid here as in manufacturing, particularly self-regulation, which here will take form in automation in warehousing and transport and decentralization which will take form in what I call Uberization of logistics.

A few other important trends will take place where digital enablement will have a key role to play. Reverse logistics will become an important area of growth considering both e-commerce returns and recycling needs. Consumer's demands on sustainability will also affect the logistics space, particularly with a push towards green supply chains. And finally, global trade will undergo a major shift, with implications on imports. Digital will have a role to play in helping companies make money while guiding the world through these changes. In this section we will discuss these, look at the state of technology today and understand how some startups and companies are already making great progress in benefiting from the trends.

Automation – Automation in the transportation and warehousing space will be a strong driver of value and it will take many forms: Unmanned vehicles, Drones, Exoskeletons and other wearable aids and overall management and visibility systems. (See Figure 6.2.) Unmanned vehicles will hopefully start plying our roadways, waterways and airways, ferrying goods much earlier than they start carrying passengers. Especially in private spaces like inside warehouse complexes or ports UMVs have already been in operation in some

FIGURE 6.2 Unmanned supply chain

form and it will not take long for this to spread to our public transportation infrastructure. The consensus here seems to be that there will still be a human "driving" the UMVs albeit with a much higher man to machine ratio. So, imagine a captain of a trucking fleet sitting in the cabin of the lead truck and commandeering an entire fleet of trucks, not necessarily always driving in a train, all at once. Drones have been spoken about for a while now and I think we will start seeing small scale commercial usage very soon. Amazon's MK27 drone development is exciting to see as both from the tech feasibility point of view and regulatory understanding point of view we are likely to reach a consensus in the coming few years. The industry will follow and while the first implementation will be in the sub-5-pound weight range over shorter distances, the movement could gather momentum relatively quickly.

Inside the warehouse itself robots have already started taking on a significant amount of work, once again led here by the e-commerce giants. Amazon acquired a robotics company called Kiva Systems in 2012, it's now called Amazon Robotics and has more than 200,000 Kiva robots working inside Amazon's warehouses.[1] Over in China, Alibaba does not seem to have bought a robotics company yet, but Cainiao, its 51% owned logistics company works with Chinese startups like Geek+ or Quicktron and has similar robots in operation in its warehouses. In addition, scanning devices and smart RFID tags are enabling easy findability and stock keeping inside the warehouses. Exoskeletons allowing workers to literally do the heavy lifting are increasing labor productivity. And finally, big data and AI driven warehouse and logistics management systems are making warehouse and transport performance easily visible and allowing managers to optimize the supply chain end to end for better delivery times and lower costs.

Uberization – I think it's altogether amazing that a startup has had such an impact on the world of business that it has become a verb, to Uberize is to take an existing asset and make spare capacity available on an open marketplace to monetize the asset better. Logistics infrastructure, especially where companies have built their own, requires high Capex and must constantly respond to uncertainties of demand. In the transportation sector, digital marketplaces have started emerging in all the different modes of transport and will continue to grow stronger over the next decade. Startups like Lalamove and Gogovan in China have Uberized last mile delivery through Vans. Amazon has been operating its flexible last mile delivery model Amazon Flex since 2015 and by 2019 it operated in 50 cities, where anyone can register and make deliveries for Amazon and a make a couple hundred bucks in a day. There are several emerging Uberization platforms for trucking and freight forwarding as well, including Flexport, BlackBuck in India or Next trucking.

In the Uberized warehousing space too, we have startups like Flexe that essentially stitched up an open and standardized network of warehouses, all layered with a unified software which allows brands access to warehouse space, as needed on demand. The benefits of having warehousing as a service instead of sinking millions of dollars of capex are obvious and we will see this space grow encouragingly in the next decade. What's more is that companies like Flexe, can take an e-commerce order directly from Google search and fulfill it to the consumer for any brand; this is what I was talking about in the e-commerce section earlier when we talked about disaggregation of e-commerce services.

Reverse logistics – Everything that goes in must come back at some point, one way or the other. There are two different flows here or two different value propositions to look at; one of e-commerce product returns and one of recycling. We will study the recycling topic a little further down in this chapter and for now let us focus on return logistics. Return rates in e-commerce have averaged around 10% or so for a few years now and the cost of shipping normally makes up to 15% of the product cost. These are averages, of course, but give a fair order of magnitude. What this means is that e-commerce players spend a whopping 1.5% of their margin on bringing back products if they choose to bring them back, excluding the product cost itself. And remember, we are talking about retail margins here which are, in any case, very thin. Having the ability to return a product, however, is an important driver of e-commerce purchases so not allowing returns is not an option.

Advanced analytics and AI will play a role in driving return costs down as will automation and Uberization. Consumers like to return items to stores because that gives them immediate confirmation of the return and their money back and we have seen e-commerce players Uberize item return (and pickup) locations already. Drones and unmanned vehicles could pick up directly from consumers and drive down cost of return transport considerably. But perhaps more importantly, retailers will develop and use advanced analytics models to predict the likelihood of a consumer returning a specific product and price a part of the return cost into the product. They will match returned products to other similar SKUs and review the listing to reconsider if they should still sell these. Or even use return prediction models to sell return insurance to consumers. If an e-commerce player can predict well, who is likely to return what kind of items using AI, then they can make a pretty profitable business out of selling insurance against product dissatisfaction.

Green supply chain – Companies will commit to ensuring their supply chains are green and sustainable, or in other words, carbon neutral, non-polluting and energy efficient. This will take significant investments in technology and new assets and most corporations will make it a point to claim their achievements to consumers for strengthening their brand equity, along the lines of the ethical voice that we discussed in the previous chapter. Apple, for instance announced a few months ago that in ten years it will have its entire supply chain running on renewable power and this difficult and commendable goal would mean that "by 2030, every Apple device sold will have net-zero climate impact".[2] Wouldn't it be amazing to make a claim like that? The answer is "Yes" and therefore we will see many corporations follow.

Extreme traceability will be another huge breakthrough where consumers will be able to perhaps scan a QR code on the product and get a detailed and deep overview of where and how sustainably the product was put together. You would, for example, be surprised at how many products you use regularly that contain palm oil, and you would hopefully not be surprised by the controversy surrounding palm oil with regards to the impact it has had on deforestation and exploitation of labor. Digital enablement can make information readily available in the most up to date form for consumers to refer to before making a purchase decision. Perhaps blockchain might have a role to play in establishing the veracity of this record of sustainable transactions within a supply chain to make sure there are no fake narratives built around topics that really matter to the consumer.

Import model of the future – And finally I want to spend a bit of time reflecting on the future of imports and international trade in consumer products. There is absolutely no doubt that cross-border e-commerce is booming and will continue to grow for the next five to seven years for sure, there is so much obvious value in exposing products from all over the world to eager consumers thousands of miles away. But as we start nearing the end of the decade, I think this trend will start reversing or abating somewhat as a few things happen. A lot of international trade over the past has relied on labor cost arbitrage and this still exists and will continue, but the benefits of this arbitrage will start becoming less and less compelling. Most markets will also by then start becoming self-reliant in the knowledge and technology needed to produce the right goods. Domestic markets in today's major exporters like China are also the biggest growing consumption centers and a time will come when there is so much demand in these markets that companies will be maxed out serving that local demand instead.

This is not bad news, according to me. The fact that we are shipping cheap products from thousands of miles away and using up the world's resources while doing so makes absolutely no sense from the society's ultimate well-being point of view. Reflecting back to the value creation logic we discussed in the first chapter, I think there is absolutely no value created or in fact net value is destroyed when a small town factory in China manufactures an iPhone case which is then shipped to someone in another country and sold for a throwaway price.

Three practical things you should do now

And thus, it is time to wrap up this topic on the future of logistics and there is again some simple advice I can give:

- As far as robotics and automation is concerned, this is just the right time to make investments in this space if you have not done so already. I think we are just a couple of years away from a breakthrough in unmanned technology and you ought to get your foot into the door now.

- From an Uberization point of view, there are likely some startups in this space in your market who have set up a transport/ warehouse platform and you should start working with them even if it is on a small scale now.

- And finally think of your supply chain and if it is green or on a good pathway to being green, use digital to create transparency and engage with the consumers on this topic. Beyond the market benefit, there is the wonderful cognizance in doing this that you are making the world a cleaner and healthier place to live in.

Digitization of the Route to Market

Nuno's weekend of sin

Ed was off on a business trip to Europe. Business trips in general these days were fewer and harder to come by. The pandemic had taught the world that business travel was quite frivolous and more of a luxury than a necessity, and consequently Ed had to travel a lot less these days. Nuno did not mind at all, it was nice to have Ed around more, gave them the opportunity to really spend more time discovering things together. Like recently they had started watching cooking shows together and begun experimenting with doing some cooking themselves. People seldom cooked these days and while food was easier, cheaper and better to just get outside, the experience of feeling the ingredients with your own hands and smelling the smells and having the feeling of having created happiness by yourself in your kitchen was irreplaceable. On this weekend, Ed was not around because he decided to stay back in Europe over the weekend for further meetings the week after and Nuno decided he was going to be a homebody. This meant watching TV all day and indulging in his three favorites: Chips, Ice Cream and Beer.

Back in the days, when he was in his teens there used to be a "tienda de barrio" or a corner shop literally right next door as he stepped out of his apartment. And another one across the street in case he could not find what he was looking for in the first one, which still existed. Now of course there was a D1, an Ara and a Justo & Bueno, all on the same street and that was convenient because there were more products available, although with a lot less character. He walked into the D1 and grabbed some German beer which was always available at a great price here, what with the strong import capability that D1 had. He would not get that in the tienda.

He walked over to the tienda, he liked shopping here because it always ended in a ten-minute conversation about Santa Fe with the storeowner, Juan, who was in his late twenties. Juan's father had passed the store on to him but still sat at the back, watching TV, drinking coffee and finding faults in Juan all day. The store itself, according to Juan made a lot less money selling goods anymore, considering the modern stores up and down the street, but he still had a hundred or so loyal clientele like Nuno, who he did free deliveries to, within around a kilometer or so. The e-commerce pickups and returns, mobile and iTunes credit, bill payment, vending and coffee machines up front, plastic bottle return, the KFC mini-franchise at the back etc., made up more than 80% of the store income which was enough for his family to have a comfortable life. There were thousands of stores like his in Colombia and, in fact, while they were all branded independently, they all ran on Google's storefront platform which helped them keep operational costs low so there was more money for them to take home.

Nuno bought two bags of chips and two pints of ice cream from Juan. The chips, Juan bought from a nationwide snack distributor who gave Juan a lot of great additional benefits like store merchandise material and helped set up a POS machine for him. In fact, Juan bought around 40% of all his products from this distributor. He even won an award last year from the chips brand for being a top 100 store in Colombia and he probably owed that to Nuno considering all the bags of chips he bought. The ice cream was a special kind, and that he bought on the big e-commerce platform and sold to Nuno. Nuno could of course have bought it himself on the same platform, but Juan was able to buy in bulk and sell it to Nuno for a lot cheaper.

Nuno rushed back home, looking forward to a binge watch the entire Lord of the Rings extended edition trilogy from back in the days. Sure, he missed Ed, but this was going to be a good day, he thought as he cracked open an ice cold Hefeweizen.

Key elements of the evolution

The way our products get distributed to the different storefronts for them to be snapped up by consumers will also change over the next decade. The Industry 4.0 principles of transparency will apply here in a big way and eventually add value to the end consumer. Particularly in markets with a large share of fragmented retail and many different routes to market, lack of visibility on what is happening in the marketplace has been a constant source of frustration for brands and digital enablement will have an answer. While the advent of modern retail is inevitable, I think the modernization of traditional retail itself is another pathway to efficiency. This was hitherto not possible but is now, because technology is further ahead and a lot more scalable than it used to be. In this topic we will examine that evolution by looking at five items. First, we will look at the advent of modern trade and how this will change the marketplace, we will then look at the mom-and-pop shop of the future and how it would evolve. We will look at how digital will enable distribution to the store to become more efficient and how the store owners will also find more store services being offered to them. Finally, we will understand how B2C and B2B marketplaces will likely converge in the end state.

Consolidation of fragmented trade – There is no doubt that modern retail will continue to grow in developing markets and catch up with developed markets by the end of the next decade or a bit more. And within modern retail the channel that is more likely to retain its relevance is the smaller format convenience channel. Looking at the consumers FMCG shopping needs, I think the full weekly stock up trip will move to e-commerce because the convenience is just unbeatable, and ten years is more than enough to establish a habit. There will still be a role for large format destination modern retail outlets, the type we discussed in an earlier chapter for that once a month leisurely visit. But for the quick mid-week top-up visit, especially while consumers are in any case out and about, the convenience store format will stay relevant and even grow in its footprint. But within convenience itself, we will see a gravitation towards larger stores with a bigger assortment where it becomes more of a mini supermarket than a small convenience store and evidence of this is already seen. So, we will have exceptionally large destination supermarkets for the monthly visit, e-commerce for the weekly stock-up and large convenience for the mid-week on the go occasion. So how about the mom-and-pop shops? I think there will still be a role for the mom-and-pop shop to play, especially for micro-trips and micro-e-commerce, and I might have just coined that term here for the first time. Shopping trips which are just a quick dash in and out, where it's not worth paying a shipping fee on a single item because it was completely unplanned, could still be serviced by small neighborhood shops not because convenience stores cannot but because purely of location proximity. So, Nuno goes to the mom-and-pop shop across the street instead of the D1 shop because it is just closer. As for micro-e-commerce too, Nuno will get Juan to do a free delivery of a small basket of products because D1 or Ara would not do the delivery for free. But why would this be possible and affordable for Juan to do if it is not for D1 and Ara?

Mom-and-pop future store and store economics – The answer to the above question lies in the fact that the store's value proposition to consumers will need to be different, as would the underlying economic model of running a store. Let us start off by looking at the value proposition of the store. The mom-and-pop store of the future will, like Juan's store likely make 80% of its income from ancillary services and only 20% from FMCG product sales. The most valuable asset a mom-and-pop had in the past was their ability to source products and merchandise them for consumers, this will go away in the future as modern retail and e-commerce do the same, except with more products and at better prices. The advantage mom-and-pop stores will still maintain is their location and character, and the successful small business owners, likely the sons and daughters, will know how to play this asset up to their advantage.

So, the sons and daughters store will sell a variety of services for which proximity is important, this could be a subset of what is available in the convenience store but for which there is no scale advantage per se. For example, having a vending machine placed in the store would help monetize the store location or an e-commerce pickup/return spot or an e-Wallet loading point and any number of services for which proximity to consumers is a key benefit. For the 20% products that are then also sold, almost like an up sell to consumers who are there for the services, mom-and-pops will participate in large buyer networks who will ensure great pricing and good profitability. Finally, from an economics point of view, a mom-and-pop shop owner will always be willing to accept a lower return on his store asset, compared to what a large modern trade chain is willing to accept on its stores. This is an important factor because it will enable families to own and operate stores in places and at a scale at which big corporations would just not be able to run their own stores.

New routes to market – Growing up in Nashik, my west Indian small town, there were families who had amassed impressive wealth within a generation by simply "getting the agency" for a specific brand or product. The folks who got the biscuits agency, the petrol and gas agency, the branded apparel agency, the paints agency, the motorbikes agency. This was the first phase of the route to market evolution back home and it was similar in all developing markets. Over time this changed a bit as brands started appointing better equipped and trained sales reps into their key distributors and a massive wholesale channel emerged as more entrepreneurs sought to further deepen a brand's reach and profit from consumer demand. This established the route to market that I grew up with and still exists in most markets. With the turn of the millennium brands went on a modernizing spree and now we have better distributor management systems, sales force automation, in-store sales promoters, third party salesforce etc., and a lot of companies are still in this phase. The true disruption is coming now, general trade is suffering as consumers move to e-commerce and modern trade, distributors are running out of business because margins are shrinking, sales reps are churning out for better opportunities and wholesale remains a black box. So, what next?

Digital enablement will help modernize this route to market. We will see large, efficient, multi-channel, multi-brand distributors emerge that will consolidate distribution across brands, geographies and channels, both offline and online. The scale advantages coupled with focus on better technology enablement for better sales resource utilization, warehouse and fleet resource utilization including open platforms, like we discussed in the earlier topic, better transparency on data and store insights which are monetized with brands etc., will allow for large distributors to make reliable margins and brands to essentially get out of the business of distribution. Unbeknownst to a lot of brands, large e-distributors have already emerged to manage online channels with much better technology, and it won't take long for these online distributors to realize what an incredible opportunity lay in modernizing offline distribution for the same brands they serve online.

Store aggregators and store services – Over the last few years we have seen the emergence of, and much discussion over, eRTM players in China, predominantly with Alibaba's Lingshoutong (LST) and JD's Xintonglu (XTL) being at the forefront and now between them claiming to cover upwards of 3 million mom-and-pop outlets. We will continue to see the emergence of store aggregators and service providers in this space over the next decade the world over, either acting as technology enabled distributors for brands to mom-and-pop shops or as ancillary service providers to mom-and-pop shops such as the ones we spoke about earlier or both rolled into one.

A store aggregator distributor platform will be able to present to mom-and-pop stores the same advantages of scale in securing inventory that a modern retailer today has and will also be able to help the store owner do a much better job of merchandising and selling. (See Figure 6.3.) More importantly, such a platform will be able to capture the institutional knowledge of the store owner, synthesize and transfer it across the marketplace to benefit from it. Quite often the store owner is seen as a key benefactor from such platforms as a recipient of technology and better prices but the platform itself, being a novice to the offline retailing space stands to gain as much in return from insights and actual data from, for example, a smart POS machine that would be installed by the service provider.

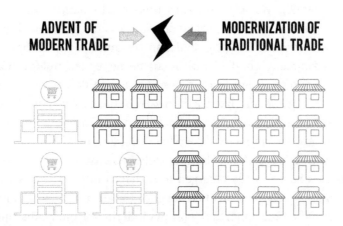

FIGURE 6.3 Modernization of traditional trade

B2B marketplaces – Finally, I also envision that there will at some point be a complete convergence between B2B and B2C e-commerce marketplaces. While most e-commerce players will not admit it, a large share of e-commerce purchases are made even today by small businesses that then sell it further down the value chain. This because the level of discounting on e-commerce sometimes makes it more affordable for resellers to buy online and sell to consumers than to buy through the local distributors. Brands will, together with the platforms, figure out a way to maintain the price differentiation between B2B and B2C sales potentially by launching membership privileges for outlets and offering better rates on bulk buys and bring this "under the carpet" trade out in the open and legitimize it.

Three practical things you should do now

So, this is how I see distribution evolve over the next decade, particularly in the fragmented trade. For companies affected by this I have the following key recommendations:

- Firstly, create and launch an outlet program for your best outlets. You can partner up with providers of technology and e-distributors and start converting your access to outlets into a real business model. The alternative is to lose that access to a third party and having to pay a fee to the third party to be able to access your own outlets in the future.

- But understand that the outlet's own world is a lot bigger than your brand, so you will need to build a proposition for the outlets that far exceeds your brand itself. Also focus that proposition for 80% on value added services, where you expect the outlets to get the most future income from. Merely providing product supply will not be enough for the outlet to stick by your proposition, that is something that is easily replicated by a competitor who is willing to absorb bigger losses for outlet recruitment.

- Find a few e-distributors or some of your biggest distributors and start discussing with them a major transformation and digitization of your route to market. There is obvious benefit for the brand and the distributor to make a proactive move towards a likely future than to get dis-intermediated by an outside player with deep pockets.

The Circular Economy of the Future

Bart loves being the Hulk

It was Saturday morning, 10 am and Bart heard the familiar ice cream cart jingle, this time it was appropriated by P&G as they sent their dispensing truck around Long Island. This was part of P&G's package-less initiative where a mobile refill station would do the rounds and consumers would fill up their perma-packs with the right product, the billing was based on a subscription service and based on actual consumption. And, of course, this was much cheaper for Bart compared to buying off the shelves. He filled up some Ariel, some Downy, some Head&Shoulders for himself and some Pantene for Jill. He also picked up some Tide pods while he was at it. "Ping!", he heard a green star being added to his score.

Later that day, Bart received some new Golf apparel from Titleist and some new Golf balls all of which was very carefully packed in layers of plastic, cardboard and bubble wrap. Bart carefully sorted it all and binned it the right way, just like it said in the "Sort it! Bin it!" campaign that took the world by storm a decade ago. They say the campaign was comparable to the "Just say no" campaign from the 80s, except it was a lot more effective in that there was a lot less waste on the streets, he couldn't say the same about drugs unfortunately. With all the e-commerce that was happening these days, Bart was sorting and delivering an amazing amount of recycled waste every week and it felt good to know that most of it was recyclable material. As he hit his 100th kilo of the year he heard another "Ping!". Bart understood that all the waste he delivered was valuable, in fact in some countries he had heard some companies had literally made millions "mining" the ocean and mining landfills for plastic waste. It was especially interesting how the Saudis, in anticipation of running out of oil immediately bought up the biggest landfills and ocean mining rights for the largest rubbish dumps in the world.

Later in the evening he stopped by at the local CVS and realizing he had forgotten to bring his own bottle, a rarity, decided to buy a bottle of water. It was PET and said "Waste neutral" on it which basically meant that the cost of picking up a similar bottle of PET from the environment was included in the price he was paying for the bottle of water. It was barely a few cents and he did not mind of course; part of that few cents charge was credited back to him in the form of green stars and he heard another "Ping!".

Back home Bart decided to just sit back on the deck and see the sun set and enjoy the peace and quiet of their beautiful backyard. He remembered the difficult years, after the pandemic with the economy out of balance and discrimination on the rise, he remembered being worried about the world and then he saw something happening, a change in human humility. That was the beginning of the end for waste and he sure hoped it stays that way. He looked at his phone and realized he had hit 1000 green stars and now was qualified to level "Hulk" in the green superheroes program. He loved being the Hulk.

Understanding the evolution in the circular economy

How we reduce the rate at which we produce waste, and deal with the current waste we have already added to the world is such an important topic that of course I wanted to include it in the book. And this not only because I believe it is important, but also because I think within the next few years the impact of the problem will become so acute that the world will have no choice but to deal with it. And digital enablement will have an important role to play in that mix. I think it's important to mention here that I think while there is a clear need to make the world aware of the problem, there is a much bigger need to get the world's resources, particularly capital to focus on solving the problem. As we discussed earlier, capital flows where there is value and people go out of their way to do something if it makes them money. While opinion leaders scream doomsday scenarios in rallies, and deniers yell back even louder, I hope there is a lot of us who will just roll up our sleeves and start creating ways for value creation which result in recovery of waste. The elements I will discuss here are package-less solutions, consumer education, return logistics and recycling capacity, consumer pricing and general transparency. (See Figure 6.4.)

Package-less solutions – Eliminating the packaging altogether is probably the first thought you would have and there is an absolute spectrum of experiments in the world today going towards this. For example, Starbucks is committed to introducing a new cup for their iced drinks which does not need a straw but has an elongated spout on the lid; you might have used it already.

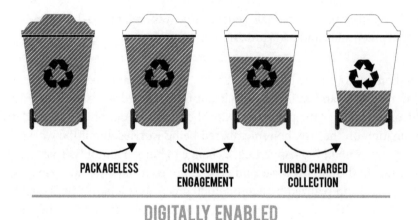

FIGURE 6.4 Progressive reduction of plastic waste

This eliminated the straw, not the packaging. There's dissolving packaging which would melt always when it's used or packaging made of natural materials like wax and seaweed and some seaweed packaging is even edible. While these experiments are important and need to continue to receive attention, I am personally much more hopeful with multi-use containers like returnable glass bottles making a comeback and refill stations like the one Bart used becoming more widespread. Companies like MUUSE in Asia or Goodless in Belgium have created smart containers with RFID which can be traced, refilled and consumers can be charged based on the fill.[3] The MIWA experiment in the Czech Republic has created an entire system around the smart container which is a precursor to what I think is going to be a revolution in package less solutions.[4]

Imagine always carrying your own bottle around, with a chip inside which you can literally use at any dispenser and with the chip ensure you only pay for what you buy. Or even always rent a container sort of like the bike sharing apps and get fined if you do not return in. These and such digitally enabled use cases would go a long way in making sure less plastic is needed in the first place.

Collection systems and recycling plants – Most large corporations have made ambitious pledges towards getting to a zero-waste status by 2030.

There is also a decent amount of plastic already being collected, nothing close to what needs to happen but the starting point is not zero. In fact, if all the companies in the world put aside a big chunk of money, we can probably collect every last bit of plastic and the problem will be solved, except this will take an insane effort and money and we will probably have to do this over time. For starters most corporations will attempt to artificially raise the price of collected plastic; in other words, they will attribute a higher value to the act of collecting plastic in the hope that this will bring more entrepreneurs into the plastic collection business and more capital to set up necessary collection infrastructure.

The garbage collection business also unfortunately happens to rest in the hands of some of the most opaque organizations in the world and digital will have a big role to play here by establishing a transparent, reliable marketplace where brands and recycling plants can buy recycled plastic from collection companies, and where there is absolute transparency in the price and source of plastic. Perhaps blockchain can play an important role here. The same marketplaces can also serve to allow consumers to reverse their plastic footprint, not unlike the carbon offset platforms. So, imagine that you buy yourself a carton of bottled water and are able to go onto a plastic collection marketplace and buy a carton's worth of "collection" essentially engaging someone in some other corner of the world to go out and collect a dozen empty bottles, in the process not only creating value but also employment.

Consumer education and sourcing – The further down the chain the plastic gets and the more distributed its location is, the harder and more expensive it gets to mine it. At some point companies will have to pay higher and higher prices for recycled material and it makes sense to work on the entire chain of disposal from the consumer down to the recycling plant to make collection easier and cheaper to perform. The best way to do this is to recruit consumers to do as many steps of the collection operation as possible and companies will find a way to educate and incentivize consumers to play their part. QR codes on packaging would, once scanned, direct consumers with clear instructions on how to dispose of the packaging, and even direct consumers to the nearest bin.

Companies will also rely on consumers to do the collection, a great example of this is Plasticbank[5] which allows registered members to collect plastic and receive groceries, schooling and health insurance in return. While this is directed also to drive affordability for the less fortunate, I think it will work even in developed markets. We will see brands riding on the wave of strong opinions on this topic to engage consumers to "do the work" in collection and get rewarded in return through promotions or loyalty points. Digital can enable such a collection engagement platform along the lines of what we discussed in the consumer engagement frontier. Consumers could bring waste that they collected to waste deposit centers, simply bin the waste and sync their devices with the smart bins to get credit.

Consumer pricing and building status – Beyond lending a helping hand in collection and in sortation most consumers will just pay for the collection when they buy the product itself. Historically, if we look at packaged goods, consumers got themselves a loose portion wrapped at the grocery store and paid for it. Then there came a time when someone figured out that products could be packaged and shipped. So, consumers were now buying not just the product but also the portability, so a product and a service bundled into one. Fast forward a few more years and enter plastic packaging and now consumers were buying the product, the portability and the lightweight and easy disposal convenience of plastic.

Now, rightfully so, consumers are demanding that they should not be given the opportunity to pollute the environment but at the same time are reluctant to stop using the lightweight affordable packaging. Brands need to add another layer of service to the product so now the consumer gets not just the product, and the portability and the lightweight convenience but also the assurance that the plastic will be collected somewhere soon. And like they do for anything that has value to them, consumers need to start paying for that extra service. This might sound a bit like avoidance of responsibility, but most companies are serious about solving the plastic issue and are even willing to take a financial hit to get things off the ground. But the fact remains, unless consumers agree to pay for what they are getting, they will not get it. Sort of like free deliveries on e-commerce that we have spoken about several times.

Brands can use digital engagement platforms to give back some of the value to consumers in the form of promotions or even by acknowledging status, like the green superhero concept I imagined earlier.

Transparency – As this entire sector emerges over the next decade in a major way, we will need platforms that create complete transparency on the underlying activities involved. For instance, a go to platform for consumers to learn about how a specific product packaging was put together, and what would happen to the packaging after consumption. This will help consumers make more appropriate purchase decisions. A platform for consumers, companies and governments to see the different streams of waste and how much waste inventory there is at any specific place so this can be addressed. A platform for collectors to see the bid pricing from recyclers and for recyclers to see the source and quality of the waste on offer on the sell side. A platform to see the ongoing sales volumes and prices so companies can make appropriate sourcing decisions. A platform that surfaces the fringe benefits of sparking the collection industry including employment generated. But most of all some sort of a global dashboard, that's perhaps constantly displayed at Times Square, at the Eiffel Tower and at the Burj Khalifa counting down the millions of tons of garbage that is being recovered, as we collectively set on the task of bringing it down to zero in the next few decades. Digital enablement will obviously have a major role to play in bringing all this data together and ensuring it is fair, accurate and well represented.

Three practical things you should do now

For companies affected by this and I am sure most companies are, a few pieces of advice:

- First, think of waste recovery not as a problem but as an opportunity; consumers want us to recover waste and this is a value creation opportunity that we need to figure out how to provide while making money. Educate your consumers and get them involved, not just as opinion leaders but more from the crowd sourcing point of view by creating engagement programs to do a value exchange of status or credits for waste.

- Invest in package-less solutions; it might seem like a gimmicky thing to do, the ice cream truck, but at scale there is a potentially break through business model there which you'll need to evaluate for your business.

- And finally, invest in transparency; the issue will only go away once the problem is solved and not knowing if the problem is being solved and to what extent is even worse than not acting on it at all.

So, there we have it, the fifth frontier, all about how products are manufactured, warehoused, transported, distributed down through the value chain to the consumer and then how the packaging is brought back again for recycling. We covered a variety of different topics under this umbrella, and the traditional monolithic way of manufacturing and distributing products will be seriously challenged in the future. Disaggregation in the supply chain and introduction of open platform marketplaces at every stage will make the manufacturing and distribution process much more complex but a lot more efficient. With that, we are now ready to move to the last of the six frontiers, this one about how a corporation will operate in this digitally enabled future along with its various stakeholders.

Notes

1. https://www.wsj.com/articles/SB100014240527023047244045772919032447962214
2. https://www.apple.com/sg/newsroom/2020/07/apple-commits-to-be-100-percent-carbon-neutral-for-its-supply-chain-and-products-by-2030/
3. https://www.goodless.be/ https://muuse.io/
4. https://www.miwa.eu/ We are a Czech company that decided to make the waste-free shopping a "new normal" by helping it make its way into the regular shops and supermarkets
5. https://plasticbank.com/ We are turning plastic into gold by revolutionizing the world's recycling systems to create a regenerative, inclusive, and circular plastic economy

CHAPTER 7
HOW COMPANIES WORK TOGETHER

We should be thankful for the times we live in. For the most, a pretty sizeable percentage of us have the luxury of waking up in a comfortable bed in warm homes, have three square meals a day. We have the facility of taking the weekend off from work, and with work itself we can work from nine to five, or thereabouts. There are rules on how we are allowed to behave at work which keeps all of us safe, and there is enough money being spent on us by our employers in training us and buying us laptops and paying for corporate trips and all kinds of other benefits.

If we were living in say 1905, in the thick of the Industrial Revolution life would have been a bit different for us. For starters, our children aged ten and 12 would have gone to work with us on 12-hour night shifts, in production factories and mines, earning 10–20% of the adult male wages in return. If we were living in France in the year 1800, under the French Revolution, we would have a ten-day week called a decadi, with only one out of the ten days being a leisure day. Interestingly, the modern two-day weekend started as an informal arrangement between factories and workers, so that workers who would want to drink themselves to oblivion on Saturday night could stop working at 2 pm on Saturday, on the promise that they would be sobered and refreshed for work on Monday morning. I also recall a curious conversation with a Japanese colleague in my consulting days. Me, living in the Netherlands, "I've got 25 days of vacation in the year". Japanese colleague, "That's it? We have 50 in Japan; every Sunday is off!". If we were living pre-Industrial Revolution, our working hours would have been 12 to 16 hours long and working conditions dire, no air conditioning and no heating, unless you were standing directly in front of the blast furnace. We would earn around 10 cents per hour and we would be far more likely to have an accident at work and die.

But people complained and things improved and they complained again and things improved again and we continue to complain; we want free food, higher pay, better titles, three-day weekends, flexible work conditions, nicer office space etc., and there is nothing wrong with that. Complaining and creating a nuisance loss for the employer is a perfectly valid lever to pull to re-set the price of our time and effort that we offer to the company we work for. But it's important to understand that it's still a marketplace and an employer, who is the buyer, has an obligation to his shareholders, which for a small business could be his family or for a large company could be you if you own shares. It is an obligation to provide as good a return as possible by employing the best ROI people they can. In short, no one is naturally entitled to have a job, I am yet to read a scripture where God said, "Let there be jobs and let everyone have one".

Of course, since the Industrial Revolution working conditions have improved and the world has become more civilized and modernized and bigger but startlingly little has changed in the job market ever since and, if anything, it has become a lot less free than it used to be a century ago. And that is primarily because the job market is now inextricably linked to the market for Government. The market for Government being essentially politicians, who will want you to sell them your democratic support in return for social services and safety etc., while making a "margin" for themselves either in actual pay, or through corruption, or through status and fame or through some ideological goals that give them self-actualization. In places where employers and Governments collaborate to mutual benefit, employees win and this works well, sort of like the co-dependent example of airlines and credit cards that we looked at earlier in the book.

Digital will change some of the underlying infrastructure of this three-way relationship over the next decade or so and we will talk about that in this frontier. We will start off by looking at the future of finance and look what being the future CFO in a company will be all about, we will then turn to employment and employability and see how that will change over time. We will talk about leadership in the next decade and how employee mindset will need to evolve to deal with all the changes. And finally, we will look at the future of government. Let us dive in one last time.

The Future of Finance

The life of Odin the CFO

Odin's dad was a finance professional as well, back in the 2000s and Odin grew up admiring the clean cut, hyper professional image his dad portrayed, and that is when he decided he wanted to also be in finance. Ironically though, what Odin remembers most were the late evenings when his dad would come back from work looking totally worn out; it was hard to believe the battering a suit and a shirt could take within a day's work. Odin thought it was cool, this romanticized 90s image of the finance guy who gave his all to his job. If only he knew what it really was like – Odin's dad for the most part hated his job. Sure, he spent maybe 20% of his time doing the really strategic stuff, but most of this time was spent trying to desperately find any two numbers that actually matched in the organization, and around the end of the month for the monthly closing, his life became an absolute hell. These days when Odin and his dad get together and reminisce about those days, he cannot identify with any of it. Odin is now the CFO of a mid-sized company and it's almost like his dad and him were in two completely different professions.

Mondays are performance days for Odin. He sets aside a few hours to spend with his market leads in their data room to understand the details of how the business is doing. It almost looks like a control room at NASA with the screens and live feeds, everything is fully automated and completely accurate. They even have an AI which surfaces all the key topics they need to look at and he loves that the conversations are all about why something happened a certain way rather than trying to understand what happened in the first place. Seems like the order volume in Munich had dropped last week, they did a quick drill down and saw that it was in one district of Munich and especially on the falafel-based meals. The AI suggested it might have to do with the recent press about sanitation issues in kebab places in the local news that might be turning consumers away from that type of cuisine. The team decided to dial up visibility and promotions on Indian food instead as the AI suggested a good correlation between Middle Eastern and Indian taste preference. Odin did this every week and for the most important cities every day. With increasing competition, smarter consumers, more taxes etc., margins were contracting every year and Odin and his team had to find small bits of efficiencies every day to keep profits coming.

The month was about to end, and this was going to be an easy week for the finance team, closing was fully automated and monthly targets were already met so they decided to all take a few days off for the month end. Odin himself was going to spend some weekend time working on their fifth ICO, the last two were very well subscribed and they were looking forward to raising some more money soon, specially to finance their Soy-milk maker business. Completely different business line where they were going to market with an appliance in partnership with a niche appliance maker and had to work out a high-quality soybean supply chain and brand. Different shape of the P&L, different shape of the balance sheet and different levers to pull to deliver value. But that was how things were in today's businesses.

He had none of the operational hassle that his own father had to face when he was in business but needed a much broader vision to be able to drive performance on so many kinds of businesses all under one roof. And Odin loved it, loved being the CFO.

Key elements of the evolution

The CFO and the finance function of the future will be quite different to the model we have today, and this future is unraveling quite fast, so the next decade will be critical. In general, the finance function will move away from being a process-oriented hygiene function to a more strategic, contributing function in the organization and in this topic, we will discuss a few of the main areas where this change will happen. For starters, a lot of the tedious repetitive activities done by the finance function will be hyper-automated freeing up time from employees engaged with these. Next, we will look at how data availability will become seamless and the burden will shift from making data available to doing something with the available data. Especially important will be the role in improving profitability which will be severely challenged in the coming decade. Companies will run a variety of business models under one roof and the finance function will have to deal with that. Finally, we will look at new ways of raising capital which will hit the mainstream and provide a great opportunity to companies which the CFO of the future will need to know how to capitalize on. (See Figure 7.1.)

Hyper-automation – Robotic process automation was another buzz-phrase that started showing up a few years ago and it will be an important component of the evolution. RPA is essentially the act of observing how humans work at a specific repetitive task and emulating a similar workflow digitally to then relieve the human of doing this repetitive task. This is different from the bottom-up build of a software solution that consists of modules that perform a specific service and communicate via APIs. The advantage being that unlike a big software implementation which can be complex, those of you who have done an "SAP project" will understand, RPA just layers on to existing ways of working and can help progressively relieve people from repetitive jobs instead of doing a big onetime software implementation. We talked about Low-code in the first section of the book and companies like Outsystems[1] have built strong

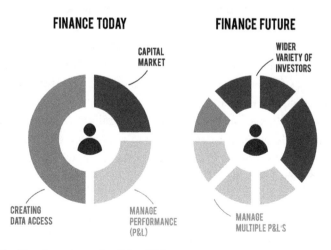

THE CFO'S CHANGING MIND SHARE

FINANCE TODAY

FINANCE FUTURE

CAPITAL MARKET

WIDER VARIETY OF INVESTORS

CREATING DATA ACCESS

MANAGE PERFORMANCE (P&L)

MANAGE MULTIPLE P&L'S

FIGURE 7.1 The changing role of the CFO

businesses based on platforms that allow companies to build their own apps to support internal processes literally by dragging and dropping functionality into a template.

As companies adopt RPA, there are three questions they will need to answer. First, where to use standard automation and where to use custom automation, because the more customization you would do to processes specific to your company, the more it will cost. We see a lot of startups for instance just buy RPA modules off the market and model their organization around the software rather than the other way round and save themselves millions. Second, how much human intervention to design for. Of course, there is a need for human intervention as a last check, but to be honest a human is perhaps already far worse equipped than a software on seeing if things are done right. So, I think having human interface would be more from the point of view of assigning liability than driving efficiency. And finally, to outsource or to insource. Over the years most corporations have used BPO to the max, in this case, instead of an automation being a cheaper alternative a person in India was the cheaper alternative. Perhaps there will be a future where RPA is a more cost-effective solution than BPO and we will see hybrid models emerge where companies do outsource but require BPO providers to use RPA to demonstrate progressive cost reductions.

Real-time performance management – Much of the value add to clients during my time in consulting was based on the ability of the firm to deploy heavily equipped data crunchers into the client's organization who would spend the first four weeks of the project just digging, analyzing and visualizing data into a 200 page deck. And that would just blow away the management at the client because most clients were and still are in such a data poor and insights poor state that it takes a specialist team and half a million dollars a month to get insights. This is less true for newer companies and will over the next decade be not true for most companies, perhaps not great news for consulting firms who will now have to rely on the quality of advice to differentiate themselves.

So imagine a weekly performance drill down session where you sit with your team and look at the world map with reds and greens on which country generated the most cash flow, because you're wise enough to know that cash flow is what really matters in your business. You double click on China because it's red and your Chinese colleagues say, "But China is different". You say it surely is, and double click on a specific category, and then on a specific brand that is red, and then the specific province that's red. And you find the one customer that is underperforming for that brand and category. And then you double-click, and you see a variance analysis which shows that the drop in performance is not because of lack of advertising, or bad pricing or the product not being nice enough but because your shelf share has dropped. You click on a video call button and call the sales rep responsible for the customer and ask him to explain the drop and he tells you that the trade terms negotiations have gone badly. You can tell him that he has the freedom to increase terms by 50 bps because that would be a cash neutral play for you as a company. Next week the reds are gone. This ability to consolidate performance data from several sources and automate the search for root causes and solutions to drive speed and efficiency in doing the right changes in the market will become an important value driver for companies. This involves aggregating from a lot of different platforms and sure enough, companies like Fivetran[2] have emerged successfully that spend all their time and effort on developing standardized connectors for different data sources for you to pipe it into a data warehouse and a dashboard like Power BI or Tableau.

Focus on productivity – Move over growth, productivity is the new number one priority, or rather will be in a few years from now. The last decade was an incredible one for corporate margins, in fact the last few decades have seen a steady expansion in corporate margins. But that is about to change for a few reasons. Firstly, the traditional go-to place to lower operational costs, outsourcing for cheaper labor is likely not going to be possible any more as China and India's supply of cheap labor is becoming fast exhausted. The alternative is to hire more expensive labor at home which by the way populist governments will push corporates to do. There will probably be higher taxes as well, again driven by popular governments and corporates will have to accept that. Competition is getting more and more fierce, especially from local players who are willing to accept much lower margins. And finally, corporate debt yields are so low that it's unlikely companies will be able to continue to raise cheap debt at the same pace at which they did in the last decade. So, expansion in margins is going to be hard to come by and so is growth. Naturally, companies will turn their attention to better asset productivity and that will be, according to me the key focus of the next decade. Enter COVID19 and that very imperative just got a major shot in the arm.

Digital enablement can help here in a few ways. To begin with, the incredible transparency that digital enablement will help create in business performance and asset utilization will help companies highlight exactly where there are productivity gains to be made; for example, better measurement on media deployment and performance will help brands understand where they are over spending on ads. Open platforms that offer much more transparency on supply and demand for specific services will help companies pay for exactly what they need and what they get; for example, sourcing creative talent off platforms will help companies avoid large agency fees on blanket contracts. Companies will be able to sweat their assets much better; for example, having the right assortment and inventory replenishment in vending machines will drive more sales from the same vending asset. And finally, companies will be able to monetize assets better; for example, putting an OOH display screen on the vending machine itself will help create an addition source of revenue.

Alternative business models – We have discussed throughout the book the need for companies and brands to expand beyond their current single product, single occasion businesses to include additional use cases. We have also repeatedly spoken about partnerships and alliances. All of this has severe implications on how a company plans it finances and this will be a big challenge for companies in the future. The most influential leaders in any company today are in the core business, and they are influential because they stem from the core. Going ahead, companies will need to have the courage to allocate more of their funds to the long-term, away from their most influential leaders. And beyond that, companies will have to gain the capability to evaluate their business as a collection of connected but different business models.

So you might have an FMCG business that compares to other FMCG companies, and a content business that compares to a Disney, and a retail business that compares to an e-commerce player, and a Services business that compares to a Utility all under one roof but all with financials that look completely different. The CFO of the future needs to be able to manage all of this. One of the fundamental reasons why corporates have not been able to build businesses in the digital age is because, when push comes to shove, these businesses are held to the same financial benchmarks as the core business. It is such an obvious miss from a resource allocation point of view but has been extremely hard for companies to orchestrate, perhaps because of the constant need to generate ever more cash to fuel the stock market rally.

ICOs and crowdfunding – I am not proposing that there will be some sort of tectonic shift in the coming decade in the sources of funding for companies because of digital enablement. I think it is much more likely that we will see an upsurge in private investment in public companies because of the productivity opportunity we spoke about above, and also because of the eventual realization that the startup space doesn't always provide reliable returns. But that has little to do with digital. Over the last three-odd years there has been a lot of speculation about ICOs and while I don't think this will become a major disruption just in the coming decade, I think we will see the share of ICO fundraising leading into perhaps double digits. So, what are ICOs?

ICOs allow companies to raise money directly from consumers by completely surpassing bankers, regulators and exchanges in return not for a share of the company but for a token that allows the ICO buyer access to the company's product whenever it is ready. Most successful ICOs today are made by companies in the blockchain space which makes this concept harder to understand using a real example. So, let us imagine a fictitious ICO by a fictional coffee chain which says it is going to need 10 million dollars to build up 100 stores and writes a project plan and a white paper about this plan. Consumers will buy tokens in an ICO and help raise the 10 million dollars and when the project is ready, their token will allow them say 20 million dollars' worth of free coffee. As the project nears completion, and confidence in the project grows, most ICO holders will end up selling their tokens for progressively higher prices.

The world of ICOs is a dangerous world marred by complexity, fraud, and regulators and bankers unhappy with disintermediation who will pull out all stops to stop companies from eliminating the middlemen while raising funds.

Countries like China and Korea have banned ICOs altogether. I do not know where this will go, but they say you cannot keep a good thing down forever. There is a clear value in making fundraising easier, cheaper and more transparent than what today's capital market intermediaries offer and I do hope we find a consensus for this channel for fundraising to evolve and become more mainstream.

Three practical things you should do now

And that is how the future of finance will evolve. We spent a lot of time in this book reflecting on consumer and supply chain evolution, and our finance colleagues not only have to deal with the implications of that but also have to orchestrate a transformation in the way they themselves work. But it is an exciting space with the good guys like RPAs and the bad guys like ICOs both together revamping the way we do business. Here's my advice to companies:

- Think about your finance function in two distinctive sub-functions – first, a services function to commoditize and automate all your repetitive tasks which uses RPA and outsourcing to the max and is staffed with technologists who are incentivized to achieve productivity in service delivery.

- Second, a value-creation function that steps away from an accounting and budgeting driven mindset to a value creation advisory mindset. Equipped with the ability to drill down better than anyone else in the organization and incentivized to find and unlock marginal sources of value in growth and in productivity every day every week.

- As your demand for funding fragments into several different businesses and business models which have a completely different risk and return profile, your sources of funding also need to change to match this new risk return profile. It doesn't make sense to fund high risk early-stage businesses with the same investors as your core business and you'll need to work out corporate finance structures to match the right investors to the right business units inside your company.

The Future of Employment

Wahad and Wahida's walk through life

The sun was about to set, and it was that wonderful dusk in Mumbai, when the air felt a bit electric from the days' worth of action that the city had seen. It was almost like all the energy trapped in this dense urban environment was now starting to seep back into the atmosphere and into the sea. So, the city could have some respite and get some rest and refresh itself before the early morning rumblings start again. Wahad and his wife decided to have a long walk on Marine drive, starting all way at Nariman point down to Chowpatty. Millions of couples across generations had done this walk before and Wahad wondered what exciting plans and what wonderful reflections had happened just along these few kilometers over its entire history.

They were so different the two of them, Wahida went to a good school and one of the best colleges. Wahad dropped out of high school and never really got any formal education. Sure, he learned a lot observing his father do his bike repairs, but just did not have it in himself to sit through school. For years he wished it could be different and wished he could go back and change the past and get his schooling done. He then discovered online learning and was instantly hooked. The self-paced learning suited him well as did the ability to pick and choose and construct his own learning agenda. But most of all he was glad his ability to learn was not held hostage by a teacher who had incredible powers over how he was assessed. When he came to Mumbai, he was not quite sure how he was going to make ends meet in the beginning. Living with his aunt in Byculla, he spent the first couple of months delivering food and groceries but soon discovered the handyman marketplace. His gentle personality, quick problem solving and his approach to fixing bikes, learnt the hard way from his father, served him well. He kept up to speed by taking every repairman online course he could find and soon he had a great set of ratings and a reputation and was making very good money.

Wahida's situation was altogether different, it was hard for him to pinpoint exactly what her role was, she seems to move around every few months from project to project. But clearly, she was someone important and they appreciated her capabilities a lot. He was glad she was doing so well, especially because it gave him the opportunity to work whenever he wanted and spend time with the girls. Although Wahida also worked pretty much wherever and whenever she wanted. She could even take as many days off as she pleased, just as long as she delivered what was asked of her. What was even more interesting was that she could decide how much she wanted to earn. She could take on more tasks and more responsibilities if she wanted to earn more money, she did that last year for a few months, they wanted to put a down payment for the apartment they bought and for five to six months she worked six days a week for ten to 12 hours and made a year's worth of salary in half a year. That was helpful!

As they reached Chowpatty, Wahad caught that look on Wahida's face, the one that said – I want some Kulfi, but I don't want to be the one that suggests it, so please suggest that we have some Kulfi and allow me to say no, so you can insist and then I'll finally relent and we can have some in the end.

"Kulfi?", he asked.

Understanding the evolution in education and employment

I think the entire journey of education and employment is going to be heavily disrupted in the coming couple of decades and the 2020s are going to be where it starts in earnest. Here in this topic, we will look at this evolution from five different angles. To start with we will look at the changes in vocational education as consumers start gearing up to establish the basics that make them ready for employment. Then we will look at employment practices and employability and how that will change. Once in the company people will experience work very differently and we will also see the trendy "Agile" methodology find its rightful form in the organization. The way employees are compensated will change as well and we will discuss that here.

De-institutionalization of education – In the first section of this book we talked briefly about how growing up in India, from a higher education point of view, there was just a couple of viable options: you became a Doctor or an

Engineer. And there are two interesting insights in there. First, from the hundreds of thousands of Engineers that graduated back then and perhaps even now, only a small fraction still have anything to do with the core engineering education that they received. This is not necessarily a bad thing and what it tells us is that employment opportunities have become so proliferated in the specific capabilities that are needed, that you can't have a degree for every job that is out there. On the other hand, it tells us that it is possible to equip our labor force with a base load of skills like critical thinking, collaborating, creating hypotheses, planning work etc., and there are probably a hundred of these that we all learnt in engineering school, that would help them take up employment in any kind of job.

I think this is where we will end up in the end, basic schooling could potentially absorb the base load of skills that higher education degrees today impart. We can stop pretending that higher education degrees are linked to employment and allow prospective candidates to pick and choose courses in a self-designed patchwork of learning which might make them ready for a target job. And there could also be a Lego model here – so a bank might say that for a credit risk analyst position they recommend the following ten courses to be completed, and the candidate is free to have that done on their time. In this new scheme of things, there is no role to play for the institution, unless it is for allowing the government to incentivize students to study specific courses by providing financing. I think online learning will become the mainstay of education soon and then it will extend to offline. A bit like the destination supermarket vs e-commerce idea we have explored a couple of times. Students will use remote learning "e-commerce" for most of their learning needs but for the in person experience they will still want to visit a college or an institute, but even offline it will be a completely modular and on demand learning marketplace. Perhaps all the campuses of the present will then serve as co-learning spaces for independent learning operators to use for their offline activities.

Employability and employment – In an earlier chapter we spoke about services marketplaces, and this trend will become a key focal point on how the definition of employment changes over time. Most companies today operate under a somewhat binary definition of full-time head count and contract employees. Going ahead I think the full-time head count will be less and less full time and the contract headcount will also have a variety of archetypes. To begin with there will be far fewer employees on the books as full-time employees. These roles will be reserved for employees who have a large enough or broad enough mandate that they need to be fully occupied, or employees that are part of a vital competitive function in the organization. Most companies today have a large bench of contract workers or temp workers who serve as an important extension of their talent pool. This group of employees will start receiving similar benefits and facilities as full-time employees if indeed they are fully dedicated to the company and employers will need to extend these benefits if they are to choose to keep the contract workers within the franchise.

Much more interesting, however, will be an entirely new group of contributors, the qualified freelancers. Companies will have the ability to carve out critical tasks which do not require full-time employees on to marketplaces where they will be picked up by available freelancers. This could even be something critical like devising a market entry strategy or writing a business plan or developing an RPA application. Freelancers will be rated by employing companies on jobs and will be compensated for their tasks. And will expect the marketplaces to perhaps cover benefits like health insurance so they continue to participate on the marketplace in return. So, your employability then will also depend on the experience you have delivered, and you can seek flexible employment when you want with whomever you want and with whoever wants you.

Agile at work – Yes, it is time to talk about Agile. Clearly, it has become much of a buzzword over the last few years and you have most likely participated in an agile team yourself at some point. Results have been mixed, it works sometimes and it doesn't sometimes and always the idea of thinking about an outcome as a product and thinking of iteratively launching one to the customer and progressively improving upon it becomes very confusing for companies when the project objective isn't exactly prototype-able. The euphoria around Agile has also spawned a whole industry of Professional Scrum Masters and Agile coaches who will gladly evangelize any unsuspecting leader into thinking the Scrum 3-4-3 is the answer to all problems. Consulting firms too have jumped on this bandwagon and it is hard to not find a consulting article which does not include "Become agile" as a key recommendation. It is a bit like saying "Make money". But that aside, just like we did with Industry 4.0, it is important to unpack Agile and see what makes it tick and adopt the underlying approach in whatever mix makes most sense for our company and our specific problem. (See Figure 7.2.)

THE 7 WHYS OF AGILE

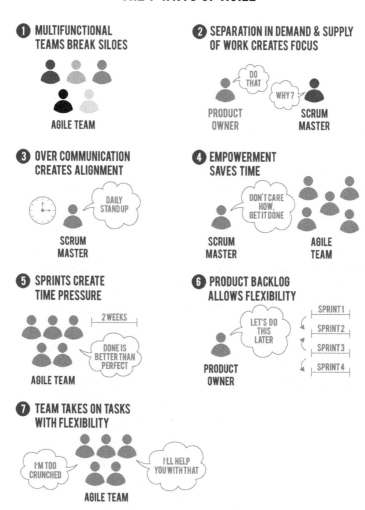

FIGURE 7.2 Benefits of Agile in action

What makes Agile click are a few principles it brings to the organization: Multifunctional teams, Separation between demand for work and supply of work, Over-communication, Empowerment, Time pressure, Flexible agenda and Flexible work. The obvious one is multifunctional teams, ensuring any skill that is needed to do a complete piece of work sits in the team so there is no need to wait for each other. The separation between the Product owner defining what needs to be done and not bothering with how it's done, and the Scrum master focusing on getting it done once a deal has been struck between them makes the mandate clear and stable. The teams over-communicate every day and there is no time lost in bringing each other up to speed and everyone is always working in sync. The team most often has a direct link to the key decision maker, no steering committees and long approvals needed, decisions are made on the spot. Time pressure created almost artificially by Sprints makes sure the team does not spin its wheels and does a good enough job instead of wasting time on perfection. The entire work, or Epic, being broken into Sprints allows to maintain flexibility of the team's agenda in the mid-term while fixing the long-term objective and the short-term tasks. And finally, because the team is in it all together, tasks can be cross allocated to whoever has capacity so in sum the total team utilization is far higher and more gets done.

The Scrum approach might not apply to all problems of the future but the above principles are very valid for a wide range of issues most companies deal with, and we will see over time that organizations stop working in strict structures and move into more flexible semi-permanent teams which exist for a year or so and then dismantle and flow to the work.

The workplace itself – The office space will be dramatically different ten years from now compared to what it looks like today. COVID has accelerated remote work and a lot of opinion pieces now think of it as a permanent mode of interaction, but we do not really understand remote work well enough to think of it as the new normal. I think a few things will happen over the next decade.

Remote work will become of course very acceptable, and in most companies, it will likely be an "always on" offer to allow people to work from home. To balance this out however, companies will need to have a much more explicit definition of what needs to be done, shared by each manager with each employee. There are also likely to be some instances where in-person presence is required, because the risk of long-term separation could be a loss of commitment and engagement, both contributing in a big way to discretionary effort from employees. Office spaces will most definitely be smaller, they had already started to be smaller before the pandemic. The space that is left will be more communal in its nature, mostly meeting rooms and large gathering spaces. Work travel will reduce dramatically. High-definition video conferencing facilities have been around for a while, but it is a significant Capex requirement which now companies might see the benefit of making. Even consumers who love to work from home, see the need to step out once a while and I think this is great for the "work from cafe" sector. I am personally looking forward to Work oriented cafe models where you potentially pay by the hour for a semi-private workplace. The payment might be nominal, potentially chargeable on a corporate account and the price point will hopefully keep 13–14-year-old schoolkids out while us adults go about our important business.

Compensation models – Finally, the way we get compensated might change as well. The traditional Base + Bonus + Equity model has many problems. The base salary itself is exceedingly difficult to benchmark because job descriptions are so different, and any benchmarking effort ends up with people up in arms about the fact that the benchmark is wrong. Going ahead, having open services marketplaces and even better transparency on salaries afforded by the likes of Glassdoor will make it a lot easier for both employees and companies to have the right benchmarks while discussing base salaries. Bonuses need to go through a transformation both from a process and from a mentality point of view. The underlying premise with bonuses is that it is possible for a company to objectively differentiate between high performers and low performers and use bonuses to compensate them differently. But it is exceedingly difficult to have an objective way of segmenting performance across markets, functions and seniority so most bonus allocations are somewhat fair but also somewhat absurd. The same goes for equity awards. Better transparency on activities and outcomes will give companies a better ability to differentiate performance.

Three practical things you should do now

And that is that for the future of work and the disruptions we can expect within it. For companies, a few key pieces of advice:

- Think actively about smaller organizations that rely on freelancers and out-sourced agents, even picking a couple of marketplace partners to collaborate on a pilot. You will need to build the internal capabilities in assessing and handling the right type of agents and starting now will help you benefit from the quality and efficiency gains that will come.

- Get rid of your office space proactively and find a distributed location model, employees will likely dislike it at first but will soon see the benefit and you will save a ton of cash.

- And finally, be open to rethink your compensation model and start studying what some of the newest companies really do and some of the newest employees really care about. You have a decade to move to a new normal and this is as good a time to start as any.

The Future of Leadership

Jaden the "Conductor"

"Welcome back boss!", said one of Jaden's Analysts to him as he walked into the office from his week-long break. It made Jaden cringe a bit every time someone called him boss, it seems like such an outdated way to refer to someone and it almost felt sarcastic. He felt like telling the associate to not do that, but he did not want to be that guy. "Thanks Bro", Jaden said, marveling at how the term "Bro" was so useful in diffusing so many complicated situations, and in this case, it was him taking a step down from the pedestal his analyst put him on, in the coolest way possible. That was a win.

Jaden's dad had set the business up, a small brokerage firm which over the years grew into a midsized brokerage firm. When online brokerages started becoming mainstream the business was at risk of closure, and Jaden came in a set up the Robo investing service which was now the main contributor to the company. His dad had taken a step back and Jaden was now the CEO. Ever since he took over the business, other than changing the nature of the business itself, Jaden had made a few fundamental changes to the way the organization worked together. For starters he rightsized the organization; it was a difficult decision to make but it was the right thing to do. It is not that people were sitting around; it was just easier to contract people from the local talent marketplace as and when needed. It was more cost effective and he had the pick from some of the smartest professionals out there. The organization became a lot flatter too and there were, outside of him, only two others who had any direct reports. He worked hard to establish an approachable image, he absolutely detested being treated as some demi-God being the CEO and wanted the team to treat him like an equal; he delegated a lot, allowed people to make decisions and also stepped in when needed. He paid his expert individual operators as well as he paid his team leaders. This was important to him, because he didn't think it was some kind of badge of honor to have a bunch of reports that made you more deserving of status or better compensation, it was merely a different type of responsibility. For the team itself, he made sure to challenge them, and he saw them working together and overcoming those challenges. Only to be set another challenge. The team initially complained about him never being satisfied but soon realized that they themselves were happiest when they were solving challenging problems rather than just pushing papers. The team was very close-knit, and the office atmosphere were always convivial, he made sure of that. This was where he and everyone else spent a big chunk of their awake hours and he wanted it to be the most comfortable, go-to place in everyone's mind.

Jaden was nothing like his dad; he was his own leader and he had decided what his own personal leadership brand was – he called himself "The Conductor" like in an orchestra.

Understanding the evolution in leadership

The people who will be leading our organizations, say ten years from now, are probably in their mid–late thirties right now, the "almost millennials". And much as difficult as it is for someone twenty years older to understand the strange way the millennial mind works, it's important because over these next ten years it's up to the older generation to develop the leadership talent that will steward our companies, and most likely our stock options. And it is not going to be enough to teach young leaders how the older generation did things, the millennial mind does not work that way. So here, I'll offer up some insight into how we will need to tweak our leadership model going ahead by looking at the change in the corporate demographic to start with, we will then look at what it means to be an "equal" leader and discuss horizontal organizations as opposed to vertical organizations. We will then delve into a couple of topics on how leaders ought to manage their employee's mindset and motivation in the coming decade.

Smaller organizations – Over the next decade, organizations will become smaller with a lot less people. The main driver of this will be continued outsourcing of tasks and capabilities to marketplaces, on the other hand we might see a big increase in freelancers and contractors. Automation will absolutely take away the need for people and that will further contribute to the organization shrink. What that will entail is the progressive concentration of responsibility from several people into fewer people. In other words, leaders will go from wearing one hat to two hats to eventually wearing several if not all hats for a specific area of responsibility. (See Figure 7.3.)

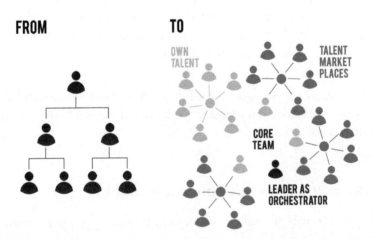

FIGURE 7.3 A new type of organization

So, we will end up with fewer, more accountable leaders and we will need to get used to handling that kind of responsibility. There are two sides to this, or two ways in which today's leaders are ill equipped for this which I want to highlight. Firstly, today's leaders mostly pick a functional career path sometime early on in their careers and have had a couple of decades of experience thriving in that specific function, but in many cases their desire or courage to step outside of their functional area of expertise is minimal. This will have to change, as we will need for example commercial leaders to take on responsibility for marketing and within marketing, brand and category leaders to take on responsibility for media and within media TV and offline guys to take on responsibility for digital media and within digital media the marketing science guys to take on creative, etc. Now I am not saying all leaders need to know how to do all things, but all leaders have to know how to define what needs doing, get it done and assess if it was done to the satisfaction of the initial work definition. Secondly, a great many leaders have over the years lost the ability to get into the trenches and work on things themselves. Worse still, leadership has started to be looked at as a profession in itself where a lot of leaders see their primary job as that to lead, which was definitely the right thing to do when there were big teams that needed direction and momentum. In tomorrow's world, we will have smaller teams and a lot of leaders will be expected to just roll up their sleeves and work alongside the team members.

Orchestration over Synthesis – The future organization will be a lot flatter and broader than today's organizations. Most large corporates today have some sort of multi-layer geographical structure and another multilayer category and function structure, with the lowest level being the operational entities which spend money and make money. The layers in the middle between the team on the ground and the leadership in the headquarters is essentially a layer of synthesis and summarizing. The traditional mantra of "span of control not more than seven" I think needs to be junked. It was the right thing to do in a context where there was little automation, a lot of information asymmetry and a lot of people working very removed from each other. In tomorrow's organization as the team is smaller, more uniform and more connected across functions, the leader would not need and should not have the unnecessary luxury of multiple layers of summarizing.

Jaden's orchestra conductor analogy is very apt here – a leader who conducts an entire team of people with multiple skill sets, all of which are important. Of course, there is a first chair and a lead in most instrument sections and the leader does not play their instrument for them. Their job is merely to conduct the proceedings and show everyone what they need to do and bring it all together in a beautiful composition. But to do so the leader must have some understanding of how each instrument works and sounds but more importantly there can only be one conductor. If the conductor decided that he would have a sub-conductor for the strings section or one for the orchestra sitting to the left and one for the right and he would conduct the leads who would conduct the musicians, it would be impossible to make music.

Celebration of non-leadership – One of the less talked about endemic issues in modern organizations are the frustrated middle, and I am sure every single person who works in a large enough company knows exactly what I mean here. The issue is simple; most employees start their careers being enamored by the company they work for and just being pumped about that fact that they have an income and can buy stuff. That lasts seven to ten years and then they hit middle management, and most people who want to stick around eventually make it here. The pyramid gets very steep and narrow from here on and maybe two out of five actually ever make it out of the middle, which makes three out of five very unhappy, frustrated and emotional until they decide to just live life listlessly in the company or move to the middle somewhere else to take their chances. There is a real problem here of supply of senior leadership roles being far lower than the demand for senior leadership roles and this problem is about to get a lot worse because the supply of roles will be less, there will be fewer leaders.

The only way to solve this is to take away the false and artificially created notion that the only way to succeed is to move up. In my startup days, one of the most important enablers of success was the fact that there was a good founder CEO, and everyone worked for him. The knowledge that no one wanted to replace him, mostly because he was very good, was really what kept us going and kept us together. There was no upward mobility to worry about, so we spent all our time trying to outdo each other in our own areas of responsibility and ended up being extraordinarily successful. We will need to create pride and wealth for leaders who do not sit on the apex of large teams but sit on areas that add value for the company.

Creating difficulties – Frederick Herzberg's theories on motivation and job satisfaction are sixty years old, but never truer than they are today, in my experience. In a nutshell, he proposed that hygiene factors like job security and pay do not drive motivation, although the lack of these could destroy motivation. Motivation, engagement and satisfaction lies in giving people the opportunity to gain a sense of achievement that can only come with overcoming challenges. I think beyond the promise of stock options and the overall cool factor which are key contributors to recruitment for startups what keeps people in the startups is exactly this. Early stage or even some established startups are not comfortable places to work. There is a lot of ambiguity, immaturity, constant risk, a general lack of objective performance management, and a lot of business challenges to overcome. But as you start knocking things off one by one, something happens inside you, that in my early days I mistook for just relief that the problem was solved but I soon grew to realize was really at the heart of the matter and had to do with how we are wired as humans. So, leaders will need to make this transformation in the mindset of their teams because this is different from the way companies operate today. Challenges equal satisfaction and challenges do not equal problems, this is the new way of the world.

Affective balance – Millennials are obsessed about being happy all the time and that is such a wonderful thing. This is not a generation which has had to give up their lives for freedom, or in a war, or for the most part in the pursuit of social justice. They just want to be happy. Subjective well-being theory, in other words the theory of how humans perceive their own happiness, states that happiness should be measured in two components: Life satisfaction and Affective balance. We talked about life satisfaction and therefore job satisfaction as being a function of overcoming challenges, but what about affective balance? And what is affective balance?

An affect is the experience of a certain emotion and there are positive emotions like Excitement, Interest, Pride, Attentiveness or Strength and negative ones like Hostility, Nervousness, Fear, Distress or Irritability and a person's real time experience of happiness depends on the extent to which at any point in time they are being affected by positive or negative emotions. It is going to be important for companies going ahead to be able to provide the promise of a work experience and environment full of positive effects and devoid of negative effects. I have in my entire career not been asked often enough, what makes me feel Proud or Alert and what makes me feel Ashamed or Upset but such emotions have shaped my perception of my workplace more than anything else. Companies will need to get a much better handle on how daily life affects their employees and take proactive measures to address this. Happiness is not something you deliver to the organization once a quarter in a feedback discussion or once a year in a bonus award. It is something that must be earned every day in each experience and interaction that happens under our watch. The best talent in the world will choose their employers based on this.

Three practical things you should do now

As companies start embarking on this transformation of their business and seek to transform themselves in the process, my top three suggestions are these:

- Start defining leadership not as people leadership but as topical and business leadership. To change the mindset of an entire generation that moving up is not the only way to grow will take time, consistent effort and demonstrable action. Perhaps pay your topical leaders more than your people leaders to show how the company's attitude has shifted and perhaps the organizations attitude might shift as well.

- Secondly, have a long-term plan on whittling down the size of the organization. These are of course such difficult decisions, and I believe having a long-term plan to build a smaller company in small progressive steps would significantly reduce the friction of downsizing compared to a big bang lay-off.

- Finally, think about employee satisfaction through a new lens of overcoming challenges in an always happy environment. Start building tools and infrastructure around these concepts of subjective wellbeing, I guarantee you will end up with a better performing company.

The Future of Government

Nuno joins a movement and Bart pays a parking fine

Nuno was concerned these days; there was an increasing amount of violence and discrimination against immigrants from the USA who were coming down, sometimes illegally, for a better future into Latin America. Immigration was the backbone of any competitive economy and allowing people to settle into a life where they want to, was one of the fundamental freedoms that humanity should protect according to him. Especially since Colombians had had the reverse immigration experience for so many decades, he thought they should be more empathetic towards these new entrants.

He knew the government had an incredible amount of data on not just all Colombians now, but also every individual who came in through its borders. There was a lot of resistance against this, and there is still a lot of discomfort in spite of the promise that this data is well guarded and not misused. He was glad that there was particularly good trackability and the government was able to provide clear data points on what was really going on. So much damage can be done by fearmongering based on incorrect information. He also likes how big tech companies had answered the call in the right way this time, being very responsible in banning disruptive comments and fact checking diligently. He really thought the Googles and Facebooks of the world wielded much more influence than the politicians and it was important that they do the right thing.

A few thousand miles away Bart woke up to a message from the local authorities saying he had extended his allowed parking slot by 30 minutes and therefore owed a 20 USD fine, which was annoying to say the least but at least he could pay it with one click with his tokenized credit card. He was looking forward to the new platform that they were about to launch which needed all cars to have an IoT device onboard which was linked to a central system and had payment details tokenized. So, you would find a free parking spot on Google Maps, then you could reserve it and park. Payment was done automatically for the exact amount of time your car spent in the parking spot. The more important thing was that parking rates varied based on the estimated number of cars looking for parking using an AI algorithm, except in this case the county was optimizing for lowest possible "time spent looking for parking".

Later that day, Bart was going to the city again to attend a stakeholder's convention for a large multinational corporation he invested in through an ICO. This corporation was in the business of mining plastic waste and converting it back into resin for recycling, and primarily operated in emerging economies in large cities like Manila and Mumbai. He was looking forward to the session, getting to know the company better of course and understanding the status of some of the big infrastructure projects they had just taken up in Laos and Bangladesh for which he had bought the ICO tokens. He was thinking about voting on some key topics in the meeting on a couple of important investment allocation decisions and thought this vote mattered perhaps as much as his vote in the US elections.

As he walked in through the hotel entrance, he saw the poor homeless man on the sidewalk across the street and wondered what will need to happen for all the beautiful benefits new technology has brought to him to find their way to improving the state of these poorest and most desperate sections of society.

Understanding some of the evolution in Government services

I wanted to round this whole section and the discussion on frontiers up by looking at how government services and people's interaction with government will change with digital enablement in the future. Of course, this is a big topic and one could dedicate an entire book to it and in fact, there are some great theses on this topic out there. But I will highlight a few items here, perhaps not in the same degree of detail as the other topics we have covered so far. These are all things happening around our companies and there is not an awful lot we can do about it. But important to acknowledge that this will affect how our consumers interact with us.

Citizen database – Like it or not, governments will start gathering and storing data on all its citizens. This involves digitizing available data which has not been digitized already, but also maintaining detailed citizen profiles on where people have interacted with any government service. This will include video captures from public CCTV cameras and other forms of data that consumers end up passively providing to the government. You might remember the 2018 case, where China arrested a criminal using facial recognition at a pop concert. Critically, I think over time there will also be much more transparency over how much consumer data companies must share with the government and under what circumstances. There is no good scenario here with a bad government, and with a good government there is a lot of upside on safety, security and other services one would expect. I think, we are likely three decades away from the market for government becoming much freer and more rational. Until then concentration of citizen data in the hands of the government will continue to harm persecuted sections of the society.

Role of big tech – Never has any entity had such a deep and immediate hold and influence on such a large percentage of the global population as Facebook and Google do today. Even more than the biggest religions or the biggest ethnicities, perhaps only rivalled by China and India with their mega populations. It's left to be seen if big tech maintains its stronghold on the consumers and if so, how governments will react to this concentration of power. The Cambridge Analytica example already exposed how much influence Facebook can have on the existence of specific actors in regular government and we have started seeing regulators now flexing their muscles with talk of breaking down large tech companies into smaller ones. I think in a decade from now there will be more even competition in the tech space and I do not think Facebook's and Google's monopoly on social media will remain indefinitely. But we need collaboration, as we discussed earlier, the market for government, the market for employment and the market for products and services are inextricably linked.

Alternative movements – #MeToo, BLM etc., could not have existed without digital enablement and where traditional governments fail to provide the right form of protection and services to all its citizens, alternatives to government in the form of popular movements will continue to do so. The next decade will for sure be one of turmoil, I think we will see a major change of guard in the world as political power changes hands from socially conservative hands to more socially liberal hands merely by virtue of a demographic shift. What will continue to be a polarizing debate is the one between the economic left and economic right. There will be consensus eventually but, as always, there will always be losers. But there will be a facility for minorities to raise their voices through parallel movements and find likeminded people from around the world. I am not talking about issues like racism, gender equality or the idiotic antivax movement for which there can be no two sides and there is only one right way. But much more so on gray areas like say vegetarianism or nuclear power, people will have the ability to live in a society, have minority views but at the same time find their place in a world along with other fellow global citizens.

Smart cities – Our cities will be much more connected, and ever better to live in. We will see innovations in transport like autonomous vehicles, electric cars etc., and in the environment like green buildings, solar power and pollution control. We will have evolution in the way public buildings are managed, and security and access to different parts of the city is controlled. Access to and usage of health infrastructure and waste management infrastructure etc. will be digitally controlled for efficiency and quality. Utilities like electricity and water will also be completely digitized in the consumer experience. The entire city would likely be fully Wi-Fi enabled, everything that provides a service will be on IoT and location enabled, and the sharing economy will have extended itself into all corners and all use cases. In the smart city of the future, life will be a breeze.

The digital have-nots – Finally and unfortunately, there will still be a lot of poor people in the world. There will still be 600 million people in the world in 2030 living in extreme poverty. One of the sad deficiencies of digital enablement is that it does extraordinarily little to lift people out of poverty, while it does incredible things for consumers who are already doing well. In fact, all signs point to more job losses and even less opportunities for the extreme poor to raise their lot and rise out of their misery. Perhaps the only way for this to change is to have a direct transfer of wealth from the beneficiaries of digital enablement to the people in extreme need. Be it through consumer donations enabled through digital platforms that find their way traceably through to those who need them, or be it through large scale philanthropy from the likes of Bill Gates and Tim Cook, who have pledged their wealth, created by providing value to the well-off consumers, to the ones in need. If there is ever a value exchange that was irrational for the capital markets but still made complete sense, then it must be this.

We have finally covered the six frontiers, and in the six frontiers we covered 24 key topics and in those 24 key topics we covered 120 key areas of evolution. Did we already consider everything that needs to be considered? For sure not. Did we need to consider everything that we did so far? Perhaps not. But are we better equipped now to start thinking about our digitally enabled future in more realistic and believable terms? I hope so. In the next section I will start prescribing a simple approach for companies to make something out of all this that is staring down at us. This is by no means the only way to succeed, neither is it by any means the only language and framework to describe the pathway that I will highlight. But I think it will be a pretty self-evident way of proceeding through the work of deciding how to create value through digital enablement. See you over on the other side.

Notes

1. https://www.outsystems.com/ At OutSystems, we change the way software is built so you can rapidly create and deploy critical applications that evolve with your business.
2. https://fivetran.com/ Simple, reliable data integration for analytics teams. Focus on analytics, not engineering. Our prebuilt connectors deliver analysis-ready schemas and adapt to source changes automatically.
3. The number of extreme poor (living on less than $1.90/day) will remain above 600 million in 2030
   http://documents1.worldbank.org/curated/en/765601591733806023/pdf/How-Much-Does-Reducing-Inequality-Matter-for-Global-Poverty.pdf

CHAPTER 8
MAKING THE TRANSFORMATION HAPPEN

Now that you have made it thus far, welcome to what I always found to be the most boring chapter of any business book – the "How to" chapter, riddled with endless frameworks and theory. Where the readers arrive with great expectations for a silver bullet and leave disappointed that they actually have to do some of the work in thinking things through themselves.

But consider this. If I read everything there is to read about playing the Piano, will I be able to play the Piano? Of course not. On the other hand, if we just stop reading anything about climate change and never think about it ever again, will climate change disappear? Also not. I guess what I am trying to say is, we have to do this together, give some of the "How to" stuff a go with me here in this book, and then go ahead and try some things out there in your world. What I promise to do is to make these last 30 pages a fun read for you.

Achtung! Sports analogy coming

2016 was an incredible year in sports moments and three teams did some unbelievable things in three separate sports. Leicester City FC, the Foxes, won the English Premier League for the first time in the club's 132-year history after spending most of the previous season at the bottom of the league table. The Golden State Warriors had the best regular season in NBA history, beginning the season with 24 straight wins and ending it with a 73–9 record, strangely they lost the NBA finals to the Cavaliers but incredible achievement, nonetheless. And the Chicago Cubs won the baseball World Series after 108 years, in an extra innings, in Game 7. What a year! I started wondering if indeed anything was possible and then Donald Trump was elected president and I was convinced.

So why did this happen? Let us look at the Leicester City Foxes' case a bit more in detail, trying to understand how they defied the 5000–1 odds of winning the championship and actually made it happen.

The simple answer is: They found a strategy, did everything right and in the end made their own luck. The Foxes had a quite different first half of the season compared to their second half; in the first half they scored a lot of goals and conceded a lot as well. In the second half they took a much more clinical approach, conceded less goals and racked up several 1:0 victories. They stuck to their team composition and made very few changes to their starting eleven – just 27 through the year compared to an average of 95.4 for previous Premier League champions. Their goal-scoring strategy too was different compared to other premier league champions, they had relatively low possession of the ball, passed the ball less and passed it less accurately. Essentially they let the opponents have the ball but when there was a reversal in possession, Jamie Vardy with his pace took it all the way and scored. And they did some noteworthy high ROI player recruitment, head of scouting Steve Walsh found Riyad Maher at Nottingham Forest, a second-tier club, for around half a million dollars and post season he was worth ~50 million dollars.

So you have to imagine that Claudio Ranieri and Co. started the year with an aspiration to stay out of relegation and developed a playbook with some good signings and a preferred style of football. Then midway they started seeing a different possible outcome and pivoted their playing style. All through the season the team stayed together, motivated and in good humor and created history. But of course, there was also luck – some real luck and some fantasy. Arsenal, which was the closest rival, did not have the mettle to deliver in the most crucial stages of the season, both Manchester United and Manchester City were having a dismal season. A late header by Robert Huth against Tottenham or Leonardo Ulloa's penalty in the final few seconds against Arsenal all came at the right critical points in time. People talk about how Leicester's billionaire owner Vichai Srivaddhanaprabha built Buddhist temples and supported ordained monks to bring good karma to the team and that helped bring the luck when it was needed. Perhaps that is the fantasy bit, but the fact remains – the Foxes had a playbook and they followed it to the T and then made their own luck. There is of course the whole team spirit thing, and it is glorious and there will be a movie sometime which we will all doubtless enjoy. But the lesson I want us to take here is this: In the complexity of a transformation that spans several years and involves several hundreds of people it is impossible to anticipate how things will turn out but if we have a plan which we follow with discipline and build resilience to pivot when needed, then we too will make our own luck.

The 3^3 Framework – Nine Steps to Build and Execute a Digital Transformation

My recommended approach, on doing an end-to-end digital transformation, has three Epics and within each Epic has three Sprints. I am using Agile Scrum language here because it sounds cool, but also because in a way I'd like you to think of this as a large-scale Agile transformation of your business. Using the Scrum thinking here will bring you all the benefits of Agile as we discussed earlier, mainly the ability to just move through the steps with momentum without spinning your wheels but still build flexibility in the way you treat each of the three Sprints. You are encouraged to move things around between Sprints inside an Epic but I'd recommend you finish an Epic before moving into the next one. (See Figure 8.1.) So here is the 3^3 model:

EPIC 1 – **IMAGINE** your digital future

   Sprint 1 – Define your **CURRENCY** and ambition of value

   Sprint 2 – Explore your own digital **FRONTIERS**

   Sprint 3 – Prioritize the available **VALUE POOLS**

EPIC 2 – **BUILD** your transformation unit

   Sprint 4 – Blueprint your **PLATFORM** idea(s)

   Sprint 5 – Recruit your transformation **TEAM**

   Sprint 6 – Setup your transformation **ENTITY**

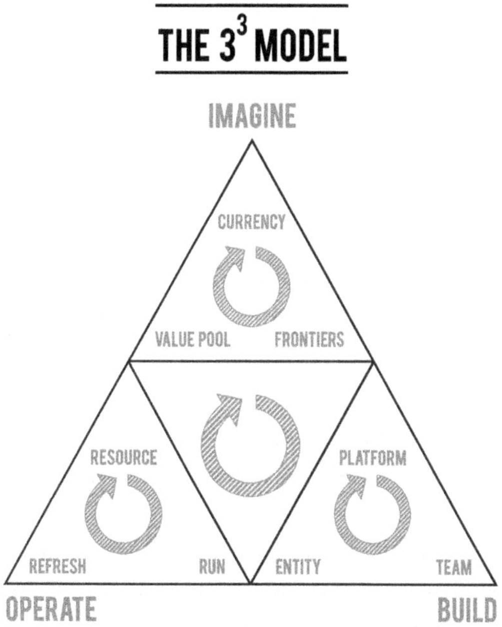

THE 3³ MODEL

IMAGINE

CURRENCY

VALUE POOL   FRONTIERS

RESOURCE   PLATFORM

REFRESH   RUN   ENTITY   TEAM

OPERATE   BUILD

FIGURE 8.1 The 3³ model of digital transformation

EPIC 3 – OPERATE the digital transformation

  Sprint 7 – RESOURCE the entity appropriately

  Sprint 8 – RUN the platform everyday

  Sprint 9 – REFRESH the platform every year

There. Through the next 20-odd pages I will run through these EPICs and SPRINTs, talk about what each of them mean, what the expected output should be and share some examples as we talk through these. But before we jump into it, I wanted to share some thoughts about the number of steps in this framework. Why are there nine steps? Could there be 10? Should there be seven? The answer to all of that is – "Yes", also possible.

Why 3³

Ohmae's 3C model, 4Ps of marketing mix, Porter's five forces, McKinsey's 7S framework, nine-block business model canvas, etc. The list can go on forever, and these are just the ones that are relatively well known. If you have been or have interacted with a management consultant, you would know the inside joke that everything always comes in threes. So I asked myself, how many steps should there be? What was clear to me was that there was no deterministic outcome to this question. A topic as complex as organizing a corporation to do a transformation has so many variables, I could come up with any number of dimensions by adjusting the granularity and moving activities between boxes. So, I thought the structure of the framework ought to be based on ease of comprehension and ease of implementation rather than attempting to be deterministic.

Consider the decimal system for instance – there is no mathematical basis that suggests that the decimal system is superior to other number systems with different bases. There is also no consensus on why the decimal system came to be the most popular system, although some say it's because we have ten fingers and that is how we started counting. In early civilizations there were only four measurements: One, two, three and many. The ancient Babylonians used a sexagesimal system with a base 60, which is why we still measure time with 60 minutes to an hour and 60 seconds to a minute. But technically there is nothing that would stop us from all deciding one day that a day will be ten hours and each hour will be 100 minutes and each minute a 100 seconds long. So, simplicity and habit are key.

Another interesting notion in Cognitive Psychology that offers some explanation of the Consultant's predisposition to advising in threes is that of "Chunking". Chunking theory says that we remember individual items better when they are bound together into a whole. There was also some research done on how many new chunks the human mind can process, store and recall at one time and it was found to be between two and four. And maybe that's why it feels so comfortable to think about new topics in three buckets, so I thought three EPICs would be good. The other beautiful thing about the number three is that it has self-similarity, you could pick one and double-click into three more and go on and on in a fractal-like deep dive into whichever topic you'd want – like a Sierpinski triangle, which looks like the illustration above.

So, armed with all of this incredible science I concluded that a 3^3 would be the ideal way to articulate the transformation framework. If you see my point, that is great. If you are thinking, "This was completely irrelevant, let's just get on with the nine steps because I am okay with it", then that is great too and let's do just that.

EPIC 1 – IMAGINE Your Digital Future

It must have been my second or third week at McKinsey and as a new entrant in the firm I was asked to help a group of leaders organize the Global energy and materials conference, which for a young analyst like myself involved doing whatever needs to be done from making slides, to coordinating with catering, to ensuring cabs are booked etc., you get the gist. On the final day of the conference there was a slew of speeches by industry leaders in front of a packed crowd at the Hotel Okura in Amsterdam and all the way at the back of this massive convention hall I sat at a little table with my laptop hooked up. With the unenviable task of loading up the slides and clicking next in case the clicker stopped working.

Busy doing my thing, I felt a soft tap on my shoulder and turned around to find the CEO of one of the world's largest Oil companies standing behind me. "Can you put this on a slide?", he said handing to me a few yellow post-it notes from his pocket. "Also, on this USB stick there are some scans, I want to present those", he instructed me as he started walking to the stage. I had less than seven minutes to get this done. I did some insane seven-minute magic, and he went onstage. Those scans were from his personal notebook, hand scrawled the night the board of the company called him to tell him he would take over as the next CEO. It was a few simple bullet points spelling out his intent and the future he imagined for this giant company. Just simply like that, maybe 15–20 words saying how this massive machinery of a company will do things for the coming decade. You can imagine how wonderstruck and starstruck I was as a 24-year-old.

And in this Imagine Epic, that is what I would like you to do. Build a vision complete with an ambition, backed by your carefully curated understanding

EPIC 1

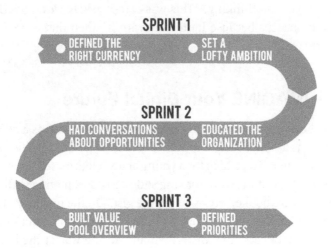

SPRINT 1
- DEFINED THE RIGHT CURRENCY
- SET A LOFTY AMBITION

SPRINT 2
- HAD CONVERSATIONS ABOUT OPPORTUNITIES
- EDUCATED THE ORGANIZATION

SPRINT 3
- BUILT VALUE POOL OVERVIEW
- DEFINED PRIORITIES

FIGURE 8.2 Imagine your digital future

of the context surrounding your business and some wizardry in thinking through where exactly you stand to make the most money. (See Figure 8.2.)

Sprint 1 – Define your CURRENCY and ambition of value

Digital transformation must be about creating value, there can be no two ways about it. Now of course, sometimes the value a digital initiative might give you would be very direct in the form of an extra sale or lower costs, and there might be times when it's a bit harder to discern the immediate value add. If you cannot make a link or an argument of how an initiative impacts the return on invested capital in your company then you should not do it. Unless you are a charity or a pure science researcher or an artist then by all means you should.

Value creation itself means only one thing; does what you create bring a benefit to anyone in the marketplace which they are willing to compensate you for? But even if it means only one thing, there are many ways to express it and you need to decide what is yours. You might say that for you it is enterprise value, which is probably the most all-encompassing way to think about it.

Or you might say revenue, or cash flow growth which are linked to enterprise value. Or you might want to be razor focused and talk about asset productivity improvement or operating expenses reduction or higher media reach, or some such component which also eventually leads to enterprise value. My recommendation is to always go broader rather than more specific because it helps to be unconstrained and you never know where the big upside might come from, unless of course you are certain about where the value is.

Once you have defined the currency, say enterprise value, you'll need to come up with a level of ambition for your organization. And you do not want to be too bearish when you do that. I have seen transformation attempts deliver mediocre results because the ambition was mediocre and it wasn't mediocre because leaders were not imaginative, it was mediocre because it wasn't culturally appropriate for the organization to claim a growth expectation unless it was suitably "underpinned". I find it amusing, this focus on underpinning growth aspirations. It's like proclaiming that you will not allow your enterprise to grow beyond what is fathomable to you personally. So my advice, think big and don't let your own limitations also become limitations for the company you're trying to build. And when in doubt just say, "Double the company's valuation in ten years". Which is another way of saying, you are going to attempt to build your company anew entirely in the next decade.

Perhaps we can draw some comfort by looking at how Netflix acquired its USD >200 billion market cap over the last 23 years of its existence. I'd say you could break up those 23 years of existence from Netflix into four distinct transformations or phases. The first build phase from its founding in 1997 through to its IPO five years later in 2002, at which point its market cap had reached ~250 USD million and a little over a year after that it crossed 1 USD billion. So, Netflix built a billion-dollar company in five-odd years which had an interesting business model but was by no means incredibly breakthrough. Then came the first growth phase with DVD rental driven growth which took it from a billion-dollar company to USD >10 billion by 2010. This was again a period of growth in subscribers led by the same great value proposition based on convenience. Then, the second build phase as Netflix carved out DVD rentals into another company and started focusing on streaming and in 2013 it streamed House of Cards, its first original content. This started the dream run as Netflix rode the wave of production quality improvements, much improved connectivity and streaming speeds and of course affordable debt to finance content creation and by 2015 it was worth >50 USD billion. And for the last five years it finds itself in its second mega-growth phase in subscribers which has resulted in a market cap of >200 USD billion when I last checked.

You need to decide if your company is either where Netflix was in 2002, with a great value proposition which is poised for growth or it is where Netflix was in 2010, just embarking on a business that would ride a massive wave of technology and consumer change. I sure hope it's 2010, what is at stake here is the difference between 10 USD billion and 100 USD billion. Unless you take on an aspiration of this nature you won't think unconstrained enough to actually end up with anything groundbreaking.

Sprint 2 – Explore your own digital FRONTIERS

We spent a substantial amount of time in this book looking at the six frontiers and I tried to be as generic as I could so as to cover as wide a scope of consumer facing companies as possible. You don't need to do that, you can go narrow and deep as it relates to your own specific business. But how?

I am not a huge fan of having a third-party consulting firm come and write up your digital transformation plan for you. Not because consultants are not helpful, they are, especially in bringing in temporary capacity to just bring momentum and diligence around the process. But there are three sides to getting the required understanding of trends: There are the technologies and trends themselves, there is the understanding of the business and there is the understanding of the company's culture. What's needed here is to trawl the world for technology and insights in the context of what the company does and how the company operates and there is no alternative to having your leaders spend the right amount of time to understand for themselves what technology evolution is underway and how other companies and startups are building businesses based on it. The culture of outsourcing the understanding of our own business to agencies and consultants is widespread and shocking to me.

So, my suggestion, take a week or two out of the time of everyone in your company, maybe it is a whole week all at once or maybe it is a day a week for a quarter. Maybe stagger it so everyone does not go missing all together and educate the organization on a broad range of technologies in-depth. Study the technologies themselves, bring in futurists to talk about the potential applications of the technologies into the six frontiers we talked about, look at examples of other companies and startups, study the history behind the evolution. Think of it as if it were a new capability that no one in the company can go on without and educate and certify everyone. Do not think of solutions yet, that can come later, just focus on understanding what is happening around you. And make sure there is enough breadth and depth to the education. There are a lot of cookie cutter programs out there which focus on digital marketing or e-commerce but not enough that cover a broad range of topics with sufficient depth. Buy thousands of copies of this book and gift one to everyone in your company!

And then let people go back to work and ruminate on it and start conversations in the company around value creation opportunities. Use a platform to record and create transparency on these ideas and conversations. I believe, your own employees, as long as they actually understand the technologies well and are given time to digest and internalize the implications, will come up with far more robust value creation opportunities than any third-party consultant. Of course, a consultant could help orchestrate the whole process and it is probably a great idea to hire one to do that.

Airbnb wasn't built in a day, or in a month for that matter. Brian Chesky, Nathan Blecharczyk and Joe Gebbia would have wished they had the luxury of time and deep experience in the home rental space and all its intricacies like you probably do of your business. In the absence of this they learnt all their lessons along all their frontiers the hard way. Take the consumer frontier for instance, Airbnb started in 2007, with an idea the founders had about allowing designers to sleep on air mattresses and acting as city guides to them, at some point they tried a room-mate matching service but that wasn't breakthrough enough. It was not until over a year later in 2008 that they realized the true problem facing consumers was the chronic shortage of hotel rooms and that insight led the company to create a simple experience centered around three clicks to book a room and opened up a big value creation opportunity. On the hosts frontier too, they spent time early on helping hosts' by making professional photographs and writing reviews but it was only later that they realized that many hosts were just fed up with their places being totally trashed after a stay leading Airbnb to come up with the "Host Guarantee" coverage of 1 USD million in 2012. The frontier they hugely missed early on was the regulators who were accustomed to earning hotel tax revenues and this has been a major headache for the company globally and they have continued to deal with it by collecting hotel taxes and launching community programs with mixed results.

Build your own deep-dive on your frontiers and take your time to examine all sides of the digital transformation. You do have time – much to the contrary to what you've been led to believe in terms of the urgency in this space, I have not seen opportunities converted or lost because of a one-year advantage or disadvantage in the market.

Sprint 3 – Prioritize the available VALUE POOLS

As your study of your frontiers nears completion you will realize that there is altogether too much opportunity and it is everywhere. From digital media to e-commerce to new products and Industry 4.0 and you will need to create a believable though not precise perspective on how these initiatives stack up against each other. As you start gravitating towards a portfolio of ideas you will need to be watchful of what I like to call the "Bright shiny object" mentality. Take for example something like Chatbots, there was an incredible euphoria around Chatbots a couple of years ago and every company was asking itself, when can I have Chatbots? It almost did not matter if they were needed or useful, we just had to have Chatbots. Fast forward two years and we are not really talking to Chatbots as much or talking about Chatbots as much either. So how do we avoid this bright shiny object thinking?

Two pieces of advice: Be exhaustive and be data driven. Digital enablement opportunities are truly everywhere and it's important you allow your organization to take a broad 360-degree view of where digital will add value. I have seen companies lose out on value either because their digital agenda is built in siloes or because they haven't been able to evaluate competing opportunities along a unified framework of value. So the marketing team, for instance, runs with digital marketing innovation on its own and the commercial team pushes the commercial agenda while the manufacturing team works out the Industry 4.0 implications and the distribution team deals with digital in the supply chain and each prioritizes for itself and in the process opportunities are just lost. What if the #2 opportunity in marketing is bigger than the #1 opportunity on commercial? Shouldn't you do that instead? Or what if the true breakthrough is in selling all office space and moving into an on-demand office model; who will look for that type of value? Your digital transformation needs to include everything, no exception.

Value all opportunities along the same valuation framework. For any initiative you should put together your best possible estimate of incremental operating income expected to be earned by the initiative in a reasonable period, say ten years. This could be productivity gains or additional business or something that delivers employee satisfaction, whatever it may be – it needs to come down to your bottom line. When startup investors are confronted by business plans from eager founders, they use a combination of valuation methods to put some comfort around what they are investing in. Broadly there are four different approaches: Look at comparable transactions, Calculate the DCF value or book value, Scorecards to decide relative risk compared to a comparable business or simply applying an expected rate of return to a future expected valuation. A lot of math to essentially rationalize what is more often than not a gut feeling. My recommendation is to compare initiatives against each other according to their incremental OI contribution and to score each initiative against each other along a risk scoring framework which considers the relative strength of your team, your capability of building the product you imagined, the consumer's willingness to buy into your idea and the competitive context. You can then apply your risk scoring to the initiative to right-size them for comparison.

As I write this, Ant Financial, which owns Alipay was poised to hold the biggest IPO of all time, of all time. This before the Chinese Regulator put things on hold. And while the WeWorks of the world have been busy with the hype around their bright shiny objects, this incredible company has been quietly identifying one value pool after another and creating value for shareholders out of their unassuming offices in Hangzhou. Starting with a simple escrow service for buyers and sellers on Taobao, then moving to a mobile payment and e-Wallet service connecting to almost every bank in China, then allowing bill payments, then starting an easy-to-use investment fund and then building an easy to get credit product Alipay has consistently identified the right opportunity and given it all they have to comprehensively win consumers every single time. No surprise that they're being valued upwards of 300 USD billion as they IPO. Your organization will need to build this capability to convert great ideas into great business plans which can then be prioritized and delivered against.

So you've come to the end of this first EPIC and now you've started to imagine what your company could achieve over the next decade. You have a bold ambition; you've done your research and you understand where the opportunities are. And you've done a valuation and you know how much this whole thing could be worth to you. It is time for you to move to the next EPIC where you will build the transformation vehicle that will get you there.

EPIC 2 – BUILD Your Transformation Unit

As I am writing this section, one of my favorite shows on Netflix released its third season. *Suburra: Blood on Rome* is what it is called, and it is in Italian, so I watch it with sub-titles. The show is a portrayal of the criminal underground in the city of Rome which is very rich in its fabric considering the different frontiers in crime and the variety of stakeholders involved including the local Roman criminal families, the gypsies of Roma, the police, the local government, the Vatican church, Italian bankers and of course the Sicilian mafia. What comes out of this is an incredible tale of violence, intrigue and high drama set to an ultra-cool soundtrack of Italian hip-hop. Other than the beautiful Roman backdrop the interesting thing about the series is the fact that no character is really perfect and you feel like you're really aligned to someone and then that very person goes and does something very irresponsible, like murder five people for instance, which makes you wonder if you were really backing the right protagonist. You have Aureliano the young scion of the Adami crime family, Spadino the young hopeful from the Roma gypsy clan and Lele the son of a police officer and a new corrupt entrant into the police force. Together they make up a youthful team sourced from adversarial parties united by the common cause of winning over Rome. All under the watchful eye of the reserved, networked and all-powerful mastermind called Samurai.

The reason why I wanted to open with this example was that I see a lot of similarities here with the team you will build for your digital transformation and the leader you will appoint which we will talk about in this Epic. The way this criminal syndicate builds alliances and acquires territory could be a lead into your own build or buy decisions as you set up your digital transformation entity and the way the loathsome trio prop up different vehicles to smuggle contraband and siphon money from the taxpayer could exemplify the need to build platforms which we will discuss here. Disclaimer – don't commit crimes. (See Figure 8.3.)

Sprint 4 – Blueprint your PLATFORM idea(s)

Platforms are the building blocks of a digital transformation. That's probably as critical a notion as one can have when it comes to driving targeted success

FIGURE 8.3 Build your transformation unit

in digital. But what are these platforms that one talks about? This gets mentioned a lot and thought leaders will drop an odd statement about platforms being the future, but no one ever explains it so I'll try here. Etymologically it doesn't offer us any clues; the word Platform comes from the old French *Plateforme* which in turn from ancient Greek *platus* meaning flat and Latin *forma* meaning shape. So, we're dealing with a flat shape.

I am going to take a leap and define a platform for our purposes as a marketplace where two entities directly adjacent to each other in the value creation chain find each other and then go through a transaction involving an exchange of value. So, when you build platforms you build marketplaces. This may sound like a stretch but that's what I'd like you to do, stretch the concept of marketplaces to go beyond the visual of an e-commerce website or even a wet market. So in the frontiers when we talked about digitized OOH media we talked about a marketplace for smart screen inventory to be sold from screen owners to brands, when we talked about consumer engagement we talk about a marketplace to exchange loyalty for added value between brands and consumers. Even in the context of Industry 4.0 manufacturing an interfacing platform between two manufacturing units can be imagined to be an internal marketplace where the units exchange parts along a pre-agreed schedule. So with this in mind we next need to examine why platforms are important? And there are three main reasons for it; ease of build, flexibility for changes and ease of monetization. Building up an initiative as a platform allows you to resource it in its entirety, effectively letting it develop independent of the matrix in the rest of your organization. Having it built as a platform allows you to let it self-regulate and focus on driving up quality of outcomes. And, of course, having it built as a self-contained platform lets you monetize it with external parties and as we learnt throughout this book, better asset monetization will be a key driver of value creation.

Practically as you execute this Sprint the key outcome you need to solve for is your prioritized list of maybe three-odd platforms to invest behind. You might have finished the earlier sprint with many more ideas of course and at this point you are going to have to run through two exercises. First, you need to look at your list of value pools and convert it into a list of platforms. Articulate the platform idea in the form of a marketplace with a clear exchange defined and the source of value or incremental operating income clearly spelled out. At this point you should look at your long list of platforms and see if it makes sense to put some of these together under one larger platform especially because of the nature of the team, partners, customers or other stakeholders being similar. And of course, you'll need to prioritize, depending on the size of your organization you should decide how much you can take on but I am yet to find an offline native company deliver more than three successful platforms at once.

Let's take a look at this platform idea from the point of view of food delivery players with the example of Grubhub. Grubhub started in 2004 essentially offering online menus for restaurants that did delivery so the marketplace here would have been one where restaurants exchanged menu information with consumers and Grubhub being compensated for it by the restaurants. In 2015 Grubhub added delivery services to its platform for restaurants which didn't do their own delivery and here the marketplace was the offer of delivery services to the consumers who then paid for it. Grubhub has rolled out a point-of-sale integration platform allowing restaurants easier management of online food orders or a virtual restaurant platform allowing restaurants to sell food online without actually having a bricks and mortar presence. All of these and much more could be independent platforms which Grubhub has chosen to aggregate into a larger marketplace to sell services to restaurant owners and consumers alike in the meal ordering and delivery space.

You should aim to finish this sprint with a similar blueprint of up to three platforms that are most valuable and interesting for you to build over the coming decade.

Sprint 5 – Recruit your transformation TEAM

Who should oversee the digital transformation in the organization?, is probably the most critical question and there is no right answer. No right answer does not mean there are no good answers, and there are some bad answers. The ideal candidate would need four personalities: A commercial value creator, a technologist, a strategist and an evangelist. The perfect candidate is all four, but impossible to find. A great candidate has three but not just any three. Most leaders out there only have at the most two of these three and unfortunately some only have one – those would be the wrong answers. So, if you had to pick one with three, which one should you drop? Ironically, to build a tech enabled business, I think the one quality that the leader does not necessarily need is deep tech knowledge. So, my simple suggestion is to find within your leadership, one such charismatic, strategic thinking and commercially focused individual and equip him with technology learning and support. Unless of course you find someone who has all four.

As you build your internal startup it will come to this, how confident you are in your vision and how confident you are in the underlying trends and how compellingly you are able to translate that confidence into a business plan that investors or your company leaders will look at and tell themselves two things: (1) This seems like a good idea, and looking at prevailing trends there is a good likelihood it will work and (2) All experience tells us that it's not going to work precisely the way the business plan spells it out, but the people behind the idea will find a way. And that's why startup founders are mega-charismatic, and even the introverted ones when placed in front of investors become church-leader like in their passionate appeal. So, if you think you are onto something, get it out there, find the right people to build it and sell the idea and maybe, just maybe you'll build the next Facebook inside your company.

Next comes the team. Find the right leader and the team will follow him. Remember, the leader in this case needs to be a snake oil salesman as much as a keen strategist who really understands the business. It is hard to motivate employees to tie their lot to something that does not exist and that's where charisma and storytelling comes in. And with the right narrative, staffing the rest of the team will likely be absolutely no issue, corporate offices are packed to the brim with people who are dying to get into more interesting situations where they can learn more. The sheer number of experienced professionals who throw away security and join startups with massive pay cuts is a testament to this. Perhaps you could dip into the frustrated middle. Bring in some outside hires to complete the team's functional expertise and you are ready to go.

Let's look at LinkedIn, a company that needs no introduction. Started in 2003, today it has over 20,000 employees worldwide and is now owned by Microsoft who bought it in 2016 for a little over 26 USD billion. Starting with the founder Reid Hoffman who had an incredible Silicon Valley career before joining PayPal in early 2000 as the COO and then founding LinkedIn in late 2002. Co-founder Allen Blue likewise followed Hoffman from Socialnet and LinkedIn, Jean-Luc Vaillant from Socialnet. So, Hoffman, a seasoned professional himself built and brought his own team along from his network including classmates and colleagues from his past, and we see this story repeat over and over again in the startup space. As you build your own digital transformation team, don't let go of this organic, founder-led way of building the team up. In the early days of the crunch it is the personal relationships which will motivate your team to rely on each other and collaborate to deal with all the challenges of building a new business together.

Sprint 6 – Setup your transformation ENTITY

You have to play the startup game with startup rules. Throwback to the business school lesson, finance 101, enterprise value is the net present value of all **expected** future discounted cash flows. I am not going to start explaining valuation here, I am more interested in the less talked about word in that definition which is "expected" and all the world's unicorns and decacorns were built on the basis of that word. So, while fueling revenue and profitability growth are great levers to grow enterprise value, so is the act of fueling expectations. And it's a lever companies definitely haven't used to its full effect as well as startups have, perhaps because of the risk that a highly uncertain part of the business with a lot of expectations might go bust, deflating the value of the entire company including the rock solid and reliable core business along with it. But no risk, no reward so companies need to decide if they want to play the expectation game, the startup game. And if the imperative is to think like a startup then you need to act like a startup. You cannot play the startup game with corporate rules. It is a bit like trying to tee off on the Golf course with a putter, it will work somewhat but it will not work anything like having a nice driver. By the way, the converse is true as well, you cannot really play the corporate game with startup rules and the attempts to do that were what gave us the WeWork debacle. And the easiest way to play the startup game is to start a startup, which is a HUGE supporting argument for nesting your digital transformation in its own entity.

Another argument is to just keep out of the way of the transformation. As you embark on this transformation, you'll have different reactions internally and a lot of non-believers that come in different forms. You have the unconvinced "This won't work in our business", the risk-averse "I think we should wait and see" and the worst of the lot, the "Excited to do this" fake supporters who say a lot but do little. This kind of implicit pushback comes more often than not because while people sort of understand that not working on these topics is not an option, the urgency is not felt strong enough for them to actually bother with doing anything about it. And I think it is important to think of separating out the transformation use cases into a separate entity for this reason.

It's irrational to expect leaders who are incentivized with short-term performance to go out of their way to contribute to initiatives that only bear fruit in three, five or ten years, far beyond the bonus window and potentially also far beyond the specific leaders' remaining tenure in their role. Altogether too much time is being spent in getting people to do things they haven't been hired to do. Carving out your most willing and capable leaders in a daughter entity and funding and incentivizing them to build the new digital enabled platforms is a much more appropriate path to success.

Google's Alphabet (or actually Alphabet's Google) is an excellent example of how a strong incumbent with a successful product, in Google's case it was Search, has over the years built new businesses and left them in a related yet carved out structure integrating them when the time is right but leaving them on their own until they are built out. Think of products like Android, Maps, YouTube etc. which are now deeply integrated but then newer entities like Waymo or Calico which remain at arm's length while the company builds these out.

You will need to strike this balance between allowing for freedom to build while at the same time ensuring the businesses strategy remains aligned with your company strategy and firmly embedded within your corporate governance. And this will bring you to the end of this second EPIC. You now have an architecture of your platform priorities which will be the building blocks of your digital transformation. You also have a leader in place and he has worked with you in finding your startup team and you have carved out an entity to build this platform within. In the next EPIC you'll resource or fund this entity appropriately, create the right environment to run it on an ongoing basis and wire up your organization to refresh your digital agenda repeatedly.

EPIC 3 – OPERATE the Digital Transformation

September 06, 2020 at Autodromo Nazionale di Monza, the temple of speed as it is called, where Formula One cars are able to rev up to the maximum speeds that they are capable of. This year's car had gone up to 360 kmph at the end of the main start–finish straight. This year the race had high drama and delivered to us an unusual result, a win for Pierre Gasly of the Scuderia AlphaTauri racing team. This result was unusual but very welcome and widely celebrated for a few reasons. For a sport dominated by three teams over the last decade it was refreshing to see a new team winning a race. AlphaTauri is also the "junior" team to the Redbull racing team and Pierre Gasly was unceremoniously relegated down to AlphaTauri last year after a low performing half season at Redbull, this was his redemption. And the thought that a junior team could trump the main team made it all the more exciting.

There are a few reasons why this analogy is interesting for us. Firstly, both Redbull and Alphatauri use a few of the same important car components. They have the same engine supplied this year by Honda, same gearbox, same front and rear suspension and probably the same of everything that regulations allow. But beyond that and most importantly in the critical area of aerodynamics they follow completely independent approaches. Sure, the Redbull team has far more investment and they get the pick of the best drivers but that has made the Alphatauri team hungrier for success and every once a while they pull out an ace like they did at Monza in 2020. Having this second team also creates more monetization opportunities for Redbull racing, and part of the reason why they maintain it as a separate team is for any eventual carve-out and sale, be it partial or complete. So interesting lessons for us to learn here as we start building our own sister entities to drive digital businesses keeping

EPIC 3

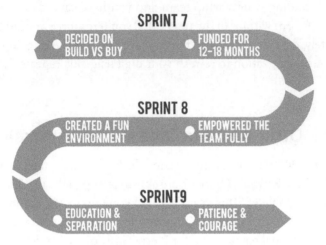

SPRINT 7
- DECIDED ON BUILD VS BUY
- FUNDED FOR 12–18 MONTHS

SPRINT 8
- CREATED A FUN ENVIRONMENT
- EMPOWERED THE TEAM FULLY

SPRINT9
- EDUCATION & SEPARATION
- PATIENCE & COURAGE

FIGURE 8.4 Operate your digital transformation

them tied to our main business yet allowing them to operate the way they deem fit to win in the market. (See Figure 8.4.)

Sprint 7 – RESOURCE the entity appropriately

There are two key decisions you need to make as you start carving out resources for this new digital transformation vehicle. Should you build, buy or invest with a minority stake or invest with a controlling stake? And if you do decide to build, how much funding should you provide to this entity? Let us dive into the first one first.

There is no definitive answer here of course and I won't make a blanket statement which says definitely build or definitely buy or definitely invest, but let's examine the plusses and minuses of the different approaches and see if we can come up with some learnings together. Let's start with the buy vs build question – the clear advantage here is the time to market, a startup that is already built is of course a much faster path to value compared to one you have to build from scratch yourself. It is also already built and has lower risk of making it to market, whereas your own plans might or might not materialize. So if you are convinced about a platform and the underlying opportunity and if you think the available asset is reasonably valued compared to your own assessment of the value pool then you should buy. Next, let's consider the three possibilities – buy 100%, buy a controlling stake or buy a minority stake. I am not a huge believer in buying a minority position in an asset or a platform that you are serious about making an integral part of your organization. Having a board seat in a startup gives a sense of control but in my startup tenure I have seen how little influence minority investors wield on the strategy and operations of the company and while it could be a hugely profitable exit for you if you were investing purely with the aspiration to make money on an exit, I am assuming that's not what you are after. Which brings us to the question of 100% investment or a controlling majority and there are two sides to this reflection as well. Buying say 70% of a company which you eventually intend to fully own essentially means you'll end up buying the rest of the 30% later at a higher valuation. On the other hand, not having a management which still holds say 10% of the company and not having the added motivation and pressure that external investors bring, both strategic investors and purely financial investors, can really just take the wind out of the sails of a startup. The idea of platform monetization to external partners which we discussed earlier combined with the notion of playing the startup game with startup rules makes this for me the most preferred option. So, find the right startup, make a controlling investment, maintain management share, invite external investors now at a valuation that is much higher because you're associated with the company and the risk is lower and aim to carve-out the business completely in a few years.

If you're building the startup how well should you fund it? I'd say fund the team for eighteen months the first time around. Most startups in the first few years have not more than 12–18 months' worth of funding available which they tend to reinforce by fundraising every year. I am generalizing and averaging a bit of course, because more often the mantra in the startup community is to raise money all the time and raise as much money as you can. Timing the fundraise so that you raise as late as possible and get a longer runway to get a better valuation, but not so late that it's obvious you're close to running out of cash and play right in the hands of hawk-like investors and end up with a down round, is a valuable skill. My startup founder boss for example had the courage to say no to a potential investor with less than six months of funding left and managed to get us all a much better deal when the investor came back to the table. But not everyone is cut out for this. In your digital entity however, your employees do not have to worry about running out of cash and I think this is more of a disadvantage than an advantage which once again points to the importance of having management holding shares and raising funding externally. The fear of dilution in own shareholding drives management to make more prudent decisions in usage of funds and brings more aggression in finding growth, this is a part of the startup game which you want to keep playing.

When it comes to make, buy or carve-out type of plays a great case in point here is TripAdvisor which, despite changing hands over its existence, has not changed its leader. Founded in 2000 by Stephen Kaufer and his co-founders it was bought by IAC in 2005 which combined it with a few other travel companies and spun it off as Expedia, Stephen Kaufer continued to lead Tripadvisor. In 2011, Expedia, which was then led by Dara Khosrowshahi who now leads Uber, carved out TripAdvisor which listed on Nasdaq then at a valuation of about 4 USD billion and of course Stephen Kaufer continued to lead the company. There are many moving parts here but what I wanted to demonstrate was that you can build or buy and integrate businesses which mutually benefit each other only to carve them out again at a later stage, all the time keeping the management and the core growth pathway of the company intact.

Sprint 8 – RUN the platform everyday

Affective balance, which we discussed in an earlier chapter is really at the heart of how a start-up runs every day and in your digital entity you want to capture all of that positivity in the way people work and the way the company is run. Four things made the startup I worked at tick for me and I think these were also major contributors to our eventual success. The expected payout, total empowerment, focus on performance and a truly fun environment. Let's look at these a bit more. I joined the founding team because I was given the opportunity to make more money in a few years than I ever would in consulting where I came from or in a corporate where I went later. This I think was true for almost everyone and even when people talk about the experience of it all, no one would have signed up for it if the expected payout wasn't big. It's important that you construct a similar compensation mechanism for your transformation leaders because this will get you the best talent out there but also keep this talent on its toes in driving value. We were all a 100% empowered and free to take whatever decisions were needed to be taken. Which did not mean we could be irresponsible, quite the contrary, the expectation was to make decisions fast under ambiguity and by definition that would cause conflict. The CEO took me aside three months into my stint and said he was not happy about that fact that no one had complained about me – he wanted me to be more provocative in my approach. And having that freedom helped us all take risks.

We were VERY performance focused. You could be the most talented person on the floor but if your numbers weren't good, you were out. People were not rewarded based on potential; they were rewarded based on results. A lot of ex-consultants, like myself felt this immediately as we struggled through our first few months. Coming from an environment where your performance evaluation is almost purely subjective, basically a bunch of people who work with you provide feedback and that makes your "rating", in the startup you were how much you sold. And that did away with the notion of "I support my people" and the cronyism that is endemic to performance evaluations in a lot of companies and had the right folks end up in the right places. Of course, it's not always perfect and the founder in any startup always has his "crew" and proximity to the founder becomes a sort of a key success factor but that aside, we had a much more objective performance culture than I had seen before or have seen since. And lastly there was the everyday experience, the fun no frills office environment. Most of our offices were essentially huge rooms with hundreds of tables and chairs and everyone sitting in the same space. You want a meeting with marketing? You walk 20 meters to their table. You want the CEO to know something? You stand up and shout out. Every day in the office was like joining a movement and it definitely helped that the average age was in the late twenties and early thirties. But does that mean you can't run the company without young people? Or that older leaders don't have the ability to be non-hierarchical and fun? I don't think so and the CEO of my current employer is easily the most approachable and relatable senior leader I have ever met in my career. But flattening an organization involves a massive cultural change which attempts to negate two decades worth of conditioning for leaders in the company and dramatic change needs dramatic steps.

Let's look at Spotify, an amazing company I have referenced several times in this book which is now well on its way to top 50 USD billion valuation. One of the cornerstones of its success has been "The Spotify model" which came out of Spotify's engineering team as they organized themselves to deliver a high-quality product with agility, all while creating an excellent environment for their employees to operate within. People from different functions work in Squads together on a specific feature and multiple Squads in a specific area form a Tribe. Each Tribe has a Trio of tribe lead, product lead and design lead to keep these areas firmly aligned. Senior technology leaders lead Chapters which maintain best practices and engineering standards in specialist areas. Then there are Guilds which employees can join based on personal interest and Alliances where multiple Tribes come together to work on a key objective. All of this might sound convoluted and you don't need to copy it. The lesson is that just like Spotify did, you would need to innovate on how your digital venture receives the empowerment and agility benefit that it will need, to be able to create value for you.

Sprint 9 – REFRESH the platform every year

This final Sprint, I want to start with one final example, that inescapable startup success story called Zoom, valued at >140 USD billion as I am writing this. Zoom was founded in 2011 by Eric Yuan in the videoconferencing space which included Microsoft's Skype, Google's Hangouts, Cisco and other well-funded startups like BlueJeans. But with a superior product and great partnerships Zoom continued to refresh its value proposition and executed subsequent fundraising rounds until its IPO in 2019. Come COVID, Zoom's usage and share price went through the roof and at once as security concerns became priority Zoom started focusing more on encryption. With the world making what looks like a long-term shift to remote work Zoom is now further refreshing its value proposition to include hardware partnerships. It's crazy to think that something as seemingly trivial as videoconferencing has seen such incredible innovation over the last decade by a company that has focused relentlessly on constantly finding ways to make video calls better.

So how does one make digital transformation not a onetime event but a long term always on capability in the company? With complete empowerment to decide the direction in which the company goes, subject to "board" approval of course, your internal startup will learn and evolve itself, so you do not have to worry about that. But you do need to keep the pipeline open, the ideas flowing and the transformation alive. A well-structured, well incentivized organization with the right education will independently refresh itself and get a life of its own.

Make digital transformation a separate function, do not embed it within marketing, sales, supply chain or IT. Have your digital leader report directly into the senior leadership of the company, at par with your business lines or business units. If you have an organization that deals with new business ventures etc., that could also be a rightful place for the digital team. Putting digital under the functions will completely jeopardize the value of thinking about platforms end to end and your priorities and urgency will be lost in internal governance. It will be painful for the existing organization, but I strongly believe this is the best way to make a major transformation work.

This we discussed before, and I will stress it here again. Invest heavily in educating your organization in depth in the technologies. You can do it as a roadshow all year round so at any point in time there is a learning ongoing somewhere in the world with a cohort. Make sure there is ample depth in the learning and the learning leads immediately to a forum that encourages and refines ideation. An important mindset to reinforce here, digital is not your technology team learning how to do business, it is your business team learning how to do future business using technology. Incentivize your internal startup based on pre-agreed targets as you likely do with the rest of your company including value created by monetizing the platforms and services built, with outside clients. But incentivize them even more to raise external funding. Fund raising is a beautiful thing, it pushes the team to always think about value creation and do whatever it takes and at the same time it could unburden you from your total funding obligation to the startup. The other important thing is patience, digital platforms are a game of accumulation. Accumulation of consumers one at a time and accumulation of knowledge and experience week after week. A startup only winds down when the money runs out and you must treat your internal startup that way as well.

But most importantly, while you attempt to do all this, demonstrate courage. Growing up in the 90s during a time of relative peace, I did not get to experience much hardship. I'd hear stories about the World War and about Communism and about the Mafia and about Terrorism and it would fascinate me that there were people, just like me all flesh and skin and bones, all around the world that go through such dramatic experiences. I spent a good part of my childhood and early adulthood thinking, maybe your ability to go out and do something extraordinary depends on the circumstances around you being extraordinary in the first place. Great moments bring out the greatness in people, I guess.

I think that probably applies to companies as well. And we are living in a period of profound change, it is almost like there are several Cold Wars in progress all at the same time. There's a generational change ongoing and millennials are solidly in their thirties, there is an economic rebalancing from the west to the east in motion, there is a clash of values between the socially liberal and the socially conservative, there is a clash of entitlement between the have nots and the ones that have too much. There is trash in our oceans and our lungs are filled with exhaust smoke. There are incredible changes in technology every few years and devices are becoming obsolete and making lifestyles obsolete together with them. And bang in the middle of it all we have a global pandemic which shows no signs of relenting quite yet. Yeah, make no mistake, there is a war afoot, and with it has come to us an opportunity to drive change. You have to imagine that every founder of every mega company, someday before they got up and made that first phone call, or wrote that first line of code or started typing out the first paragraph in a business case or met a friend over a coffee to speak about their idea for the first time, had a moment's hesitation and wondered if they were just day dreaming. But something inside them made them go ahead and make that first move anyway. It is also highly likely that whatever idea they shared; their business today looks nothing like it. But if they had not had the courage to make that first move, they would not have changed their own life and the lives of billions along the way. So there you have it, the final Epic where you resource and run your transformation and set it up for continued success with a healthy dose of courage.

This is the end. We started our journey a few hundred pages ago understanding value creation and then looking at the top ten technology trends and the top ten consumer trends. We then went through the six frontiers of reach, engagement, commerce, products and brands, manufacturing and distribution and companies in general. And finally, we explored the 3^3 framework where I offered you a blueprint to base your digital transformation from. And this is where my journey with you readers ends for now as I eagerly look at the coming decade with bated breath, understanding and learning from the moves you will make and capturing the essence of why things end up the way they do.

EPILOGUE

A November day dawned in 2060.

In Berlin, Odin was just waking up at 6 am. He was going to turn sixty next month and was feeling reflective about the last 25 years. He thought back at the first date with his companion at the Shell stop gas station and was looking forward to the short 100km drive to the beach later that day. They still lived separately and on a spectrum of marriage and friendship they had spent the last 25 years comfortably somewhere in the middle. Odin got himself ready and sat comfortably into his travel pod which accelerated in the direction of what used to be Rostock, now completely under water. We weren't able to stop global warming in time and now most of the world's resources were being poured into building giga-dams and recovering land. A few minutes into the ride, her pod came in view, ran parallel to his and then eventually joined up. The partition slid upwards and the pods combined as she slid next to him into the seat and gave him a quick kiss on his cheek.

Over in Mumbai it was 10:30 am and Wahad had just had his breakfast. His daughters still lived with them and he was so happy about that – one was an Ocean mining engineer and the other had taken up a career in Law, specializing in Centenarian rights. He switched on the third projector to get an update on the latest news up in the North of India. For three years there had been major food riots all over the North and he was living in constant fear that it might flow over to Mumbai. Life as a minority had still not improved anywhere in the world and anger always quickly got re-directed to the most vulnerable. He watched for a bit and then decided to disengage – he felt like wanting to be transported back to their life in the 2030s so he keyed in a few parameters in his content device which artificially rendered a one-hour memory of a Sunday in 2035 in their home within five minutes and launched on the 3D projector.

It was a little after lunch in Seoul and Jaden sat in the balcony of his 400th floor apartment in Gangnam. He stared up in the sky and there was no sunlight glistening on his still porcelain face – by now retained in its youthful form with multiple grafts and other cosmetic procedures. There was an absolute swarm of drones and small satellites up in the sky blocking out his sun – the government had made regulations around no-fly zones, but it wasn't making much of a difference. He needed them as well, he didn't leave his building much anymore, it was more than a skyscraper, it was an entire little town crammed together in a massive 500 floor building which extended many blocks in what used to be the trendy Gangnam neighborhood.

It was getting to midnight in Bogota and Nuno was just about to call it a night. It had been a decade now since Ed took his own life and Nuno blamed law enforcement. Unfortunately, the government had continued to take a very strong-armed approach towards immigration and Ed had joined a massive global movement against this protectionist policy. Nuno thought Ed had been targeted in the ensuing civil war not directly but indirectly with hyper-surveillance and, in the end, this was too much for him to bear. This had been a turning point in his own life. The civil war was won, and the country had changed for the better, but the activism bug had bitten Nuno. He had given up the violin and turned all his efforts to a new passion – Reforestation and just last year all Amazon tropical forests were completely restored to their state 150 years ago. Ed would be proud.

A few thousand miles north, Bart was also about to go into sleep mode, it wasn't exactly sleep anymore. Bart was ninety this year and according to his calculation, he was only about 65% human by weight. He had a new artificial stomach, esophagus and parts of the large intestine. Those Rennie pills stopped working after he turned 75. He also had limb-support in both legs and a few other small implants in his body. He still played golf – but not the real thing anymore. All virtually. In fact, last month he took an entire five-day virtual vacation in the Bahamas. He was 45 years old in this vacation and he went virtual diving, that was fun. Pity that the Bahamas didn't exist anymore. Jill joined him on the vacation – and it was nice re-living their original real Bahamas trip. The real Jill was sitting right beside him, and he thought she still looked as beautiful as she had when they first met.

So much has changed in this world and this November day is full of delights and pain, togetherness and desolation, love and tragedy, optimism and destruction. But I guess those have been around on every November day just in a different form and will likely be around forever. The unexpected intrigue of life continues as the earth spins on and on.

INDEX

INDEX